PAUL ON PREACHING

PAUL
ON
PREACHING

JEROME
MURPHY–O'CONNOR, o.p.

SHEED AND WARD — NEW YORK

© JEROME MURPHY-O'CONNOR, O.P.

NIHIL OBSTAT: FRIBOURG (SWITZERLAND) 27 MAY
   1963 C. SPICQ, O.P.   H. STIRNIMANN, O.P.

IMPRIMI POTEST L. COFFEY, O.P. PRIOR PROV. HIB.

NIHIL OBSTAT: JOANNES M. T. BARTON, S.T.D., L.S.S.
   CENSOR DEPUTATUS

IMPRIMATUR ✠ GEORGIUS L. CRAVEN,
   EPŪS SEBASTOPOLIS VIC. GEN.

WESTMONASTERII, DIE 23A DEC. 1963

The Nihil obstat *and* Imprimatur *are a declaration that a book or
pamphlet is considered to be free from doctrinal or moral error. It is
not implied that those who have granted the* Nihil obstat *and*
Imprimatur *agree with the contents, opinions or statements expressed.*

Library of Congress Catalog Card Number 64-19908

Manufactured in the United States of America

ordination of two texts, each of which if taken in isolation might give rise to a false interpretation.

> By sending his Son in the likeness of sinful flesh in view of sin, he condemned sin in the flesh. [Rom. 8.3]
>
> For our sakes he made him to be sin who knew nothing of sin. [2 Cor. 5.21]

Through Adam's fall the whole human race was contaminated by sin (Rom. 5.12, cf. 3.23); it was sinful flesh.[11] The reality of Christ's human nature made him part of a humanity thus deformed. To such an extent, at least, was he "made sin".[12] But, Christ "knew nothing of sin". It is not a question here of speculative knowledge of the nature of sin, for the negative form of the statement is intelligible only if we understand this knowledge to be experimental. Christ never experienced the reality of sin within himself, even though he experienced to the full the punishment due to sin. (Rom. 4.25.) That is why, despite the reality of his humanity, his flesh only "resembled" ours. It possessed a purity that ours does not enjoy. The purpose of this solidarity with sinful humanity was the conquest of sin and the redemption of men through the conferring of the adoption of sons.

How was this mission accomplished? In the first place by Christ's redemptive death on the

Cross, "by means of the redemption which is in Christ Jesus, whom God has put forward as an instrument of propitiation [*hilastērion*] through his blood." (Rom. 3.24–5.) Christ was the Paschal Lamb immolated for us. (1 Cor. 5.7.) In virtue of the blood of Christ shed on the Cross (Col. 1.14,20), our sins have been wiped out (Eph. 1.7: Titus 2.14), and we have been reconciled with God. (Eph. 2.13.) All the effects of redemption are attributed either directly to the blood of Christ,[13] or to his violent death.[14]

Christ's death was not only a reparation for sin but also the inauguration of a new life in which the relationships between God and man have been changed. The risen Christ is the cornerstone of the new order of salvation, and it is in this perspective that the deepest significance of the Resurrection is seen. Paul does consider other aspects of the mystery: it is the starting-point of the apostolic preaching (1 Cor. 15.14–17), the exemplar of our bodily resurrection (1 Cor. 15) and the type of our resurrection from sin (Rom. 6.3–11), but these are overshadowed by his conception of the Resurrection as an essential element in the work of redemption and, together with the Ascension, inseparable from the Passion. This is the understanding that all the Greek and many of the Latin Fathers have of the famous affirmation of Rom. 4.25, "[Christ] was delivered up for our sins and rose

again for our justification."[15] The Resurrection
has a salvific value—a fact which appears only
natural when we remember that Christ did not
become incarnate, die, and rise again for his
own sake, but in his capacity as Redeemer.

The life restored to Christ by his resurrection
was not that which he laid down on the Cross.
(Rom. 6.9–10.) Through his resurrection Christ
inaugurated a new mode of existence, that of
"Son of God *in power*". (Rom. 1.4.) According
to Cerfaux this is "the true efficacious life of
Christ, the Saviour and sanctifier . . . Everything
preceding the resurrection from the dead is only
the establishment of a humanity, insertion into
the human race and into history, with a pejorative nuance."[16] In 1 Cor. 15.45 Paul declares that
by his resurrection the new Adam became "a
life-giving spirit", that is, by his resurrection the
humanity of Christ passed, not only from a cor-
poreal state to a spiritual state (as will ours), but
also to a state that is a principle of spiritual life.
By his resurrection Christ was established "Son
of God in power" (Rom. 1.4), i.e., constituted in
his messianic function as Saviour with the power
proportioned to such a role.[17] Even before the
Resurrection Christ was endowed with the fullness of divine life but did not possess it in his
role of living and life-giving Head. In the divine
plan, the spiritual existence of his glorified

humanity was the necessary condition for the bestowal of this new life on his members.[18]

Insertion Into the Salvific Plan

Christ in "giving himself a ransom for all" (1 Tim. 2.6) provided indisputable testimony to the universality of God's salvific will and to the reality of his desire "that all men be saved and come to the knowledge of truth". (1 Tim. 2.4.) But does this mean that the individual members of the human race benefit passively, that the riches of the Passion are bestowed on them automatically without effort on their part? A text such as Titus 2.11, "The grace of God has appeared bringing salvation to all men", might well incline us to reply in the affirmative, but there are others which give us pause and Paul's teaching on baptism definitely shows that his reply is negative.

> According to the grace of God bestowed upon me, like a skilful master-builder *I laid the foundation* and now another is building thereon ... Other foundation can no man lay than *that which is already laid* which is Jesus Christ. [1 Cor. 3.10–11]

The object of Paul's preaching, the foundation-stone which he lays, is Jesus Christ. (1 Cor. 1.23.) Yet before his preaching that foundation was already laid. Despite the apparent inconsistency both statements are needed in order to get at the truth. The foundation is already laid in so far as Christ died and rose. He is now the life-giving Spirit (1 Cor. 15.45), the meritorious and efficient cause of all grace. Grace can flow from no other. He is the Head of the Body, which is the Church (Col. 1.18), the sole and inexhaustible source of all its riches. Yet that foundation has still to be laid in so far as the individual has yet to enter into community of life with the risen Christ, for through Christ's death he is only potentially justified. Consequently, as far as each individual is concerned, the mystery is still being worked out, and will, in fact, be brought to full perfection only with the Second Coming of Christ, his "epiphany of glory". (Titus 2.13.)[19]

Perfect absorption of the individual into the mystery takes place through baptism, which, in conferring the spirit of adoption (Titus 3.6: Rom. 8.15), transforms his nature into "a nature in the image of his Son's" (Rom. 8.29), and so fulfils the design of him who "predestined us to be adopted as his sons through Jesus Christ". (Eph. 1.5.) Without faith, however, baptism is void, producing no fruit; and without preaching there can be no faith. Hence, in order to bring out preaching's central position as the divinely established bridge linking the subjective and the objective orders of redemption, we must briefly examine Paul's teaching on the effects of baptism, then show baptism's essential dependence on faith, and finally, establish the relationship of both baptism and faith in preaching.

THE EFFECTS OF BAPTISM

Baptism, for Paul, is both an end and a beginning, a liberation and an inauguration. Its action, which draws its power from the death of Christ (Eph. 5.25–26: Titus 3.5), both destroys and vivifies.

It destroys the "old man" by destroying his "body of sin" (Rom. 6.6: Eph. 4.22: Col. 3.9), by stripping off "the body of the flesh". (Col. 2.11.) "Flesh" (*sarx*) here does not denote human nature as such,[20] but human nature as infected by the gangrene of concupiscence and dominated by evil,[21] the prey of passions (Rom. 7.5: Gal. 5.24) and desires (Rom. 8.7) hostile to God, and so imperious as to be termed a "will". (Eph. 2.3.) The stripping off of the flesh is possible only because it is a sharing in what has already been done by Christ on the Cross. Jesus' death can be called his "circumcision" because the Crucifixion was the real and complete laying aside of the flesh of which circumcision is the partial symbol.[22] By dying Christ divested himself of his flesh (Col. 2.15); in baptism "our old man is crucified with him". (Rom. 6.6.) Consequently, we too are stripped of our flesh. (Rom.

7.5: 8.9: Col. 2.11.) Since this closes off the avenue of approach, we are in effect "dead to sin" (Rom. 6.2–11), no longer subject to its dominion. (Rom. 6.12,14.)

But baptism does much more than restore human nature to the position of favour it enjoyed before the fall of one man gave sin entry into the world. (Rom. 5.12.) Through a death similar to his own we are made one with Christ (Rom. 6.5: Gal. 3.28) and, in consequence, participate in the new life to which he rose. (Col. 2.13.) We are put into vital contact with the Holy Spirit, who, through "the waters of regeneration and renewal" (Titus 3.5), not only purifies and sanctifies us (Eph. 5.25–26), but actually takes up residence within us. (Rom. 5.5: 2 Cor. 1.22: Titus 3.6.) Possessors, therefore, of the Spirit of Christ (Rom. 8.9–10), we can be truly said to have "put on Christ". (Gal. 3.27.) The difference between the baptized, a "son of God" (Gal. 3.26), and the erstwhile "stranger and enemy" (Col. 1.21) is so great that the passage from one state to the other is presented by Paul not as a change but as a new creation (2 Cor. 5.17).

The importance of baptism for the individual must not cause us to overlook its social implications. In Eph. 5.25–6 it is the Church that is considered as the subject of baptism; baptism is the birth of the body of Christ in its members. "In one Spirit we were all baptized into one body." (1 Cor. 12.13.) Baptism is the "new circumcision of the Christ" (Col. 2.11), and thus, by implication, the rite of initiation into the new Israel of God, the Church.[23]

Preaching, faith and baptism are closely associated in Eph. 1.13–14:

> In him also, having heard the word of truth, the Gospel of your salvation and having believed it, you were sealed by the Holy Spirit of promise . . .

Here that which precedes the impression of the "seal of the Spirit" is expressed by the two aorists "having heard" and "having believed". If the sealing refers to the post-baptismal gift of the Spirit (i.e., confirmation) we should expect to find in the preceding words an allusion to baptism, since in the context it is a question of the insertion of the individual into the glorious scheme of salvation previously described. (Eph. 1.3–12.) Instead we find verbs designating the two acts of those who present themselves to become Christians. The act of sealing, therefore, belongs to a baptismal context (compare Acts 2.41: 8.12–14) and the fact that it follows the two preliminary acts of the Christian-to-be makes it very probable that the impression of the seal is to be understood as a reference to the sacrament of baptism.[24] This passage, then, establishes a chronological order between faith and baptism, but tells us nothing of their precise relationship.

The form their interaction takes is suggested in the sixth chapter of the Epistle to the Romans. The first part of this chapter (vv. 1–11) concerns baptism and concludes with the words, "Consider yourselves as dead to sin and as living for God in Jesus Christ". (v. 11.) But the very real possibility of falling back into sin remains. Consequently, the second part (vv. 12–23) centres on the idea of service: Christians must hold themselves always at God's disposal and not give their allegiance anew to sin. The notion of service immediately evokes that of obedience. Baptism is the entry into a new service and must, in consequence, include an act of obedience.[25] Verse 17 brings this out clearly: "You obeyed wholeheartedly that form of doctrine to which you were delivered." Genuine acceptance of the mystery preached implies the desire to satisfy the exigencies it imposes. An acceptance of the Gospel which does not include a desire for baptism is not true faith. The faith that justifies does so because of the perfection of its surrender to the manifested will of Christ—"He that believes *and is baptized* shall be saved." (Mark 16.16.) The Christian is justified by faith because he is, as a believer, crucified with Christ (Gal. 2.16–19):

> You are all children of God *by faith* in Christ Jesus, *because* [*gar*] as many of you as *have been baptized* in Christ have put on Christ. [Gal. 3.26–7]

The saving power of baptism is not given it by the faith of the recipient; however, his attitude of entire submission is a condition *sine qua non* that the sacrament produce its effects.

> You were buried with him in baptism, in which also you were raised to life through faith in the power of God who raised him from the dead. [Col. 2.12; cf. Eph. 4.5][26]

Only those who believe in the resurrection of Christ can participate in its fruits.

The acceptance of a doctrine is conditional upon its presentation, and the dependence of faith on preaching could hardly be expressed more clearly or succinctly than in the Epistle to the Romans:

> How could they believe in him whom they have not heard...? Hence faith comes through hearing [the Gospel]. [Rom. 10.14,17; cf. 1 Cor. 15.1–2][27]

The place of preaching in the divine plan is as essential as the death and resurrection of Christ

In him [Christ] he chose us before the foundation of the world that we might be holy and blameless in his sight in love. He predestined us to be adopted as his sons through Jesus Christ, according to the good pleasure of his will, unto the praise of the glory of his grace, wherewith he hath made us gracious *in the Well-Beloved.* [Eph. 1.3–6; cf. Col. 1.13]

Thus, man can be the object of God's love only as a consequence of, and by participating in, the love of God for his Son. One has only to read the description of the plan of salvation in Eph. 1.3–14 to recognize the significance of the repeated "in Christ" (or its equivalents; *vv.* 3,4,6, 11,12). The motivating force behind the divine plan for the salvation of mankind is the eternal love of the Father for the Son.[5]

The ultimate finality of the divine plan is just as sublime as its conception and motive. God acquires nothing by his love-inspired activity, but that which it achieves is "to the praise of the glory of his grace". (Eph. 1.6,12,14.) Every step in the process of man's salvation, from conception to execution, is due to God. (Phil. 1.6.) All possibility of conceit on man's part is therefore excluded: "Let him who boasts, boast in the Lord." (1 Cor. 1.31: 2 Cor. 10.17.) God deliberately chooses the foolish and weak things of the world, the things that are despised, the things that are not, "lest any flesh should vaunt itself before God". (1 Cor. 1.29.) The very existence of believers in Christ (1 Cor. 1.30) is, therefore, the manifestation of the divine power and glory:

> He brought us to life with Christ . . . and raised us up and seated us in Christ Jesus in the heavens to show in ages to come the surpassing riches of his grace, through his kindness to us in Christ Jesus. [Eph. 2.4–7]

In raising and glorifying Christ, God exalts those who have their very being in him. In virtue of the reality of their spiritual life, Christians are already seated with Christ in glory.[6] They are for all ages the proof of the "surpassing riches" of the divine grace. As constituting the Church they make known

> . . . to the principalities and powers in the heavens the manifold wisdom of God, as exhibited in the eternal plan he has brought to pass in Christ Jesus. [Eph. 3.10–11]

The glorious (mystical) presence of the believers in heaven is the concrete realization of the salvific plan. The celestial powers were not aware of the existence of "this mystery which from all ages had been hidden in God" (*v.* 9), otherwise they would not have moved men to crucify Christ. (1 Cor. 2.8.) But the physical death of Christ is the virtual formation of his body which

ciple, embodied centuries before in the choice
of his people:

> It was not because you [Israel] are the largest
> of all nations that the Lord set his heart on you
> and chose you, for you are really the smallest
> of all nations. [Deut. 7.7–8; cf. 1 Cor. 1.26–9]

The divine decisions are above and beyond all
human motivation. Faced with the grandeur of
God's design, Paul could have taken refuge
behind the words of the Deutero-Isaias whose
teaching he knew so well: "My thoughts are not
your thoughts, nor my ways your ways" (Isa.
55.8),[3] and so have abandoned all hope of
accounting for the divine decision. But his heart
saw the one motive possible: love.

> But God who is rich in mercy, by reason of his
> immense [*pollē*] love wherewith he loved us
> even when we were dead in our transgressions,
> brought us to life with Christ—by grace you
> are saved—and raised us up and seated us in
> the heavens in Christ Jesus. [Eph. 2.4–6]

The force of the phrase "by reason of his immense love wherewith he loved us" is to be
noted. To redouble a verb by the addition of a
noun or participle of the same root is a Semitic
mode of expressing the superlative. "To love
with love" is to love intensely and completely,[4]
but not even the superlative satisfies Paul. He
adds the adjective *pollē*, which is really untrans-

latable because it can be understood either quantitatively (meaning "vast" or "immense") or qualitatively (meaning "strong" or "powerful"). Words simply cannot adequately express the reality towards which Paul's mind gropes. All he can hope to do, then, is to evoke some idea of the limitless riches of a love beyond human comprehension. The very infinity of this love indicates that it is not drawn by our goodness, but its gratuity—"by grace you are saved" —is thrown into clear relief by a description of the state of humanity before the divine love was manifested:

> We too at one time were all living in indulgence of the desires of our flesh. We were fulfilling the promptings of the flesh and of our minds and were by nature children of wrath like the rest. [Eph. 2.3; cf. Rom. 3.10]

As "children of disobedience" (v. 2) we merited God's anger not his love. The use in Eph. 2.4 of the aorist "he loved" with its connotation of a precise moment of time, is a sign that Paul, as might be expected, conceives this love in its supreme concrete manifestation, Christ. (Eph. 5.1–2.)

But Christ is not only the expression of God's love for us; he is in a sense also its origin. Only in Christ are we the objects of God's saving love:

revelation are in a sense but two aspects of the same reality. Considered in itself the plan of salvation is a mystery, since, besides the idea of secrecy, it evokes the impenetrable depths of God's wisdom; considered as made known, it is the Gospel through which men are saved. The revelation of the mystery is itself part of the mystery.

Broadly speaking, therefore, the matter of this chapter falls into two main sections. The first consists in an outline of God's salvific design as an objective reality, that is, its motivation, finality and means of execution. The second section is concerned with the individual's contact with the saving Christ. It will be seen that the initial contact is effected by preaching, which is the bridge between the objective and the subjective orders of redemption. Preaching's pivotal role in God's plan for humanity is thrown into fuller relief by a concluding section which underlines Paul's conviction that even in the old dispensation salvation consisted in a personal response to a divine call.

The Plan of Salvation

MOTIVATION AND FINALITY

If there is a single passage in his epistles which expresses the essence of Paul's doctrine and sets

all the other elements of his thought in proper
perspective, it is perhaps the following:

> For us, one God, the Father, from whom all
> things and we for him, and one Lord, Jesus,
> through whom all things and we through
> him. [1 Cor. 8.6][2]

God is the Alpha and the Omega of everything
that is, the source of its being and perfection,
the end toward which it tends and for which it
was made. Associated with the Father in his
creative act is Jesus, "in whom have been
created all things". (Col. 1.16.) The reiterated
"we" and the appellative "Father", indicate that
Paul's attention is not concentrated exclusively
on the material order. His thought is moving,
perhaps half unconsciously, on the plane of the
new creation in grace. (1 Cor. 1.30.) The transition is all the more natural because in the order
of grace the same priority must be attributed to
the divine initiative as in the material order.
The decision to save men, to renew the creation
that left his hands as "good" (Gen. 1.12,18,21 etc.)
but which had been corrupted by the ravages of
sin (Rom. 5.12), was made by God alone in
perfect freedom. He owed it to no-one. Paul's
consciousness of the entire gratuity of the divine
action in his own regard (1 Cor. 15.9–10: 1 Tim.
1.12–17) heightened his awareness of this prin-

men. The light thus shed on the role of preaching immediately provoked the questions, What is the preacher? Is he given any divine aid in the exercise of his function? And if so, what is the immediate effect of this grace? (Ch. 2.) Having seen that the grace accorded him is the identification of his word with God's in view of man's salvation, the next step is to inquire into the relationship of the preacher's ministry to that of Christ. (Ch. 3.) Paul's view that his mission is a prolongation of Christ's led naturally to an examination of those passages in which he attributes a real efficacy to the word of God. (Ch. 4.) At this stage the question arose: If the word is really efficacious through being endowed with the redeeming power of Christ, why does it in fact sometimes fail to save? This necessitated an analysis of the factors that condition the efficacy of preaching, both from the side of the proposal of the word and from the side of its reception. (Ch. 5.) A final section rounds off our inquiry by examining Paul's global view of preaching as a liturgical act. (Ch. 6.)

It is for those who read them to judge whether the following pages represent faithfully the thought of St Paul. If they do, the greater part of the credit must go to the great Pauline scholar under whose guidance they were written, Father Ceslaus Spicq, O.P., of the University of Fribourg. This is mentioned not to involve him in the defects of this study or to make him in any way responsible for its inadequacies, but simply as a tribute to his generosity and as a gesture of gratitude for his penetrating and always constructive criticism.

Most sincere thanks are also due to all those who have helped me in so many ways, but especially to Sister M. Keverne, O.P., of the Institut de Hautes Études, Fribourg, whose patient and careful revision of the manuscript has placed not only the author but his readers deeply in her debt.

put to him are those which arise naturally from his own teaching, not those suggested by the voluminous current literature on the theology of preaching, and our whole concern has been to ensure the authenticity of the emergent pattern of thought.

For the sake of clarity, it has been thought preferable to limit our investigation to Paul's conception of that preaching whose object is the conversion of non-believers. This is commonly termed missionary or kerygmatic preaching. The use of the latter terminology is entirely legitimate, for, of all the thirty-two verbs employed by the New-Testament writers to signify preaching, *kērussō* is in itself the most apt to characterize the proclamation of the Gospel to a non-Christian world. Yet it will not be out of place to point out that in the Pauline writings it is not a technical term for this form of preaching, for besides denoting preaching to unbelievers, it is used of preaching within the community, of heterodox preaching, and even of Jewish teaching. This underlines the danger of attempting to classify passages as referring to missionary or to catechetical preaching exclusively on the basis of the terms employed. The criterion must be much more comprehensive, and is finely suggested by J. J. von Allmen: "There is a preaching which leads from unbelief to baptism and a preaching which leads from baptism to the

Lord's Table; there is a preaching which insists on the decision to be taken and a preaching which recalls this decision in order to ensure its permanence; there is a preaching of conversion to Christ and a preaching of growth in Christ."*
Very often, because of the heterogeneous character of audiences, the distinction of these two types of preaching depends entirely on the individual hearer, and so, much of what is said in the following pages will be applicable to catechetical preaching. Nonetheless, this study is formally concerned only with the theological structure of that proclamation of the word of God whose primary object is the genesis of faith.

The most fundamental point to be established was Paul's estimation of the value of preaching. This made it imperative to ascertain the place he assigns to it in the divine scheme of salvation. (Ch. 1.) To elaborate the Pauline vision of the plan of salvation in all its dimensions would need a volume to itself, for salvation is the master-concept of the theology of St Paul. Consequently, while attempting to preserve the proportions of the whole, we have had to content ourselves with highlighting the elements most relevant to preaching, showing it to be the point of contact between the objective and the subjective orders of redemption, the first conduit through which the merits of Christ's passion are channelled to

* *Verbum Caro* 9 (1955), 113–14.

renewal at all, and is in practice neither effective nor lasting. True renewal must begin with a profound appreciation of the nature of preaching, a realization of just what preaching is. Only theological reflection can give this awareness, for preaching is a saving event, not a display of human eloquence. The form this reflection should take is determined for us by the Holy Spirit. Not, however, in the form of a private inspiration. As Father Charles Davis recently pointed out, an active receptiveness to the Spirit, which should be the condition of every Christian, includes an attentiveness to his action in the Church. That action, as manifested by the movements stirring within the Church today, indicates that all renewal must be a rediscovery and a recapturing of the pattern, structure and ideals that existed at the beginning. In other words, it must be effected by a return to the sources. And when it is a question of a renewal of preaching no further apology need be made for an effort to share the insights of the preacher par excellence, St Paul.

We leave aside the peripheral problems of the Apostle's preaching method, and of the content of his sermons. These, moreover, have already been adequately studied, by Bultmann (*Der Stil der Paulinischen Predigt*, Gottingen, 1910), for example, and by Dodd (*The Apostolic Preaching and its Developments*, London, 1951). The question we put to Paul is simply, What is preaching? There is no explicit evidence that he ever put the question to himself, at least in this form, but from this it cannot be inferred that any effort to extract an answer to it from his writings is foredoomed to failure. He never treats explicitly of the activity that was his life because his mission was to preach Christ, not to speculate on his own prerogatives and power. Nonetheless, because in order to fulfil this mission he had to defend his right to preach, his epistles contain many hints of his understanding of the role of the preacher in God's design to save humanity. Our task, then, is comparable to that of the artist who builds up a mosaic from many pieces of stone, each with its own colour and texture. We have to build up a concept from numerous apparently unrelated "asides". The pitfalls inherent in this procedure are obvious. Because the need for this study arises out of a contemporary situation there is the danger of imposing our problematic on the Apostle, of assuming that our centres of interest were also his, whereas its value should lie in a confrontation of the authentic thought of Paul and the existent situation. We have tried to avoid this distortion by refusing to *impose* any system on his thought. The systematization necessarily involved in our presentation evolved from meditation on his writings. The successive questions

THE PLACE OF PREACHING IN THE PLAN OF SALVATION

PAUL speaks of the divine plan to save men as a "mystery" (Rom. 16.25–6: 1 Cor. 2.7–10: Eph. 1.8–10: Col. 1.26–7)—a mystery meditated in eternity in the wisdom of God (1 Cor. 2.7: Eph. 3.10) and for untold ages known to him alone. Knowledge of it was not shared by any other being, human or celestial. Only as God began to lay the groundwork for its execution was man permitted to perceive, very dimly, its outlines. What he saw found expression in the prophetic writings of the Old Testament (Rom. 16.26), but the plan had already been put into operation when God shared his knowledge fully with the humanity it was to benefit. In the Epistle to the Ephesians Paul includes himself among those privileged to share this knowledge in a special way:

> Surely you have heard of the gracious commission of God bestowed on me for you, how by revelation the mystery was made known to me, as I have already briefly written. From this, when you read it, you can perceive my insight into this mystery of Christ which was

not made known to the sons of man as it has now been revealed to his holy apostles and prophets in the Spirit. [Eph. 3.2–5]

The revelation of the mystery is not given for the private advantage of the recipients but rather in view of a special duty they have to perform. In Paul's case this is

... to announce to the Gentiles the unsearchable riches of Jesus Christ and to show clearly to all the dispensation of the mystery which has been hidden from ages in the God who created all things. [Eph. 3.8–9]

His task involves the communication to others of the content of the mystery, but over and above that, he has to show how the plan is being carried out.[1] To the Ephesians he says:

The Gentiles are admitted to the same heritage, and to the same body and are beneficiaries of the same promise in Jesus Christ through the Gospel of which I was made the servant. [Eph. 3.6]

The preaching of the Gospel is, therefore, the instrument whereby the Gentiles are admitted to the heritage of the Jews and, through Christ, have access in one Spirit to the Father. (Eph. 2.11–18.) The plan of salvation is not merely revealed in preaching, it is thereby actuated and brought to fulfilment. The mystery and its is the Church. (Eph. 2.14–16: Col. 1.22.)[7] Made visible on earth through the activity of the Spirit, this body, now mystically seated at the right hand of God and one day to be really present in the heavens, is the manifestation of the unsearchable depths of God's wisdom, of the plenitude of his love and of the infinity of his power. The very existence and life of the Church *is* the praise of his glory, the glory of his grace.[8] The Church is, thus, an eternal hymn of praise. And this is the ultimate end that God set before himself in the conception and execution of the plan of salvation.

CHRIST: THE MEANS OF SALVATION

Since the divine plan was conceived in love it is not surprising to find the first step in its execution presented as an "epiphany of love":

But when the *chrēstotēs* and the *philanthropia* of God our Saviour appeared—not as the result of the works of righteousness which we did ourselves, but as the effect of his mercy—he saved us by the water of regeneration and renewal in the Holy Spirit whom he poured out richly upon us through Jesus Christ our Saviour. [Titus 3.4–6]

The love of the Father became effective at a precise moment of history, characterized elsewhere as "the fullness of time" (Gal. 4.4: Eph.

1.10), and under a double form: *chrēstotēs* is
goodness in the sense of disinterested benevolence, having overtones of generosity and liber-
ality;[9] *philanthropia*, literally "love of man", is
here practically synonymous with *chrēstotēs*, but
accentuates the universality of the divine favour
and directs our thoughts to the precise concrete
expression of the Father's love, the incarnation
of Christ.[10] "When the time had matured God
sent his Son made from a woman." (Gal. 4.4.)

For Paul, Christ is always the Redeemer, and
while aware of the three stages of his existence,
viz., his pre-existence as Son of God, his mortal
life, and his glorious existence as Son of God in
power after the Resurrection, it is to this third
that he devotes his attention. Christ's terrestrial
life counted for little in Paul's estimation, though
from this it cannot be concluded that he in any
way tried to attenuate the reality of Christ's
humanity. 1 Tim. 2.4–6 shows that Christ was
the one possible mediator between God and man
precisely in virtue of his two natures. However,
as this passage also shows, the most important
event of Christ's life was his passion. Apart from
the Incarnation this is the only "incident" preceding the Resurrection that Paul considers
worthy of note.

Paul's understanding of the position of Christ
vis-à-vis the human race of which he became a
member must be gleaned from a careful co-

3.6). The preaching is addressed *to all* (1 Thess.
2.16: 1 Cor. 9.22), yet all who hear it, contrary to
what might be expected, are not termed
"called". It would seem, therefore, that for those
who do not respond, the Gospel is not a "call"
since Paul regards as "called" only those who
obey it. It follows then, that the factor which
makes preaching a "call" for some and not for
others must be extrinsic to the actual proclamation of the good news. Two texts show it to be
a divine choice. The first declares:

> We know that for them that love him God
> works all things together unto good for them
> that are the called according to his plan. For
> those whom he hath foreknown [*proegnō*],
> them he hath predestined [*proōrisen*] to bear
> a nature in the image of his Son's that he
> should be first-born among many brethren,
> and those whom he hath predestined, them he
> hath also called, and those whom he hath
> called, them he hath also justified, and those
> whom he hath justified, them he hath also
> glorified. [Rom. 8.28–30]

Paul here summarizes the plan of salvation in
five acts: foreknowledge, predestination, call,
justification and glorification. Just as in Rom.
11.2, where it is a question of Israel, ("foreknowledge" appears here as the beginning of a salvific
process) The idea of speculative anticipatory

knowledge—even though this is the most common connotation of the verb *proginōskō* and its substantive *prognōsis*[34]—is entirely out of place here.[35] Allo has well shown that when *proginōskō* has God for its subject, its object is always the elect, and that it is a question of a loving preferential knowledge.[36] The meaning of "those whom he hath foreknown" is almost "those whom he hath chosen", as Father Lemonnyer's translation brings out, "ceux sur qui son regard s'est arrêté d'avance".[37] Given this meaning of "foreknowledge", "predestination" can only accentuate the voluntary element implied and make the idea more explicit by determining the purpose of the choice. The important point for our purpose is to note that the "call" is consequent on this choice, so that only those who are chosen are called. The call is essentially the efficacious externalization of a divine choice. Only the "elect" are constituted the "called" by preaching. This is even more patently apparent in the second text.

> God chose you from the beginning for salvation in sanctification of the Spirit and credence of the truth. It is to this he called you by our gospel, unto the possession of the glory of our Lord Jesus Christ. [2 Thess. 2.12–13]

Thus, the election of the Thessalonians is manifested and made effective in the preaching of the

Gospel. Their full obedience to the truth is, for Paul, the sure sign of their election by God. (1 Thess. 1.4–5.)

Hence, not preaching as such, but preaching as the intimation of a choice made from all eternity in Christ Jesus (Eph. 1.4), is the point of contact between the objective and subjective orders of redemption. It puts individuals into contact with the merits of Christ's passion only in so far as it embodies an eternal call addressed to them.

In responding to God's summons "the called" (*klētoi*) are united with one another in the Church (*ekklēsia*). Paul addresses a letter "to the Church of God [*tē ekklēsia tou theou*] at Corinth, to them who are saints through divine call [*klētois hagiois*]". (1 Cor. 1.2.) Were etymology the only argument one would be tempted to attribute the constitution of the *ekklēsia* solely to the *klēsis* (call)—after the example of the Greek *dēmos* (assembly), whose convocation was currently expressed by the phrase (*ek*)*kalein eis ekklēsian*.[38] There is a certain amount of truth in this, but Paul did not give the name *ekklēsia* to the communities he came into contact with because they sprang into being through preaching. The term *ekklēsia* was familiar to Jewish converts in the Septuagint translation of the Hebrew *qahal* (*Yahweh*) which designated the people of Israel as the "convocation" or "assembly" of God;[39] it was the name given to those whom Yahweh called from the servitude of Egypt to be his holy people.[40] With the recognition of Jesus as the Messias, the embodiment of all the truest aspirations of Israel, the titles and privileges of Israel were assumed quite naturally to be the right of the new society he called into existence. On becoming a Christian Paul would have found *ekklēsia* in use as a designation of the primitive community,[41] and would, in turn, have employed it as a title of the communities he himself founded, in which were assembled the true (spiritual) descendants of Abraham. (Rom. 4.16–21: 9.6–13.) However, the *ekklēsia* is not constituted by those who simply believe. As has been seen the constitutive act of the body of Christ, which is the *ekklēsia*, is baptism. But the *ekklēsia* may be considered constituted by the *klēsis* (call) in so far as this call has for its object not merely an internal assent, but an assent expressed in submission to the rite of baptism.

THE CONTINUITY OF THE SALVIFIC PLAN

Mgr. Cerfaux has remarked that Paul never abandoned the religion of his fathers and that had he been questioned as to his Jewish orthodoxy he would not have known what to make of the inquiry.[42] This "aside" reveals a profound understanding of how conscious Paul was of the unity and continuity of the divine plan, points on which he meditated with agonizing intensity when he faced the perplexing and painful problem of the incredulity of his Jewish brethren.

In the long chapters (9–11) of the Epistle to the Romans Paul makes it quite clear that even though he is "the minister of the *new* covenant" (2 Cor. 3.6), he is not preaching a new religion destined to supplant Judaism.[43] He insists, at the very outset, that it is not "as though the work of God has failed". (Rom. 9.6.) "God has not rejected his people whom he foreknew" (11.2), "because the gifts and the call of God are irrevocable." (11.29.) Accordingly he emphasizes that Christianity is not an entirely new entity— it is the homogeneous continuation of Judaism. The pagans are the wild shoot grafted onto the cultivated olive (11.24) whose root bears them. (11.18.) This cultivated olive is the faithful remnant (cf. 11.5), the qualitative Israel (11.17) and with it the new converts form one body.

Hence it would seem that the New Covenant, of which Paul has been made the herald, should be taken, not as something completely new, but as new in the sense of Jer. 31.31–3:

> Behold the days shall come, saith the Lord, and I will make a new covenant with the house of Israel and with the house of Juda, not according to the covenant which I made

with their fathers in the day that I took them by the hand to bring them out of the land of Egypt . . . this shall be the covenant that I will make with the house of Israel after those days, saith the Lord, I will give my law in their bowels and I will write it in their hearts.

The New Covenant is here opposed to that of Sinai—but not in such a way as to discredit the Old Covenant completely. The Law which is the norm of the Covenant is no longer something purely extrinsic; it is interior to man, being written on his heart, or, as Paul will say, "on tablets of flesh". (2 Cor. 3.3.) The New Covenant appears not as a repudiation of the Sinaitic alliance but as its renewal in a more perfect form.[44]

In a similar way the Sinaitic Covenant is envisaged as a ratification of that enacted with Abraham. (Gal. 3.12–18.)[45] Hence it would seem that when Paul speaks of "covenants" (Rom. 9.4; cf. Eph. 2.12) he has in mind not a series of acts bearing on different objects but a single covenant continually renewed.[46] He does focus attention on the three high points of this continuing renewal—the call of Abraham (Gal. 3.16,18), the giving of the Law on Sinai (2 Cor. 3.6,14), and the messianic era (Gal. 4.24: Eph. 2.12)[47]—but it is clear that for him at least these different stages of the Covenant are only successive manifestations of the same divine decision.

This decision bears on the essential element in subjective justification: the individual is justified through faith. That salvation comes through faith alone and not as a reward due to any human achievement was irresistibly borne in on Paul by the experience of his own conversion. But on rereading the Old Testament in the light of this new knowledge, he soon saw the consistency of the divine pattern as manifested in the three great stages of the religious history of the world: the era before the Law, the era of the Law and the era of Christ.

For Paul the era before the Law is dominated by the figure of Abraham who "believed God and it was counted to him for justification". (Rom. 4.3,9,22: Gal. 3.6.) What Abraham believed was a promise made to him by God. The "call" in his case was issued without benefit of any human intermediary by Yahweh himself, whom Paul will term "he who calls". (Rom. 9.12.) Abraham's initial response, however, had to be maintained. Hence there came another call, a trial to test his faith, and once again in the Patriarch's desire to conform himself to the divine will God found the response he desired. (Gen. 22.1ff.)

In a later age the Law and the Prophets spoke of salvation through faith. (Rom. 3.22: 10.1–21.) Abraham's vocation had its parallel in that of Israel at Sinai.[48] There each individual was called

to ratify personally the response of Abraham—
to put himself as unreservedly into the hands of
God as Abraham had. The Law expressed the
conditions of this gift of self[49] and implied the
necessity for its continued renewal. (Exod.
19.4–6.) Each generation was called upon freely
to choose Yahweh. (Jos. 24.14ff.) The divine
initiative was the fundamental "call" but it was
brought to the attention of individuals of succeeding generations by the reading of the Law
and, particularly, by the preaching of the prophets who were sent to remind the people of the
exigencies of the divine love and of the punishment consequent on lack of faith.

The great prophet of faith is Isaias, who is
three times cited by Paul with reference to the
incredulity of Israel. (Isa. 10.22 = Rom. 9.27:
Isa. 28.16 = Rom. 9.33 and 10.11: Isa. 53.1 = Rom.
10.16.) In Isaias the idea of faith is closely associated with that of the Remnant,[50] as indeed it
is in Paul, who finds in the doctrine of the Remnant the principle of solution of the problem of
the salvation of Israel. An important text is that
quoted by the Apostle in Rom. 9.33: "Behold I
place in Sion a stumbling-stone and a rock of
offence; and whoever believes in him shall not
be confounded." Its interpretation is not made
any easier by the fact that it is a rather free combination of passages from two distinct prophecies
(Isa. 8.14 and 28.16). Chapter 28 *v.* 16 sounds a

note of hope in a prophecy of doom and Paul's substitution of "a stumbling-stone and a rock of offence" for the original "a tried stone, a corner-stone, a precious stone founded in the foundation" does nothing to falsify the general sense. Faith is the quality of the Messias that renders him apt to be the foundation-stone (cf. Isa. 11.5) of a community (the Remnant) made up of those whose faith is similar to his own.[51] He is a magnet drawing all those whose lives are polarized on God. But there are others who consider their lives their own and who rely on their own un-aided strength. For these he occasions the supreme moment of truth, the decision that is their ruin. Not having faith "they stumble and fall and are broken in pieces". (8.15.)

In virtue of his divine mission the prophet himself also had this capacity to provoke the crucial decision. In one characteristic and highly significant passage he recounts his visit to King Achaz on the express orders of Yahweh to remind him that his trust should be placed not in politi-cal alliances but in God: "If you do not believe, you shall not stand." (Isa. 7.9.) The overtones of the use in this short verse of the same Hebrew verb first in the *Hifil* and then in the *Nifal*, can only be brought out by a paraphrase—"If you do not believe, you detach yourself from your sole real support."[52] The very subsistence of Israel as a nation, therefore, is intrinsically

bound up with faith. Security can be bought
only at this price.

In both these passages, as always in Isaias,
faith is the attitude of him whose confidence and
trust in Yahweh finds expression in complete
reliance on divine assistance. This is the response
demanded by the divine promise. Those who
accept the prophet's reiteration of this promise
are saved; those who refuse it, by that fact, cut
themselves off from the true Israel.[53] Salvation
then, does not consist merely in belonging to a
community chosen by God. It demands, and
always did demand, a personal act of faith on the
part of each individual.

Hence, Paul is fully justified in seeing salvation through faith as the consistent element in
all stages of the history of God's dealings with
men. Faith is always the response to a divine
call. In the Pauline epistles it is always God
who calls. He can do so directly and immediately,
as in the case of Paul's own vocation, but where
he so wills his call is transmitted to men by his
chosen representatives; this is the normal procedure, both in the Old and New Testaments, as
far as the ordinary individual is concerned.

The Old-Testament concept of the function
and nature of preaching seems very close to that
of Paul. In reality they are similar only in so
far as both are related to faith, which is a key
factor in the divine plan. What can never be

overlooked is the fact that while the Prophets preached the messianic *promises*, the Apostles preach the *realization* of those promises in Christ. This naturally implies a tremendous difference in the whole atmosphere of preaching. The appeal of the Prophets leaves one with the impression of a despairing cry, because even though the man of good will responded and committed himself to a definite attitude toward God, he was not given the power necessary to maintain this effort.[54] On the contrary, Paul can speak of the triumph of the Gospel (2 Cor. 2.14) because it is a word of power, a divine force (Rom. 1.16) that communicates itself to those who receive it.[55]

NOTES

1. The presence of *oikonomia* with *mystērion* is a little disconcerting, and only fits in if taken in the sense of "dispensation in act". "The mystery is that indicated in *v.* 6, and that which was arranged or ordered as to the carrying out of this is the *oikonomia tou mystēriou*." (Abbott.)

2. The ingenuity of commentators has been much exercised in supplying verbs fully to express the thought condensed in these crisp phrases. The various efforts are discussed by F. M. Sagnard ("A propos de 1 Cor. 8.6" *ETL*, 26 (1950), 54–8), who points out that some falsify the sense by inserting a static verb, "to be", because here, in a nominal or pronominal phrase, the prepositions retain a force very similar to their original adverbial value and indicate a movement. Spicq and Leitzmann concur for the first member and translate: "For us [there is only] one God, the Father, from whom

all things [come] and towards whom we [go]." In the second member they content themselves with "to be", but Sagnard, in the light of Eph. 4.9–10 (cf. H. Schlier, *Le Temps de l'Église*, Tournai (1961), 177), preserves the idea of movement: "... One Lord, Jesus Christ, through whom [come] all things, and through whom we [go]". The idea of return is verified only in the supernatural order.

3. Cf. below, ch. 3. The context of this phrase concerns the Covenant (*v.* 3ff).

4. Cf. Spicq, *Agapé*, vol. 1, 278.

5. Cf. Spicq, *Agapé*, vol. 1, 269; St Thomas, *In Ep. ad Ephesios*, ch. 9, lect. 1, no. 16.

6. Cf. Cerfaux, *L'Église*, 266.

7. Cf. Schlier, *Temps*, 175.

8. Cf. Schlier, *Temps*, 186.

9. Cf. Spicq, *Agapé*, vol. 2, Appendix 2, "La Bénignité", 379–91. It is this generous kindness that, according to Eph. 2.7, is at the origin of our salvation.

10. Cf. Spicq, *Pastorales*, 276, also "La Philanthropie hellénistique, vertue divine et royale (à propos de Tite 3.4)", *Studia Theologica*, 12 (1958), 169–91.

11. "Paul usually speaks not of 'sins' in the plural but of 'sin' in the singular. It is a question here, not so much of particular acts, as of a mode of being resulting from past acts, or rather of an evil form imposed on men and ruling their comportment. Sin appears as a state of human nature opposed to God since the fall of Adam, and implies all the degeneracy of paganism as well as the continued infidelity of the Jews." (Cerfaux, *Le Christ*, 105.)

12. The history of the exegesis of 2 Cor. 5.21 and Gal. 3. 13 has been exhaustively studied by L. Sabourin in his *Rédemption sacrificielle* (1961), 13–160. He reduces the interpretations of 2 Cor. 5.21 to three main groups: (1) Christ was made *man*; (2) Christ was made a *sacrifice for sin*; (3) Christ was treated as the greatest of sinners, as "sin itself". The second and third interpretations

obviously presuppose the first. The arguments offered in favour of the second interpretation as the formal meaning of the verse (*Rédemption*, 153–159) are the most convincing, especially if we give to the *peri hamartias* of Rom. 8.3 the meaning "sin-offering", a value it constantly enjoys in the Septuagint (Cf. Sanday-Headlam, *Rom.*, 193, who, however, note that "we need not suppose the phrase *peri hamartias* here specially limited to the sense of 'Sin-offering'. It includes every sense in which the Incarnation and Death of Christ had relation to, and had it for their object to remove, human sin.") Sabourin, echoing St Augustine, combines interpretations (1) and (2) in a neat formula: "Christ invested himself with mortal flesh, similar to that of sin, in order to become 'sin', that is to say, true sacrifice for sin." (*Rédemption*, 137.)

13. Eph. 1.7: 2.13: Col. 1.20: Rom. 5.9.

14. 1 Cor. 6.20: 7.23: 15.3: 2 Cor. 5.15: Rom. 5.8–10: Col. 1.22: 1 Thess. 5.10: 1 Tim. 2.6: Gal. 2.21': 3.13.

15. Cf. S. Lyonnet, "La Valeur sotériologique de la résurrection du Christ selon S. Paul", *Gregorianum* 39 (1958), 297–8.

16. Cf. Cerfaux, *Le Christ*, 211.

17. Cf. Lyonnet, "La Valeur", 311; Cerfaux, *Le Christ*, 344.

18. Thus understood, the Resurrection clearly pertains to what is termed objective redemption. In a synthesis of the work of redemption based exclusively on the concept of merit this would be impossible because after his death Christ, having ceased to be a *viator*, could no longer merit. Paul's synthesis, however, is founded on the idea of efficient causality—as is St Thomas'—and to attribute causality to the Resurrection does not at all destroy the traditional distinction between objective and subjective redemption, because two stages can still be distinguished in the justification of each individual: "A first stage in which the humanity

of Christ became capable of justifying men, i.e., of being utilized as an instrument by the divinity to this end. This stage comprises all the mysteries of Christ and especially his death and resurrection in which all the other mysteries find their consummation. Then a second stage—*posterior natura*—in which this instrumental causality is effectively exercised on each one of us through faith and the sacraments." (Lyonnet, "La Valeur", 308.)

19. The building metaphor recurs in another context which also suggests the distinction between the subjective and objective orders of redemption. In Eph. 2, Christ, in virtue of his redemptive death, appears as the sole agent in the reconciliation of Jew with Gentile and of both with God. (*vv.* 13–16.) But it is due to the Gospel that men are in Christ. (3.6.) The erection of the House of God, built up of the living stones that are the Jews and Gentiles, is primarily due to Christ acting through his Spirit (2.22), but nonetheless the apostle-prophets are its foundation. (2.20.) They can only play this role in virtue of their proper activity which is the revelation of the mystery. (3.5,9.) In 1 Cor. 3.11 the role of foundation is attributed to Christ himself. Cf. Schlier, *Eph.* 142; J. Pfammatter, *Die Kirche als Bau*, Rome (1960), 73–107.

20. As it does in Rom. 1.3: 8.9: 9.5: 2 Cor. 1.17 etc.

21. "'Flesh' in another series of texts designates existent human nature, evil and stained, vitiated, infected by concupiscence, dominated by a positive power of evil; in a word: in direct relationship—of origin and tendency—with sin." (Spicq, *Dieu*, 167.)

22. Cf. C. F. D. Moule, *The Epistles to the Colossians and to Philemon*, Cambridge (1958), 96; J. A. T. Robinson, *The Body—A Study in Pauline Theology*, London (1961), 41. The Synoptics represent Christ speaking of his future death as a "baptism", cf. Mark 10.38; Luke 12.50.

23. Cf. Cerfaux, *L'Église*, 128.

24. Cf. I. de la Potterie, "L'Onction du chrétien par la foi", *Biblica* 40 (1959), 17–18. In texts of the second century the expression "seal of the faith" (or an equivalent such as "seal of the truth") is used to signify baptism. ("L'Onction", 21.) Schlier considers the baptism to be associated with imposition of hands. (*Temps*, 188.)

25. Cf. Schlier, *Temps*, 64, 132.

26. Masson translates *en hō* by "in him" and in consequence takes the passage to mean that our resurrection is attributed to faith and not to baptism. His sole argument is that parallelism is suggested by the repetition of *en hō kai*. This presumption must yield, as Abbott points out, to the natural association of *suntaphentes* with *sunēgerthēte*. This association is confirmed by Rom. 6.3–4. (If in Rom. 6.5 our resurrection is referred to in the future tense, it is only because when speaking of participation in Christ's death, participation in his resurrection appears as a future event.) Lightfoot further notes that *Christō* must be reserved to be understood with *sunēgerthēte* where it is needed. Cf. Oepke. *TWNT*, vol. 1, 543.

27. Cf. below, ch. 5, *n.* 38.

28. Rom. 1.6,7: 8.28: 1 Cor. 1.2,24.

29. Cf. Schmidt, *TWNT*, vol. 3, 490.

30. Rom. 9.24: 11.29: 1 Cor. 1.9,26: 7.17: Gal. 1.6,15: Col. 3.15: Phil. 3.14: 1 Thess. 4.7–8: 2 Thess. 2.13: 1 Tim. 6.12: 2 Tim. 1.9.

31. Cf. Schlier, "Der Ruf Gottes. Eine biblische Besinnung zum Gleichnis vom königlichen Hochzeitsmahl" *Geist und Leben* 28 (1955), 242–44.

32. Schlier, *Eph.*, 83.

33. Cf. 1 Cor. 5: 1 Tim. 1.19: 5.15: 6.10,21: 2 Tim. 4.9.

34. Cf. Bultmann, *TWNT*, vol. 1, 715–16.

35. Cf. Dupont, *Gnosis*, 95.

36. "In Pauline usage the term *prognōsis* expresses something much more limited than the 'foreknowledge'

of the metaphysicians. It comprises two ideas, knowledge and choice, and in a certain sense already implies pre-destination. Its object is never the damned." (Allo, "Versets 28–30 du chap. 8 ad Rom.", *RSPT*, 7 (1913), 273; cf. also *RSPT*, 13 (1924), 503–5). Cf. Dupont, *Gnosis*, 101.

37. Quoted in Allo, "Versets", 272, *n.* 1.

38. Cf. Cerfaux, "L'Église et le règne de Dieu", *ETL*, 2 (1925), 189, *n.* 53. *Ekklesia* in the sense of a consulta-tive or deliberative assembly occurs in 1 Macc. 5.16: 14.19. The *demos* of Ephesus gathered in the theatre (Acts 19.29) is termed an *ekklesia*. (*vv.* 32,40.)

39. Cf. Schmidt, *TWNT*, vol. 3, 531; Cerfaux, *L'Église*, 74–77.

40. *Ekklesia* in the Old Testament signifies, "almost technically, the Church of the desert". (Cerfaux, *L.Église*, 78.)

41. Cerfaux, *L'Église*, 86, 302; Schmidt, *TWNT*, vol. 3, 519.

42. Cf. Cerfaux, *Recueil II*, 455, *n.* 3.

43. Cf. W. C. van Unnik, "La Conception paulinienne de la Nouvelle Alliance", in A. Deschamps et al., *Lit-térature et théologie pauliniennes (Rech. Bibl.*, 5), Louvain (1960), 121.

44. Cf. W. C. van Unnik, "Conception", 116.

45. Cf. J. Giblet, *L'Alliance*, in J. Giblet et al., *Grands Thèmes bibliques,* Paris (1958), 25; A. Robert, "Logos", *DBS*, 5, 452.

46. God made a first covenant with Noah. (Gen. 6.18: 9.9,12.) He renews it with Abraham (Gen. 15.7ff.: 17.1ff.), Isaac and Jacob (Exod. 2.24), Aaron (Num. 18.19), Phinees (Num. 25.12–13), Levi (Mal. 2.4–5), Josue (Jos. 24.25), David (2 Sam. 23.5), and above all through the mediation of Moses on Sinai. (Exod. 19.3ff.: 24.7ff.) The covenants of Abraham (Gen. 17.7,13,19), of David (Ezek. 37.25: Isa. 55.3) and of the messianic era (Ezek. 16.60: Jer. 32.40) are characterized as eternal. (Cf. Ecclus. 44.19.)

47. In his reflections on the history of his people, Jesus Ben Sirach mentions the covenants noted above, but gives special prominence to those with Abraham (44.21–23) and with Moses. (45.1–5.) Cf. Cerfaux, *L'Église*, 19,21.

48. Cf. J. Giblet, "L'Election", in J. Giblet et al., *Grands Thèmes bibliques*, Paris (1958) 12.

49. Cf. "L'Election", 25.

50. Cf. F. Dreyfus, "La Doctrine du Reste d'Israel chez le prophète Isaïe", *RSPT*, 39 (1955), 367.

51. Cf. "La Doctrine", 368.

52. Cf. "La Doctrine", 376.

53. This idea is exactly paralleled by 1 Cor. 1.18.

54. For the Prophets one of the principal elements of the New Covenant was the intrinsic change that God would effect in man by enlightening and strengthening him interiorly. Cf. P. van Imschoot, "L'Esprit de Jahvé et l'Alliance Nouvelle", *ETL*, 13 (1936), 206.

55. A further difference between the Old-Testament and New-Testament preachers is suggested by John 15.15: "No longer do I call you servants, for the servant does not know what his Lord is doing; but I have called you friends, for all that I have heard from my Father I have made known to you." The New-Testament preachers are much more aware of the value of their work in that they know precisely what God intends in using them. They are conscious—as the Prophets never were—of the key role they play in the plan of salvation.

2

PREACHING: GOD'S INSTRUMENT

AKING up a remark made by Oscar Cullmann, Father Spicq has rightly insisted on
the intrinsic dependence of biblical theology on philological exegesis.[1] The reason is
obvious: we can legitimately attribute to the
sacred writers—and indeed to any author—only
those notions expressed or implied by the words
they use. A study of the terms used by Paul to
designate the preacher is, therefore, essential if
we are to grasp the understanding he had of his
office. Each reveals a distinct aspect of the
preacher's being. Each adds a different touch of
colour to the final picture. The insight thus obtained into the fundamental structure of the
preacher's office will be deepened and clarified
by an examination of two further series of texts.
The first deals with the adaptation of the
preacher to his function, the second with the relationship between God and the preacher's word
which is also his.

But before taking up these three points in
turn one preliminary point must be dealt with.
Since Paul considers his activity in the light of

that of the prophets of the Old Testament,[2] it will be helpful to outline briefly the essential qualities of the prophetic ministry. Having already noted that the basic purpose of the preachers of both dispensations is the same, namely, the engendering of faith, the contrasts between them will throw into greater relief the distinctive characteristics of New-Testament preaching.

THE PROPHETIC MINISTRY

The Greek *prophētēs* (of which our word "prophet" is but the transliteration), as found in the Septuagint, normally translates the Hebrew term *nabi'*.[3] There is still some doubt as to the true etymology of *nabi'*[4] but the suggestion that it means "speaker, announcer" is almost certainly false. It is now generally agreed that Hebrew itself throws no light on its derivation and, following Albright's lead, modern opinion attaches it to the Accadian root *nabu* "to call".[5] In the Code of Hammurabi the verbal adjective *nabi'* means "called". The Hebrew term, then, would mean "one who is called, one who has a vocation". The purpose of this vocation becomes clear from the usage of the word, of which we have a perfect example in the two parallel passages Exod. 4.15–16 and Exod. 7.1. In the first, when Moses complains that he is slow of speech and no fitting spokesman, Yahweh replies that his brother Aaron will aid him:

> You are to speak to him and put the words in his mouth . . . he shall speak to the people for you; he shall be your mouth and you shall be God to him.

In the second Moses again protests his weakness and Yahweh answers:

> I have made you as God to Pharoah, and Aaron your brother will act as your *nabi'*.

The purpose of the *nabi's* call, then, is that he should speak for him who calls him. This is confirmed by another instance where we find Yahweh placing his words on the lips of Jeremias, whom he has called to be his *nabi'* among the nations. (Jer. 1.5,9.)

The active element implicit in the term *nabi'* is made explicit in its Greek translation *prophētēs*, for the particle *pro-* is to be taken, not in a temporal sense (to fore-tell), but in a substitutive one (to speak for or in place of another).[6] The person signified by these two terms is clearly nothing but an instrument in the hands of a superior on whom he is absolutely dependent. The nuances of this relationship can best be appreciated by a consideration of concrete cases, for example, the vocation and mission of the prophets Isaias, Jeremias and Ezechiel.

In the account of the vocation of *Isaias* (Isa. 6) all is so perfectly smooth and controlled that one can easily imagine it in terms of the majestic unrolling of a court ceremony. The chosen one is brought before the King of Kings seated in all his glory among the seraphim, who chant his power and sanctity. Isaias' reaction is an overwhelming sense of his own unworthiness that finds expression in an immediate avowal. One of the seraphim purifies him by touching his lips with a burning coal. In virtue of this sacramental gesture the prophet is made adequate to the task about to be imposed upon him,[7] which is to extend to the nation the purification he himself received. The sudden change in his attitude and the spontaneity of his acceptance is explained by the divine force acting in him. All that remains is the reception of the message that he as Yahweh's spokesman is to transmit. The message is that the nation must have faith not in its own resources but in Yahweh. But as men's dispositions vary so will their reactions to his proclamation. Men of good will will receive it and will turn again to Yahweh. The hard of heart will reject him, and thereby cut themselves off from the true Israel, which in consequence is purified of their imperfection. Yahweh is a burning flame (Isa. 10.17), contact with which purifies or consumes. Through the mediation of the prophet, men, be they of iron or of brittle dry

wood, are brought face to face with the decision
that will be their salvation or their ruin.

Before he was even born Yahweh had chosen
Jeremias (Jer. 1) and had consecrated him to his
prophetic ministry. But in the moment of his
call the prophet protests his weakness far more
vehemently than did Isaias. Yahweh, however,
overrides his objections by promising him divine
assistance in the carrying out of his task—his
mission is, as it were, forced upon him. This element of constraint is not referred to directly in
the narrative but is obviously implied by the
way in which God effectively silences all murmuring, for the repeated assurance of divine protection would indicate that Jeremias' doubts
persist. God does not argue but commands and
then consoles for a submission that has left every
doubt alive. The rebellion seething within the
prophet is permitted to boil to the surface now
and again (e.g., 15.18), but when he tries to re-
press the divine word that Yahweh placed on his
lips—"I put my words in your mouth"—lest his
preaching bring him more suffering, the word
becomes a burning fire within his bones forcing
him to give it utterance come what may. (20.9.)
Like Isaias', Jeremias' mission has both a positive
and a negative aspect. He is sent "to root up and
pull down, to waste and to destroy and to build
and to plant". (1.10.) As if indifference and
stupidity were not enough, he has to contend

with the opposition of 'false preachers. These are those who pretending to prophesy in the name of Yahweh preach only what their listeners wish to hear. (23.17,27.) They are not to be heeded, Jeremias insists, because they have not been sent by Yahweh nor has he said anything to them. (23.16,21,32.) Only he who has received the word of God can proffer it; false prophets preach only their dreams. (23.28.) The true *nabi'* has received not only a commission but also a message that he must communicate faithfully. (23.28.)

God's transcendence and his utter indifference to the qualities of the instrument he uses are more evident in the narrative of the vocation of *Ezechiel*. The title "Son of Man" by which Yahweh addresses him (2.1) has a pejorative connotation; it emphasizes the distance between God and his creature. Yet God deigns to use man and to adapt him to his use. In the case of Isaias this adaptation had been effected by one of the seraphim (Isa. 6.5–7), while the lips of Jeremias were touched by Yahweh himself. (Jer. 1.9.) Ezechiel, however, actually eats the word of God. (Ezek. 3.1–4.) The brutal realism of this gesture gives us to understand that the word of God is assimilated to the very being of the prophet. Consequently, to hear him is to hear Yahweh. (3.7.) Our impression of the instrumental character of Ezechiel's mission is heightened by the frequent

3

repetition of the phrase, "The word of Yahweh
came to me." (3.16: 6.1: 7.1: 11.14 etc.) This
word is not a permanent possession, for more
than once it is taken away from him (3.24–27:
24.27: 33.22), but when it is present it must be
communicated to those for whom it is destined.
The prophet is not held responsible for the reception of his message—that depends entirely on
his hearers—but failure to fulfil his obligation
to preach it would be held against him. (Cf.
33.7–9 = 3.16–21.)

The prophet of the Old Testament was but
an instrument moved by the Spirit of Yahweh
(Mic. 3.8: Isa. 48.16: 61.1: Zech. 7.12) which
conferred on him the qualities necessary for the
successful discharge of his task (Mic. 3.8). Irresistible power was attributed to his word because
it was a participation in the dynamic force of the
divine word (Isa. 9.7: 55.10–11: Jer. 23.29).
Because of its unique relationship to the salvation of God's people, the prophetic message had
to be spoken in its entirety and with scrupulous
exactitude. (Amos 3.3–8: 7.15.) The great
variety, both in the manner in which the divine
message was received by the prophets and in the
ways in which it was communicated to their
contemporaries, cannot obscure a trait common
to all. Each was vividly aware that the words he
pronounced were not his alone; his speech was

INTRODUCTION

THIS book is not an instruction on how to prepare a sermon. Nor is it an anthology of Pauline themes systematically tabulated to facilitate the researches of the busy priest. What it aims to do is to share St Paul's insight into the structure of a key element in the life of the Church, the proclamation of the word of God.

The need for a reappraisal of preaching is made imperative by the link some forge between it and contemporary atheism. Just as the Reformation four centuries ago, the progressive dechristianization of society today is attributed to a failure of preaching. The factor that more than any other made the Reformation possible was the theological confusion that marked the preaching and teaching of the Faith in the early sixteenth century. Today preaching is admittedly orthodox, but it is often vapid and lacking in vitality. It no longer seems to make converts or to lead to sanctity those who already have the Faith. That this is due in part to the spiritual mediocrity and the technical incompetence of individual preachers there can be no doubt. The preference of the majority of churchgoers for the Mass which is not accompanied by a sermon, and the apathy with which even a short talk is received, must largely be their responsibility. Yet to blame the preacher for everything would be onesided. The evolution of new techniques of communication has almost imperceptibly altered the mentality of those to whom his message is addressed. "Dialogue" characterizes the mood of the moment better than any other single term. All truth is felt to be more easily and perfectly assimilated in the give and take of free discussion. The very value of preaching as an institution is being questioned, and its more radical critics would suggest that perhaps it should be abandoned in favour of something better adapted to the spirit of the age.

The first chapter of this study rules out the radical "solution" as impossible. Preaching has a perennial value, for it forms part of the essential structure of the Church. The salvation won by Christ would not benefit man were it not preached. Though not of comparable intrinsic value, the apostolate is as indispensable a means of salvation as the death of Christ—and the two are intimately connected. What is needed, then, is a revitalization of preaching, and the only question is, how is it to be achieved? Here, fortunately, we are not left to our own resources. The experience of the lay apostolate and the liturgical movement has shown that a renewal on the level of technique alone is not really a

ABBREVIATIONS

NOTE: References to commentaries on a given text are presented merely by the name of the commentator and the reference, if not otherwise explained, will be to the author's commentary on the passage in question. Where an author's work is frequently referred to an abbreviation follows his name. In both these cases full bibliographical details are given under the author's name in the bibliography.

A-G Arndt, W. F., and Gingrich, F. W., *A Greek-English Lexicon of the New Testament and other Early Christian Literature*. A translation and adaptation of W. Bauer's *Griechisch-Deutsches Wörterbuch zu den Schriften des N.T. und der übrigen urchistlichen Literatur*, 4th ed., 1952, Cambridge (1959).

ANET *Ancient Near Eastern Texts relating to the Old Testament*, edited by J. B. Pritchard, Princeton (1955).

CBQ *The Catholic Biblical Quarterly*.

DBS *Dictionnaire de la Bible: Supplément*, ed. L. Pirot and others, Paris (1928-).

DBV *Dictionnaire de la Bible*, ed. F. Vigouroux, Paris (1895-1912).

ETL	*Ephemerides Theologicae Lovanienses.*
JBL	*The Journal of Biblical Literature.*
NRT	*Nouvelle Revue théologique.*
NTS	*New Testament Studies.*
RB	*Revue biblique.*
RHPR	*Revue d'histoire et de philosophie religieuses.*
RSR	*Recherches de science religieuse.*
RSPT	*Revue des sciences philosophiques et théologiques.*
RT	*Revue thomiste.*
TS	*Theological Studies.*
TWNT	*Theologisches Wörterbuch zum Neuen Testament*, ed. G. Kittel and G. Friedrich, Stuttgart (1933–).
VD	*Verbum Domini.*
ZKT	*Zeitschrift für katholische Theologie.*
ZNW	*Zeitschrift für die neutestamentliche Wissenschaft.*

Qumran Literature

1QS	*The Manual of Discipline*
1QSa	*The Rule of the Congregation*
1QH	*The Thanksgiving Hymns*
CD	*The 'Zadokite' (Damascus) Fragments*

UNITED STATES EDITIONS OF
WORKS CITED IN THE NOTES

W. F. ARNDT and F. W. GINGRICH, *A Greek-English Lexicon of the New Testament and Other Early Christian Literature* (Chicago, University of Chicago Press, 1957).

T. BOWMAN, *Hebrew Thought Compared with Greek* (Philadelphia, Westminster, 1961).

O. CULLMAN, *Christ and Time* (Philadelphia, Westminster, 1950).

NEILL HAMILTON, *The Holy Spirit and Eschatology in St. Paul* (Naperville, Ill., Allenson, 1961).

J. B. PRITCHARD, *Ancient Near Eastern Texts relating to the Old Testament* (Princeton, Princeton University Press, 1955).

ALLAN RICHARDSON, *An Introduction to the Theology of the New Testament* (New York, Harper, 1959).

H. SCHLIER, *Principalities and Powers in the New Testament* (New York, Herder & Herder, 1961).

CONTENTS

FOR MY MOTHER

AND

IN MEMORY OF MY FATHER

dom of God and his glory (1 Thess. 2.12), which
is eternal life. (1 Tim. 6.2.) This distinction
explains how Paul can sometimes speak of the
vocation of the Christian as a thing of the past
(e.g., 1 Thess. 4.7: 2 Thess. 2.14: Gal. 1.6) and
at the same time speak of God as calling not just
once but continually: "... faithful is he who
calls you [ho kalōn]" (1 Thess. 5.24); "... such a
suggestion does not come from him who calls
you". (Gal. 5.8.) Schlier formulates the idea with
admirable concision: "Der klētos ist nicht der
einmal Gerufene und dann von dem Ruf fort
und anderswohin Entfernte, sondern er ist der
nun in diesem Ruf als einem Nachruf bleibend
Stehende."[32]

The call to glory implicit in the call to salvation may be refused. Paul's reproof to the faithful of Galatia shows them to be on, if not actually
over, the brink of such a refusal: "I marvel that
you are in such haste to desert him who called
you in[to] the grace of Christ for another
gospel" (1.6); and this is only one among a
number of parallel cases.[33] On the other hand,
the call to salvation appears as always efficacious.
Paul speaks nowhere, either explicitly or implicitly, of a rejected call in this sense; he gives
the title "the called" only to those actually
justified by faith and baptism. Now the divine
call takes place in time through the medium
of the Gospel (2 Thess. 2.13–14: Gal. 1.6: Eph.

which it proclaims, and as baptism, the reproduction of that death and resurrection in the
individual, towards which it tends. Preaching
effects the initial contact of Christ with the
Christian-to-be. This is possible only if it
embodies a divine call addressed to that individual.

PREACHING AND THE ETERNAL CALL

In the Epistles the members of the Church
are frequently termed "the called" (*hoi klētoi*),[28]
and "to call" (*kalein*) appears as a technical term
for the whole process of salvation.[29] While the
person who calls is always God,[30] it is possible to
distinguish two divine calls, or better, two
aspects of the divine call.

Christians are called to peace (1 Cor. 7.15:
Col. 3.15), to freedom (1 Cor. 7.22: Gal. 5.13)
and its perfect exercise which is sanctification
(1 Thess. 4.7), and to the grace and fellowship
of Jesus Christ. (1 Cor. 1.9: Gal. 1.6.) All these
gifts they now enjoy,[31] and for convenience we
term the divine call in so far as it is their principle, *the call to salvation* (cf. 2 Thess. 2.13–14).
But the very presence of these gifts is itself an
invitation (which we term *the call to glory*) to
the hope reserved for them in heaven (Eph. 4.4:
Col. 1.5,23), to the prize of the heavenly call
(Phil. 3.14), that is, to the possession of the King-

at the same time that of another. This unshak-
able conviction had its roots in their certitude of
their vocation and in their mystical experience
of direct contact with God.

THE PREACHER'S TITLES

We have already noted that Paul gives to himself, as well as to the other apostles, the title
"prophet". (Eph. 2.20: 3.5.) The preceding
section dispenses us from further discussion of
this title here,[8] where attention will be focused
on eight other terms used by Paul to characterize
his office and that of his co-workers. We are justified in calling them "The *Preacher's* Titles",
because Paul clearly stated more than once that
preaching was the essential function of both himself (1 Cor. 1.17: 1 Tim. 2.5–7) and his collaborators. (2 Tim. 4.2: Titus 2.15; cf. 1 Tim. 2.12:
5.17: Titus 2.1.) Five of these titles are found
together in the long section of the First Epistle
to the Corinthians which commentators entitle
"The True Concept of the Christian Apostolate": *Diakonos* (3.5); *Sunergos Theou* (3.9);
Hypēretēs (4.1); *Oikonomos* (4.1); and *Apostolos*
(4.9). Two others, *Kērux* and *Didaskalos*, are
associated with the last-mentioned in 1 Tim. 2.7
and 2 Tim. 1.11. Finally, in the superscription
of the Letter to the Philippians Paul presents
both Timothy and himself as *Douloi Christou.*

Kērux—"Herald"

With the exception of its application to Noah, "the herald of justice" (2 Pet. 2.5), the title "herald" is not found in the New Testament outside the Pauline corpus, and even there it occurs only twice (1 Tim. 2.7 and 2 Tim. 1.11), each time forming part of the triple title "herald, apostle and teacher".

In Homeric times the "heralds" were important court officials drawn from the upper classes of society.[9] They were the ruler's companions and any services they performed were of a purely personal nature (*Od.*, 19,247; *Il.*, 2,183). In this age the best translation would, perhaps, be "courtier".

The meaning of the term changed radically in later times, when the "herald" appears as a salaried servant charged with the communication of information. Merely the mouthpiece of his master (Plato, *Polit.*, 260d), he resembled the *presbus*, "legate, ambassador", in so far as he acted in the name of his principal and with his power and authority. (*Thuc.*, 4,30,5.) But there was a difference. The "legate" was given great freedom in the exercise of his mission, whereas the "herald" was entrusted only with short simple communications of the question-and-answer variety, which he had no power to modify in any way. (Plato, *Leg.*, 12,941a.) The "herald" was never employed as a negotiator, was never more than a simple organ of communication. The term had a religious connotation inasmuch as, in his diplomatic missions, the "herald" was considered to enjoy the special protection of the gods, whose anger was incurred by any violation of his immunity. (Herodotus, 7,131–6.) This sacral nuance evident in the political use of the term is even more apparent in the use of "herald" to designate the important civic functionary who prepared all that was necessary for the sacrifice and who, as the spokesman of the assembled populace, offered the prayer for the health, prosperity and freedom of the city.

Because of his special claim on divine protection, every "herald" was in a sense a "herald of God". This title is given in point of fact to Hermes, and to the Stoic philosopher. Hermes conveyed to men the messages of the gods, and the philosopher, even though connected with no religious group, was considered as the instrument through which God spoke to men.

Such religious and social connotations remained with the term in the post-Christian period.[10] In papyri dating from the first post-Christian centuries the "herald" appears as a town crier charged with public announcements.[11] When the announcement had a legal character there is evidence that the "herald" was liable to punishment if he failed to repeat it literally.[12]

The papyri testify also to the association of the "herald" with the mystery religions,[13] and with religious festivals.[14]

"Herald" is practically non-existent in the Septuagint. Ecclesiasticus does employ it in a description of the fool—"He opens his mouth as a public crier" (20.15)—thus underlining the lack of personal thought behind the "herald's" utterance. The Book of Daniel uses it, in the sense found in the papyri, of the minister of Nabuchodonosor who announces to the citizens the obligations of worshipping the idol. (3.4.)[15]

The one idea that emerges with clarity from this brief glance at the Greek usage of the term "herald" is the subordinate character of the person it designated. He was a mouthpiece, devoid of all personal significance, without power to add to or subtract from the message entrusted to him. It was his message that was all-important. The term seems so apt to describe the bearer of divine revelation that its infrequent use in the New Testament to characterize the Christian preacher is a little surprising.[16] Friedrich explains this reserve by invoking the idea of immunity included in the Greek understanding of the term.[17] Christ had warned his disciples that they would be persecuted unmercifully. (Matt. 10.16.) And from the beginning, tribulation was in fact the lot of those who preached the Gospel. (Acts 4.5–21: 5.21–41 etc.: 2 Cor. 11.23–33.) The early Christians would have found it difficult to reconcile the treatment meted out to their ministers with the respectful hearing accorded to a "herald". This contrast alone would have inhibited their use of this title.

It may, however, be doubted whether this is the total explanation. The title may have been avoided precisely because it was enjoyed by the Stoic preachers, or because it was in a sense false. While it has in its favour that it manifests the correct position of the preacher *vis-à-vis* the divine message with which he is entrusted, this is more than counterbalanced by its positive exclusion of freedom of presentation. The "herald" must repeat by rote what has been communicated to him, whereas the preacher must adapt the unique, inviolable message to diverse classes of hearers (e.g., 1 Cor. 3.2: 1 Tim. 5.1–3: Titus 2.1–10).

Apostolos—"Apostle" [18]

This term is manifestly cognate with the verb *apostellein*, "to send away or out". Although employed frequently (seventy-nine times) in the New Testament with the general sense of "envoy", this meaning was very uncommon in profane Greek, Herodotus being the only profane writer to use the term in a sense approximating the New-Testament usage. In 1,21 he employs it as a synonym for the "herald" sent to arrange for a truce. In 5,38 the chief, Aristagoras, goes himself as "apostle" to Lacedaemon. In the latter instance the meaning "ambassador" is somewhat weakened by the fact that he is mentioned as sailing in a trireme, because *apostolos* was originally an adjective used most frequently to qualify *ploion*, the phrase signifying a freight or transport ship. By degrees the adjective alone came to signify this same reality and assumed the characteristics of a substantive. It is thus used to mean a naval expedition (Demosthenes, *Or. XVIII*, 107) or its leader (Hesychius, s.v., *Anecdota Graeca*, ed. Bekker, 217,26). The usage of the papyri is altogether different and shows how sharply the ordinary everyday usage of the word differed from that of the New Testament. In these documents we find *apostolos* with the meaning "bill of lading, invoice" (*P. Oxy.*, 9,1197,13 etc.) and, in some cases, "passport". (*BGU*, 5,64.)[19] *Apostolos* occurs only once in the Septuagint, when the prophet Ahijay refers it to himself: "I am a hard messenger from God to you." (1 Kings 14.6.)[20] The adoption of the term, therefore, by the New-Testament writers does not seem to have had its origin in any current usage.

The only rationale which will cover all the instances of the term's use in the Pauline letters seems to be the basic notion of *being sent*, with a reference—in some cases very indirect—to the propagation of the Faith. Paul's own right to the title he so frequently claims consists in his having been *sent* (*apostellein*) by the risen Christ to preach (1 Cor. 1.17), that is, to reveal the mystery of Christ to the Gentiles. (Gal. 1.16: Eph. 3.8.) He had a lively awareness of the honour this implied: "I am the least of the apostles. I am not worthy to be called an apostle, because I persecuted the Church of God." (1 Cor. 15.9; cf. 1 Tim. 1.15–16.)

Others share his "being sent". For example, because of the authoritative character of their mission, the title "apostles of Christ" (1 Thess. 2.7) is given to Silvanus and Timothy, Paul's assistants in the foundation of the Church at Thessalonica. Again, in 1 Cor. 4.9 "apostles" includes Apollos (at least), and in 1 Cor. 9.5, Barnabas. These all merit the title "apostle" because of their association with Paul. Their "being sent" means, in effect, that they were commissioned by him. Paul's awareness of the validity of a mediated commission is implicitly attested to by his avowal that the peculiar character of his own mission was due to the fact that it did not come to him "through the intermediary of a man". (Gal. 1.1.)[21] The first "apostles" were chosen by God in the person of Christ (2 Cor. 5.17–20), but these in their turn, in order to extend the effective area of their preaching, could mediate this commission to others. Paul himself would surely term "apostles" those whom he sent (*apostellein*) to perform a determined task, such as Titus (2 Cor. 12.17–18) and Tychicus (2 Tim. 4.12). In order to be an "apostle" Paul accounts it absolutely necessary to be sent; merely to have seen the risen Christ does not suffice. After mentioning the "Twelve" in the list of witnesses who could verify that Christ had risen from the dead because he had appeared to them, Paul opposes "the five hundred brethren" to "all the apostles" (1 Cor. 15.6–7).[22] The difference between these two groups lies in the fact that alone the members of the latter were charged with a mission.

The element of subordination, of lack of independence, is just as perceptible in "apostle" as it is in "herald". The "apostle" has a mission to accomplish and until it is fulfilled he is not his own master. *Apostolos* is entirely Greek in form, but as has been noted, the meaning it has in the New Testament is not that which it had in the common speech of the first century. In the Pauline epistles it is always associated with the word of God[23] and its meaning is always a modality of the root idea suggested by the etymology, "envoy, one sent". Greek evidently merely provides the form. The idea conveyed is that evoked by the Old-Testament term *nabi'*, "prophet". This immediately sets the service performed by the "apostle" in a new perspective, while its grandeur is manifested by the attribution of the title to Christ himself: "Think of the apostle and high priest of the religion we profess, Jesus". (Heb. 3.1.) Christ was *sent* into the world to save sinners (*ex-apostellein*, Gal 4.4), and that sending is the Good News. Because of his commission by Christ (mediate or immediate) to preach the Good News, the apostle participates in the saving mission of Christ. (2 Tim. 1.10–11.)[24]

Doulos Christou, Theou—"*Slave of Christ, of God*"

Paul's use of the term "slave" to describe a particular social condition (1 Cor. 7.21: 1 Tim. 6.1: Titus 2.9) is perfectly conformed to strictly Greek usage which employed this word to designate one who stood in a relationship of complete servitude to another, and whose will was completely absorbed in his master's.[25] But he breaks decisively with this usage in transferring the term to the religious sphere.[26] In this the influence of the Old Testament is evident.[27]

Where it occurs in the Septuagint "slave" translates, in all but a few instances, *'ebed*, its exact Hebrew equivalent. But this term, because of the absolute, despotic character of royal power, was also used to designate the (free) subjects of a king and, in a special way, his officers and ministers, whose attachment to his service

broke all other social ties.[28] Eventually, because
man's relationship with God was conceived in
terms of the relationship of a subject to his
temporal sovereign, the word came to be used of
man as utterly dependent upon and subject to
Yahweh.[29] Consequently, it could be, and was
in fact, applied to all faithful Israelites (2 Kings
9.7: Isa. 54.17: 63.17: Ps. 34.23) as distinguished
from their erring brethren, "the slaves of Baal".
(2 Kings 10.23.) In the religious sphere, therefore, the idea evoked is not simply that of subjection and dependence, but of subjection freely
accepted in a practical way. Only the just really
merited to be called 'ebed Yahweh. The perjora-
tive nuance of "slave", already weakened by this
usage which made of it a title of respect, dis-
appeared entirely when the expression 'ebed
Yahweh came to be employed to designate those
whom Yahweh chose as his instruments in the
realization of his plan for humanity. These were
the "slaves of God" par excellence, not by reason
of any personal perfection, but simply in virtue
of the divine choice.

"Hear, Jacob, my slave, Israel whom I have
chosen." (Isa. 44.1; cf. 41.8.) Chosen not through
any merit on its part (Deut. 7.6), Israel's function
was to bear testimony to Yahweh among the
nations. (Isa. 43.10.) The title was given to the
Patriarchs, Abraham, Isaac and Jacob (2 Macc.
1.2) and to Moses (Jos. 1.2; cf. Num. 12.6–8:

Deut. 34.10–12: Ps. 105.26.) It was applied to the
Prophets as a body (Amos 3.7: 2 Kings 9.7: Jer.
7.25), to Isaias (Isa. 20.3), to David (Ps. 18.1:
1 Macc. 4.30) and to the mysterious *'ebed
Yahweh.* (Isa. 42.1.) The role played by these
men in the history of salvation demonstrates
clearly that *'ebed Yahweh* was an appellation of
the highest honour. But it was a functional, not
a personal, title. Its dignity flowed not from the
personal qualities of its bearer but from the
unique character of the function he fulfilled. It
was his choice as God's instrument that counted,
not his position or ability. This is evidenced by
the attribution of this title to an unbeliever such
as Nabuchodonosor. (Jer. 25.9: 27.6: 43.10.)
Taken in itself, the term "slave" essentially
denotes dependence and servitude, but since
God has no need of man—"Save I, all is nothing" (Isa. 45.6)—the nuance of humiliation is
entirely absorbed in the grandeur of the service.

This usage is so perfectly mirrored in Paul's
own use of the phrases "slave of Christ" and
"slave of God", that it is impossible to deny his
dependence on the Old Testament. So conscious
was he of the dignity implied in this title that
he only once applies it to the ordinary believer.[30]
As a general rule, he reserves it strictly to himself and his immediate collaborators. The
formula "slave of Christ Jesus" occurs three
times: Paul applies it to himself (Rom. 1.1; cf.

Gal. 1.10), to himself and Timothy (Phil. 1.1), and to Epaphras (Col. 4.12). In the superscription of the letter to Titus Paul introduces himself as a "slave of God". Timothy, as head of the Church in Ephesus, is a "slave of the Lord". (2 Tim. 2.24.) This usage evidences Paul's awareness of being (with his co-workers) the successor of the great instruments of God of the Old Testament. The "slave of Christ" is the *'ebed Yahweh* of the New Covenant (2 Cor. 3.6), and just as much God's agent in the execution of the plan of salvation (1 Cor. 3.5).

But what does this mean in practice?' "We do not preach ourselves but Christ Jesus [as] Lord; we ourselves are your slaves for Jesus' sake." (2 Cor. 4.5.) The preachers are set in a privileged position but, in conformity with the paradox of their title, it is a position which makes them the servants of all. (1 Cor. 3.22.) In fulfilling the charge laid upon them they are treated as "the scum of the earth, the dregs of humanity". (1 Cor. 4.13.) But it is this abasement, this willing acceptance of the "form of a slave" which was Christ's (Phil. 2.7), that permits the light of the Gospel to shine more intensely and its power to operate with greater effect. (2 Cor. 4.7–11.) The demands made on the preacher are severe, and failure is an ever-present possibility—"If I still sought men's favour I would be no slave of Christ" (Gal. 1.10)—but the humiliations are as nothing because they are for Jesus' sake. The dignity of the service far outweighs the conditions under which it is performed.

Diakonos—"Servant"

According to Trench *diakonos* probably derives from the root which gives *diōkō* "to hasten after".[31] From this basic connotation the step to the meaning "servant" is not too difficult. In the Septuagint the term is found almost exclusively (five times out of seven) in the Book of Esther, where it designates a court servant. This is also the meaning in Herodotus (4,71,72). Yet the sense "messenger" is also noted, and there is abundant evidence that the term acquired a religious connotation through being applied to the attendants or officials of a temple or religious guild.

All these nuances are found in the New-Testament usage. In its full literal meaning *diakonos* is applied to waiters at table (John 2.5) and to court servants. (Matt. 22.13.) It is also used to mean a church official. Paul employs it more frequently than all the other writers of the New Testament combined, and does so chiefly in reference to the work of preaching the Gospel. In some cases it is true that the reference to the apostolate is rather indirect (e.g., Col. 1.7) but Paul states clearly to the Colossians that he became a "servant of the Church" in virtue of the

charge laid upon him to preach the word of God.
(Col. 1.25.) Hence he can also say that he is a
"servant of the Gospel". (Eph. 3.7: Col. 1.23.)
Alluding to the evangelisation of Corinth, he
describes himself and his collaborator as "servants", and the context shows how literally this
is to be taken. (1 Cor. 3.5.) In another instance,
Timothy is advised that if he does what Paul
counsels he will be a good "servant of Christ",
and the advice concerns precisely what he should
preach. (1 Tim. 4.6: 2 Cor. 11.23.) Finally, Paul
and his assistants are termed "servants of the new
covenant". (2 Cor. 3.6.)

Paul was the first to use the term "servant" in
reference to the apostolate. In the Synoptics and
in the Fourth Gospel it is used almost exclusively in the context of an exhortation to humility. But even there the stress is on humble
service. Trench underlines the dynamic connotation of *diakonos* in opposition to the more
static concepts of *doulos* and *therapōn*.[32] Hence,
while again evoking the idea of subordination
already noted in the other terms discussed,
"servant" adds a hint of Paul's vivid consciousness of the pressing urgency of the mission
entrusted to him. (2 Tim. 4.2: 2 Cor. 5.14.)

Hypēretēs—"Servant"

Originally this term appears to have meant an
oarsman, and was in fact used for the rowers on

a war-galley to distinguish them from the soldiers it carried.[33] Gradually it came to mean anyone who did anything at the behest of another, i.e., an underling.[34]

In the civil administration of a Greek city the salaried employees (*hypēretai*), who could even be non-citizens, were distinguished from the honorary magistrates (*archai*).[35] In Athens the term designated the agents of the Council (Demosthenes, 19,17) as well as those of the courts (Plato, *Leg.*, 4,10,720a). It was used also of a military adjutant (Arrian, *Tract. X*, 4) and of a physician's assistant.[36] *Hypēretēs* occurs only four times in the Septuagint. In Deut. 3.24 and Prov. 14.35 it merely means servants of the king without any further determination. In Wis. 6.5 it is employed of the kings of the earth who, since they hold their power from the Lord, are "the *hypēretai* of his kingdom".

There is abundant material for the study of the usage of the term in the papyri. The generic meaning "employee" is attested to regularly from the third century B.C. down to, and past, the New-Testament period, yet there is much evidence that the word had acquired a technical connotation in civil service and juridical circles. After an exhaustive study of the available material, Kupiszewski and Modrzejewski concluded that the quality characterizing the *hypēretēs* in these spheres was that of an *official witness.*[37] In the juridical sphere he was not only entrusted with the delivery of various documents[38] but had to attest officially to their delivery and reception, normally by appending his signature.[39] He represented the administration in various investigations, e.g., into the extent of the damage to property,[40] into the cause of deaths[41] etc. His presence gave an official character to oaths[42] and to certain acts of commerce.[43] In the present context, the most interesting function of the *hypēretēs* was his duty to publish the official report and the administrative directions of the *strategos*, his chief.[44] In the New Testament *hypēretēs* appears frequently as a public official connected with the administration of law, the most obvious example being Matt. 5.25. That there was a difference between the *hypēretēs* and other servants is witnessed to by John's use of the two terms *hypēretai* and "slaves" to signify the totality of those present in the courtyard of the High Priest with Peter (18.18), and here, as elsewhere (Matt. 26.58: Mark 14.54: John 7.32: Acts 5.22), it designates the under-officers of the Sanhedrin. However, in the New Testament, the term also carries a religious connotation. In Luke 4.20 it is used of the synagogue attendant who receives from Jesus the scroll containing the prophecy of Isaias.

This rather material relationship of the

hypēretēs to the word of God is made more formal by Luke in the introduction to his Gospel:

> In as much as many have attempted to put together an account of the things that have been fulfilled amongst us, even as those who were, from the beginning, eye-witnesses and *hypēretai* of the word [1.1–2]

The obvious interpretation, viz., that the two terms "eye-witnesses" and *hypēretai* cover a single category, is confirmed by the structure of the phrase. Clearly, Luke is here referring to those from whom he obtained an authentic account of the life of Christ, and these could only have been the Apostles, who had been with Christ from the beginning of his public life and had been associated with him as official collaborators in virtue of their special vocation. How perfectly the "legal" meaning of *hypēretēs* fits this context needs no emphasis. It serves as an apt foundation for the religious element implied.[45]

That *hypēretēs*, as used by Paul, certainly carries a religious nuance is evidenced by the qualifying genitive, "*hypēretēs* of Christ". (1 Cor. 4.1.) He employs the term to insist on the subordinate character of his position in the Church, for he had no wish to be adopted as the leader of a faction that would destroy the unity of the body of Christ. (1 Cor. 1.11ff.) Nonetheless a certain respect was his due because his office was given him by Christ, who established him *"hypēretēs* and witness [*martus*] both to what you have seen and to what you shall yet see of me". (Acts 26.16.) In view of the legal connotation of *hypēretēs* it is tempting to see the "and" of this verse as merely explanatory.[46] This would give to *hypēretēs* its full force of "official witness"—a meaning whose aptness in 1 Cor. 4.1 (the only text where Paul applies this term to the preacher) can hardly be questioned.[47]

Oikonomos *"Steward"* [48]

In the light of what has been said in the first chapter concerning the relationship of preaching to the divine "economy" of salvation, it is entirely natural to find the preacher termed an *oikonomos*. It is usually translated "steward", but was probably as general in meaning as our modern "manager".[49] The "stewards" of the Hellenistic kings occupied positions of supreme importance in the government of large territories. This usage accords with that of the Septuagint, where "steward" translates *'aser 'al habbayt* "the Master of the Palace". The functionary bearing this title was originally the steward of the royal property, but as with time his importance increased, he eventually exercised the authority of a Prime Minister.[50] The

title is also found in use in the time of the
Roman Emperors, though then, apparently, it
did not denote a position of much power. Not
only individuals but groups had their "stewards",
and in this sense there is evidence in Paul's own
letters that *oikonomos* was the title of a city
official (Rom. 16.23) who, as far as we can gather,
was almost invariably of servile origin, if not
actually a slave.[51]

Though these "stewards" fulfilled certain
religious obligations in the course of their
duties[52] this would not suffice to substantiate a
claim that the term had a specifically religious
value. That it bore some religious connotation
is apparent from its use by private societies of a
religious nature as a title for their servants. The
Serapis and Hermes-Trismegistus cults furnish
us with clear examples.[53] In this way a common
term was given a cultural nuance, or, at the very
least, was used to describe a position of trust
and responsibility in the sphere of the sacred.

In the New Testament, "steward" is used by
Christ to denote the slave charged with the dis-
tribution of rations (Luke 12.42) and also the
unfaithful servant accused of wasting his master's
goods. A rather curious use of the term occurs in
Gal. 4.2:

> But I say that so long as the heir is a child he
> differs nothing from a slave though he is lord

of all, but he is under guardians [*epitropoi*] and stewards until the time set by the father.

The unusual feature is the use of the term in relation to a minor orphan. In this passage Paul clearly refers to a law of inheritance by which the minor who inherits his father's possessions has no right to use them as he pleases, due to his subordination to the "guardians and stewards". In rabbinic law a "guardian" was appointed, by the father or by the court, only when property was left to a minor.[54] In such a case the "guardian" became the actual master of the orphan's heritage. If appointed by the court he had to render an account of his stewardship to that body, but if appointed by the father, the only restriction on his authority was that imposed by his own sense of justice and loyalty. In content, then, the term "guardian" is equivalent to "steward", and though Paul employs two terms he is not to be interpreted as referring to two different functionaries. The "and" is again only explanatory. For one not familiar with Jewish law and its terminology "steward" provides the necessary clarification of the technical meaning attached by the rabbis to "guardian".

Though undoubtedly present, the connotation of instrumentality and subordination is not so marked in "steward" as it is in some of the other terms discussed. The "steward" is permitted much more initiative in the carrying out of his function than, for example, is the "herald". Hence, as Paul recognizes, the one quality essential to a "steward" is fidelity to the spirit of his undertaking (1 Cor. 4.2: Titus 1.7), for he has been given something, not to selfishly possess, but to use for the sake of others. In the case of the prophet, this was the word of God (e.g., Jer. 23.28); for Paul, it is the "mysteries of God" (1 Cor. 4.1), the "deposit" (2 Tim. 1.12). Both the prophet and the "steward" are administrators of a truth not theirs.

Didaskalos—"Teacher"

If we except the references to charismatic functions in 1 Cor. 12.28 and Eph. 4.11,[55] "teacher" occurs only twice in the Pauline epistles as the designation of an ecclesiastical office, and, in both instances, is a title of Paul himself used in conjunction with "herald" and "apostle". (1 Tim. 2.7: 2 Tim. 1.11.)

Though "teacher" is used frequently in the New Testament as a title of Christ,[56] it is rather difficult to determine its value. The original spoken term must have been the Aramaic *rabbi* (cf. John 1.38: 20.16: Matt. 23.8), which often instead of being translated is simply transliterated (e.g., Mark 9.4: Matt. 26.25). This title, originally a term of authority in any sphere (cf. 2 Kings 25.8: Jer. 39.13: Esther 1.8), became, after the disappearance of the monarchy, the prerogative of the new ruling class of priest-teachers.[57] Thenceforward, since their function was the communication of knowledge of the Law, *rab* assumed the meaning "teacher", but never lost its original connotation of dignity and authority.[58] The Greek *didaskalos,* "teacher", does not at all convey this latter nuance,[59] but in virtue of its essential connotation of systematic presentation of doctrine,[60] it would seem perfectly apt to render the teaching aspect of *rab(bi)*. Yet even here we notice a curious hesitation on the part of the Synoptics.

In Mark 4.38 we find "Teacher", but in the parallel passages "Lord" (Matt. 8.25) and "Master". (Luke 8.24.) Mark 9.4 has "Rabbi", and the parallels again "Lord" (Matt. 17.4) and "Master" (Luke 9.33). Where Mark uses "Teacher" (9.38), Luke has "Master". (9.49.) More than either of the others, Luke appears to have felt the inadequacy of "Teacher" as a Christological title. The conclusion which has been drawn from his discriminative use of "Teacher" and "Master" (*epistatēs*) perhaps affords a clue to why "Teacher" enjoyed so little popularity as a title of Christ, for it is completely absent from all the epistles, Pauline and Catholic. Glombiza points out that in the Third Gospel Jesus is a "teacher" only as far as strangers are concerned (e.g., 10.25 and 22.11).[61] "Teacher"

is a title based on superficial observation, and it
is never employed by the disciples, who have
experienced the real nature of Christ's mission.
They prefer to address him as "Master" (5.5:
8.24,45: 9.33,49: 17.13), and it is significant
that each time this title is set in close relation
to the "power" of Jesus. It would be typical of
Luke to adopt this subtle way of asserting both
that Christianity is not merely a collection of
doctrines, and that Christ is much more than a
mere teacher. Even during his lifetime the
attitude Christ adopted to the Law (Matt. 5.21–
48) was felt to be inconsistent with the position
of a rabbi. (Mark 1.22.) Thus, a growing perception of the partial inaccuracy of "Teacher",
coupled with an increasing awareness of its
resonance in Greek ears, is probably the explanation of the term's gradual disuse as a divine
title.[62]

And this could in turn explain both the
adoption of the term by Paul, despite the express
command of Christ to the contrary,[63] and the
rarity of its use. Its adoption in the Pastoral
Epistles was most likely occasioned by Paul's
anxiety to emphasize his personal doctrinal
authority in the face of the prevalent heterodox
teaching (1 Tim. 1.3: 6.3) emanating from
Jewish sources. (Titus 1.10.)[64] Each time he uses
it, he stresses the fact of his commission, and the
addition of "teacher" to "herald and apostle"

underlines the intellectual aspect of his function, a stress necessitated by the activity of false "teachers". (2 Tim. 4.3.) That Paul was well aware of the nuance of doctrinal authority implied in "teacher" can hardly be doubted after the use he makes of that term in Rom. 2. 20, his sarcastic castigation of the proud Jewish doctors of the Law.

In view of his awareness of the basically Jewish content clothed in the Greek form of *didaskalos* Paul could well have given himself the other title associated with it in Matt. 23.9–10, namely that of "father", because not only in rabbinic literature,[65] but throughout the East generally,[66] the communication of knowledge was considered as a form of generation. In point of fact, however, Paul never claims this title.

The reason lies not so much in the simple fact of Jesus' teaching on the divine paternity and his express prohibition of any other claim to fatherhood (Matt. 23.9) as in the importance that the fatherhood of God quickly assumed in the life of the Church. This is brought out clearly in the Epistles. All Paul's prayers that his readers may enjoy grace and peace are addressed to "God our Father".[67] Although he speaks frequently of "the God-Father" (Gal. 1.1: Phil. 2.11: Col. 3.17), he just as often says simply, "the Father" (Rom. 6.4: Eph. 2.18: 3.14). That the Apostle could use a common word so abso-

lutely is certainly indicative of the exclusiveness
of the concept it signified.

For Paul the fatherhood of God has as its correlative man's adoptive sonship (Rom. 8.15,23:
9.4: Gal. 4.5: Eph. 1.5) in virtue of which he
can cry "Abba, Father". (Rom. 8.15: Gal. 4.6.)
The setting up of this relationship is the bringing into being of the "household of God" (1 Tim.
3.15). And in this household Paul is only the
"steward". (1 Cor. 4.1.) He may act *in loco
parentis* (Gal. 4.2) but that gives him no right to
assume the title of the head of the household. To
claim the title "father" would be to arrogate to
himself a dignity which he does not possess. His
converts, however, do owe their Christian being
to him (Philem. 19), for he has begotten them
through the Gospel. (1 Cor. 4.15.) Consequently,
he has a greater right to the loving respect which
is the normal concomitant of paternal dignity
than the mere "pedagogues" who endeavour to
build on the foundation he has established. (1
Cor. 3.10ff.) If Paul does more than once insinuate that the relationship between himself
and those he has taught is that of a father to his
children,[68] it is in order to communicate to them,
in some degree, a realization of the love motivating all he does on their behalf. His exhortations,
his teaching, his reprimands are all inspired by
love. (2 Cor. 2.4: 5.14.)

Sunergos theou—"*God's Co-worker*"

This rather daring title is found only twice in the whole Bible. It is given once to Paul and Apollos (1 Cor. 3.9) and once to Timothy. (1 Thess. 3.2.) The reading of 1 Cor. 3.9 is certain, but Nestle, while adopting the reading "God's co-worker", lists a number of variants for 1 Thess. 3.2: (1) "co-worker"; (2) "servant (*diakonos*) of God"; (3) "servant of God and our co-worker"; (4) "God's servant and co-worker". A number of critical editions[69] have chosen the reading "servant [*diakonos*] of God", but Vaganay's discussion of these variants has clearly shown that the reading "God's co-worker" is to be preferred.[70] Variant (3) is obviously a harmonization; (4) is a combination of our text and (2). "God's co-worker" is undoubtedly the *lectio difficilior* and explains variants (1) and (2); the text having been altered in order to suppress so daring an expression. All unwittingly this is a valuable indication of the sense in which *sunergos theou* must be understood.

The latest to object to the translation "God's co-worker" has been V. Furnish.[71] He admits the ambiguity of the Greek and the fact that the author's use of "co-worker" elsewhere is not decisive because this is the unique instance of the qualification "of God". The meaning then must be determined from the immediate context.

Following Lightfoot and Lietzmann, Furnish considers 1 Cor. 3.8b ("... and each shall receive his wages according to his labour") as parenthetical, and so relates verse 9a immediately to verse 8a: "He who plants and he who waters are equal." Paul's intention, he says, is to stress the equality of the ministers of the Gospel in order to discourage the foolish veneration of individual apostles which had given rise to the factions at Corinth (1.12: 3.4); they are all equal, all being fellow-workers in God's service.

It is perfectly true that Paul's purpose in this passage (3.5–4.13) is to correct the distorted view of the apostolate prevalent in Corinth. The Corinthians exaggerated the importance of the Apostle. Paul counteracts this by pointing out that he and Apollos are nothing, since it is God giving the increase who really counts. (3.7.) But to stop at this point would be to merely substitute one erroneous view for another. Verse 8b is not parenthetical. The promise of a reward is important as bringing out the reality of the work accomplished by the preachers. They are "servants" not only in name but in deed, who do plant and water. (v. 6.) In carrying out the charge laid upon them, they are God's instruments in the genesis of faith. They are "servants *through whom* you believed". (v. 5.) Everything is due to God. (v. 7.) He commissions the preachers; he gives the seed its vitality; he prepares the soil for its reception. But the preachers actually do co-operate with him in bringing the seed of the word of God into contact with the soil that is men's hearts. The context, therefore, indicates that *sunergos theou* is to be understood in the sense of "God's collaborator". This finds confirmation in Allo's observation that *sun-* always implies a direct reference to the genitive following.[72] Naturally the preachers co-operate with one another, but the whole dignity of their function flows from the fact that it is primarily a collaboration with God.

The same idea is found in 1 Thess. 3.2 where Paul writes that he has sent Timothy, "our brother and God's co-worker in the gospel of Christ to establish you and encourage your faith". Here the sphere of collaboration is determined by the phrase "in the gospel of Christ". "Gospel" obviously must be taken in the active sense it enjoys in 2 Thess. 2.13: Phil. 1.5: and Rom. 1.1, that is, as the actual communication of the good news of salvation. It is precisely as a preacher, therefore, that Timothy is God's co-operator. Note, as in 1 Cor. 3.9, the reference to faith; however, here it is a question not of its genesis but of its preservation. In both operations the preacher is equally God's instrument, and a few verses later, Paul again underlines the reality of his contribution:

I held out no longer, but sent that I might know of your faith, lest perhaps the tempter had tempted you and our toil should prove in vain.

This anxiety indicates that the preservation of the Faith is a co-operative effort in which the preacher and the convert play their respective parts. The fact of this double co-operation (preacher-God; preacher-convert) makes the interpretation of 2 Cor. 6.1 somewhat uncertain, for the second party is not specified: "Co-operating, we exhort you not to receive the grace of God in vain." Either "with you" or "with God" must be supplied. Both are possible in the context, but the balance of probability seems weighted in favour of the latter by the verses which immediately precede:

On Christ's behalf, then, we are ambassadors, since God is exhorting *through us*; we beseech you for Christ's sake, be reconciled to God. [2 Cor. 5.20][73]

The preachers co-operate with God because they speak for him, or rather, because he uses them to convey his message to men.

What title could lay greater emphasis on the dignity of the apostolate! Yet there is never danger of misapprehension, for the contexts in which it is used amply attest that its splendour and nobility stem from its essentially subordinate character.

The Preacher: a Portrait

The preacher is a paradox. He is a man of destiny but not master of his own. He is devoid of personal significance but a key figure in the salvation of the world. He teaches with authority and freedom but is essentially a simple organ of communication. He can speak of the message he brings as "his", but it does not originate with him nor does he have any power over it. He is chosen from among men and given a title of honour, but his privilege is to serve and to suffer. He is a slave but motivated by love.

Seven of his titles apparently denote the lowest of functions, but the eighth, "God's co-worker", is the key to their true meaning and reveals the secret of the paradox. The preacher is only the spokesman of another, but because that other is God, to be chosen to collaborate with him, no matter what be the conditions of service, is to be honoured and not degraded. The preacher is only an administrator, but the deposit entrusted to him is the word of life.

ADAPTATION TO THE APOSTOLATE

As has become evident, Paul's idea of the preacher owes much to the Old-Testament presentation of the function of the Prophets. In the narratives of the prophetic vocation we remarked on the sacramental gesture that fitted the prophet for his mission. (Isa. 6.5–7: Jer. 1.9: Ezek. 3.1,4.) The startlingly realistic symbolism of the Old Dispensation is not found in the New, but there does exist explicit evidence that the preacher is conditioned for his function by the bestowal of special graces. These graces, in view of his essentially subordinate character, can be conceived in terms of a communicated instrumental power, making him capable of achieving the salvation of souls.

There is no proportion between merely natural endowments and such an effect. Paul was so conscious of this that he even used it as an argument to prove the divine origin of his mission:

> Am I not an apostle? Have I not seen Jesus our Lord? Are not ye my work in the Lord? If to others I am not an apostle, yet to you at least I am, for ye are the seal set upon my apostleship in the Lord. [1 Cor. 9.1.]

The basic qualification of an apostle was to have been sent by the risen Christ. (Acts 1.22.) Paul did receive such a mission on the Damascus Road but in order that his readers may have more evidence than his word alone, he introduces a supplementary proof, namely, the efficaciousness of his preaching at Corinth. He

4

adduces the Church at Corinth as a *documentum apostolatus sui.* (Cornely.) The numerous conversions could not conceivably be the result of any merely human effort. The concluding phrase of this passage, "in the Lord", may be taken as indicative of the true source of the preacher's power.[74]

In his second letter to the faithful at Corinth Paul describes his work among them in terms which, even allowing for the metaphor, are inexplicable on the assumption that any purely natural force was at work:

> Manifestly you are an epistle of Christ, drawn up by us, written not with ink but with the Spirit of the living God, not on tablets of stone but on hearts of flesh. [2 Cor. 3.3]

What is Paul, what is Apollos compared with such a work? Their only too evident humanity makes it obvious to all that the power they wield is not theirs but God's:

> We hold this treasure in vessels of clay that it may be clearly seen that this extraordinary power comes from God and not from us. [2 Cor. 4.7]

Paradoxically, it is their lack of what the world regards as necessary qualities that makes them, in God's eyes, perfect instruments, because it is part of his plan that his works should be attributed to him alone. There is no contradiction between Paul's humility when he speaks of his own person (e.g., 1 Cor. 4.9–13: 2 Cor. 4.7–15) and the pride with which he speaks of his mission. Both are unfeigned, and the reconciliation between them is effected by his awareness of having received a gift in no way merited. He terms this gift, "grace" (*charis*), "power" (*exousia, dunamis*), "sufficiency" (*ikanotēs*).

Because of his former career as a persecutor of the Church (1 Cor. 15.9: 1 Tim. 1.13), Paul was vividly conscious of God's benevolence (Gal. 1.15) in his regard:

> By the grace of God I am what I am, and his grace in me has not been fruitless. I have laboured more than all, *yet not I but the grace of God with me.* [1 Cor. 15.10]

As God's love is not drawn by the good of creatures but causes their goodness, so too his favour causes grace in man. The object of God's favour is always the recipient of a gift. In virtue of the divine action Paul (and his associates) have been made *adequate* ministers of the New Covenant (2 Cor. 3.6); the reception of this "grace" has made them "competent" (*ikanos*). It is their "sufficiency". The same idea, though expressed rather differently, is to be found in 1 Thess. 2.4: "We speak as being approved [*dedokimasmetha*] by God and entrusted with the gospel." The verb *dokimazō* means "to examine, to prove by testing", but in the context has to explain Paul's confidence and success. He is "one who has been approved". Clearly, since the subject is God, it cannot be a question of a mere verification of Paul's ability. That would be no explanation, and moreover, would imply that Paul considered his adaptation to the ministry to be a purely juridical approval. For all his acquaintance with the Hellenistic world and its patterns of thought, Paul remained a Semite for whom the divine action is always really efficacious. His quality of being approved (*dokimē*) is, therefore, something real within him.[75] The purpose of this divine act concerns the Gospel, for Paul and his collaborators have been approved in view of the realization of the plan of salvation. "Gospel" in this context has obviously an active sense (the actual proclamation of the Good News) because it is equated with the "appeal" (*paraklēsis*) made by Paul (*v.* 3) to which the Thessalonians responded. (1.6.)

The idea that this "grace" is a "power", already hinted at in 1 Cor. 15.10,[76] is found somewhat more explicitly in Gal. 2.7–9:

> Having acknowledged that I had been entrusted with the gospel of uncircumcision as Peter of circumcision . . . since he who assisted Peter for the apostolate of circumcision assisted me for the gentiles [*ho gar energēsas*

Petrō eis apostolēn tēs peritomēs enērgēsen kai emoi eis ta ethne] . . . having acknowledged the grace bestowed on me [they gave us the right hand of fellowship].

The grace given to Paul is his commission to preach to the Gentiles. The datives (*Petrō* and *emoi*) do not indicate the place of the divine action,[77] but the individuals for whose advantage or on whose behalf it is exercised.[78] Visibly manifested by his success, this grace implies permanent[79] divine assistance.[80] This is perfectly clear in 1 Tim. 1.12:

I give thanks to him who infused power (*endunamōsanti*) into me, Christ Jesus our Lord. I thank him for judging me worthy of this trust and appointing me to his service.

The aorist *endunamōsanti* refers to a definite moment of past time: Paul's vocation on the Damascus Road. There he received not only a mission but also the power which made its fulfilment possible. The New English Bible's paraphrase renders the sense well: "I thank him who has made me equal to the task."

This power is without doubt that which Jesus promised to his Apostles when he sent them to preach. (Matt. 28.28–30: Acts 1.7–8.) Because the Apostles as founders of the Church enjoyed special graces, one cannot infer that what was given them is necessarily the property of every preacher. Paul, however, by his use of the plural in 1 Thess. 2.4 and 2 Cor. 4.7, indicates that graces analogous to his own have been conferred on his assistants. It is an awareness of this power within him that he tries to arouse in Timothy when the difficulties of the latter's task seem almost to overwhelm him:

> I remind you to rekindle the gift of God which is within you through the laying on of my hands. For God has not given us a spirit of timidity, but of power, of charity and prudence. [2 Tim. 1.6–7.]

Timothy received, through the mediation of Paul, the same grace as Paul himself had received, and this grace in its triple function endows him with all the qualities necessary for a preacher. (*v.* 8.) Most fundamental is "power", the quality which makes him capable of producing divine effects.[81] The faith by which men are saved (Eph. 2.8) is a divine gift (Phil. 1.29), but its genesis is dependent upon preaching. (Rom. 10.17.) Were preaching a merely human activity the gratuity and divine character of faith would be gone. The exercise of this "power" is motivated by "charity". The preacher is God's slave,[82] completely subordinate to his will, but not treated as an inanimate instrument. God respects the freedom of the nature he has created, yet assures the activity of the instrument he has

chosen by infusing into the preacher's heart a
consuming love for all mankind.[83] This love is
the inspiration of all his activity. It drives him
to the limit of his resources, disposes him to welcome joyfully all sacrifices.[84] Take away this love
and the preacher, like the incarnation and passion of our Lord, becomes inexplicable. Thus
rooted in divine power and motivated by love,
the activity of the preacher is further governed
by "prudence". The preacher must be aware of
the individuality of his hearers. He must take
into account the differences arising from age,
sex, and social condition (1 Tim. 5.1–3: Titus
2.1–10) and adapt his presentation of the Gospel
accordingly.[85] The "personalization" of the
unique message involved in this adaptation is
not a falsification. The body of revelation transmitted by Paul to Timothy is accompanied by
the grace necessary for its integral preservation:
"Guard the precious deposit through the Holy
Spirit who dwells in us." (2 Tim. 1.14.) In his
turn, Timothy is to pass on this deposit to men
competent to teach (2 Tim. 2.2), handing on with
it the grace without which their ministry must
be inefficacious. (1 Tim. 4.14: 5.22.)

When is this supernatural aptitude for the
office of preacher given? For Timothy it was
obviously the moment of the imposition of hands.
Paul does not offer any data which would permit

us to determine with certainty when this took place. His manner of speaking of it as already ancient (1 Tim. 4.14: 2 Tim. 1.6) appears to exclude the hypothesis that it immediately preceded the appointment of Timothy as head of the Church at Ephesus. If we allow an association with the allusion to Timothy's education (2 Tim. 1.5) it seems probable that the imposition of hands took place at Lystra, when Paul took Timothy with him to replace John-Mark, and to aid him in the spreading of the Gospel. (Acts 16.1–4.)[86]

As for Paul's own grace, his consistent use of the aorist when referring to its reception (2 Cor. 10.8: Gal. 2.8: 1 Tim. 1.12) and the complete absence of any circumstantial explanation indicate that it was a point of time indelibly impressed on his memory. The obvious conclusion that the implied reference is to the apparition on the Damascus Road is confirmed by the context of 1 Tim. 1.12. His charge brought with it the power necessary for its perfect fulfilment. The mission, then, is the cause of what St Thomas calls the *gratia sermonis*,[87] a conclusion already suggested by Paul's own query: "How are men to preach unless they be sent?" (Rom. 10.15.)

The most prominent of the side-effects of this grace is the virtue of *parresia*, "audacity".[88]

Because attached to God's service, the preacher is subject to no purely human power. His sole concern being to transmit his message integrally, unswayed by any considerations other than the will of God, his activity is marked by the confidence and daring that ensure success. Without the courage and realism to translate his ideals into practice, all the preacher's other virtues, in particular his fidelity, profit him nothing. To this extent, then, is "audacity" the virtue most characteristic of an apostle.

THE WORD OF GOD

Implicit in the parallel between the preacher and the prophet and explicit in the titles "herald" and "steward" is the idea that the preacher is not the source of the doctrine he preaches. The message he communicates does not originate with him; it is the word of God. This apparently simple expression has a multiplicity of implications.

The first and most obvious is that the truth the preacher proclaims originates in God and has been communicated by him. Ezechiel's frequently recurring phrase "the word of Yahweh came to me" (3.16: 6.1 etc.) provides a perfect illustration of this meaning. Paul, in the apologies for his ministry that he was forced to make, emphasizes not only that his message does not originate with himself, but also that he has not received it from any other man:

> For I make it known to you brethren, that the gospel preached by me is no gospel of man, nor did I receive or learn it from man, but by revelation from Jesus Christ. [Gal. 1.1]

After outlining his doctrine very sketchily for Timothy, Paul concludes: "Such is the gospel of the glory of the blessed God wherewith I have been entrusted." (1 Tim. 1.11.) The same idea underlies the oft repeated "word of God" (1 Cor. 14.36: 2 Cor. 2.17: Phil. 1.14 etc.) or "gospel of God" (Rom. 1.1: 2 Cor. 11.7: 1 Thess. 2.2 etc.), or "witness of God". (1 Cor. 2.1.) The realities signified by these different terms are not precisely co-extensive, but the point to be noted is that they are all divine in origin. The word of God is also "the word of the Lord" (1 Thess. 1.8), "the gospel of Christ" (1 Thess. 3.2 etc.) or "the witness of Christ" (1 Cor. 1.6: 2 Tim. 1.8). The implication in each case is the same—the message preached is no human invention.

It is not to be thought that Paul could speak thus of the matter of his preaching simply because he received it through a direct personal revelation. (Gal. 1.11.) Throughout his career Paul prided himself on being totally unlike those who adulterated or falsified the word of God (2

Cor. 2.17: 4.2). But towards the end of his life, a worn-out prisoner (2 Tim. 1.12), faced not only with the certainty of further suffering but also with the rising tide of error, he wondered if he would have the strength to guard intact to the end the deposit of doctrine confided to him. Despite his anguish his faith finally triumphed:

> I know in whom I have put my trust and I am confident that he is able to guard the deposit committed to me until that day. [2 Tim. 1.12]

God is exigent but he is also just. For a super-human task Paul enjoyed superhuman aid. It was not in God's purpose that the deposit of faith should vanish with Paul's death, nor was it God's intention to communicate his message directly to each individual preacher. There was to be a chain of transmission, as Paul makes clear to Timothy:

> Hold to the pattern of sound words which you heard from me . . . guard the precious deposit through the Holy Spirit who dwells in us. [2 Tim. 1.13–14]

And Timothy had a similar obligation to his successors:

> The things you heard from me in the presence of many witnesses, the same entrust to faithful men, such as will be able to teach others in their turn. [2 Tim. 2.2]

Yet, because of the authorized transfer, the message always remains the word of *God*, the gospel of *Christ*.

Paradoxically, it is a phrase that has permitted exegetes of the liberal school to oppose Paul to Christ that enables us to penetrate more profoundly into the meaning of the phrase "the word of God" and to explore further its implications. Paul terms his message "*my* gospel" (Rom. 2.16; "our" 2 Thess. 2.14). Today there is no necessity to prove again that this is not a gospel different from Christ's. It is not difficult, as Allo points out, to show "that the dogmas promulgated by the Apostle of the Nations are only the explanation, or the translation into more general or to an extent more intellectual terms, of that which the Synoptics recount as performed or taught by Jesus."[89] Paul can call the unique message "his" because he made it so. The originality of his presentation was the natural result of his perception of the unity of that message in terms of one central idea, the saving Christ. The depth to which this concept penetrated his whole being enabled him to combine entire fidelity with an extraordinary degree of flexibility. Ever sensitive to the changing needs of his hearers he was never a mere canal for divine communications as were the oracles of pagan legend. Yet for all that, he was conscious that his words were, in a sense, divine. The message is supernatural not only in its origin but also in its transmission:

> We thank God unceasingly for this also—that, when you had received from us the word which you heard, God's word, you accepted it, not as the word of men, but—as it truly is —the word of God. [1 Thess. 2.13][90]

The same idea runs through 1 Cor. 3.5–4.16, where Paul takes himself and Apollos as examples (4.6) to illustrate the universal truth that the ministry as such (3.8) is completely dependent on, and subordinate to, God. The change in *v.* 6—"I planted, Apollos watered, but it was God who was giving the increase"—from the aorist tense to the imperfect is very significant. "The aorists sum up, as wholes, the initial work of Paul (cf. Acts 18.1–8), and the fostering ministry of Apollos (cf. Acts 18.24–19.1); the imperfect indicates what was going on throughout, God was all along causing the increase."[91] The divine action is not concomitant with that of the preachers as if the two were in parallel. Rather, they interpenetrate, so that the preacher's words may be said to be formally the word of God. It is thus that Paul can refer to the Thessalonians as "God-taught":

> About brotherly love you need no words of mine, for you are yourselves taught by God to love one another, for thus indeed you act to

all the brethren in the whole of Macedonia.
[1 Thess. 4.9–10]

How have they been taught *by God*? It seems
highly unlikely that there is question here of a
special divine revelation. The precept of frater-
nal charity occupied such a central place in the
Gospel message (Matt. 5.43–8: 19.19) that the
Thessalonians must have been made aware of it
the first time they came into contact with the
word of God. They are taught by God, therefore,
in accepting the preaching of Paul and his companions, whose words energized by divine power
(1 Thess. 2.13) remain within them, a permanent
living lesson. The Thessalonians have been sum-
moned from the ranks of "those who know not
God" (1 Thess. 4.5) and enter the Kingdom of
Heaven by responding to this appeal (1.6) which
is "our gospel" (1.5):

> God chose you from the beginning unto salva-
> tion through sanctification of the spirit and
> credence of the truth. It was to this end he
> called you through our gospel. [2 Thess.
> 2.12–13]

God is "he who calls" (1 Thess. 5.24), but the
words he uses are those of the preacher.

This is brought out with striking clarity in
the following passage which manifests Paul's
vivid realization of the implications of his commission:

Whoever is in Christ is a new creature: the old things have passed away, behold they have become new! But all things are from God who reconciled us to himself through Christ, and conferred on us the ministry of reconciliation. That is, God, in Christ, reconciled the world to himself, not holding men's sins against them, and he committed to us the word of reconciliation. We are ambassadors, therefore, on Christ's behalf *since God is entreating through us*. [2 Cor. 5.17–20][92]

The believers are "in Christ". Such a radical change from their former state of "strangers to the life of God" (Eph. 4.18) can only be attributed to divine power. In Christ, God reconciled the world to himself by agreeing not to take into account the sins for which Christ made expiation. (Cf. 1 Cor. 6.11: Eph. 1.7: Col. 1.14.) Why then did he further confide "the ministry of reconciliation" to the Apostles? The answer is to be found in a passage of the Epistle to the Colossians:

Formerly you were yourself estranged from God, you were his enemies through your evil thoughts and deeds. But now he has reconciled you by his body of flesh, delivering it to death, so as to present you holy and blameless and irreproachable in his sight. Only you must persevere in your faith, firm on your foundations, without swerving from the hope promised in the gospel which you heard, which has been preached in the whole world and of which I, Paul, am the servant. [Col. 1.21–3]

Here it is seen that men must avail themselves of the reconciliation effected by Christ. Each one must personally ratify that reconciliation. This is achieved through faith, which is the total dedication of self implicit in obedience to the Gospel preached by Paul. The function of the "ministry of reconciliation" entrusted to Paul and his collaborators, then, is to make actual for their contemporaries the reconciliation effected by Christ. To this end God has placed on their lips "the word of reconciliation". This is not merely a message *about* reconciliation, though naturally it does inform those who hear it of the effects of the passion and resurrection of Christ. Provided that those who hear it receive it with faith, this word reconciles them with God.[93] Thus Christ's ministry of reconciliation is prolonged in that of his chosen servants. They act "on Christ's behalf". But just as the reconciliation effected by Christ is attributed to God working "through Christ", so too is the efficacy of the preacher's words. These are laden with salvific power "because God is entreating through us".

This is the effect of the grace of the apostolate, the consequence of their being entrusted with

the "ministry of reconciliation". It is not necessary each time they preach that God place anew
on their lips the "word of reconciliation". An
authentic mission confers a stable function and a
permanent power, in virtue of which the
preacher's message is formally God's word. "How
are they to believe in him [Christ] *whom* they
have not heard? And how are they to hear without a preacher? And how are men to preach
unless they be sent?" (Rom. 10.14–15.)

NOTES

1. *Agapé*, vol. 1, 6.
2. This will be more apparent after we consider the
relationship between Paul and the Servant of Yahweh.
(Ch. 3.) Paul implicitly gives himself the title "prophet"
in two passages, Eph. 2.20 and 3.5. Joüon's classic argumentation (in *RSR*, 15 (1925), 532–4) in favour of the
identification of the "prophets" of these verses with the
"apostles" also mentioned has been revitalized recently
by J. Pfammatter who concludes: "Dabei ist nicht an
eine von den Aposteln—dort im engeren Sinn ver-
standen—verschiedene Gruppe von Männern zu den-
ken, sondern es handelt sich lediglich um einen anderen
Gesichtspunkt, unter dem dieselben Urapostel Fundament der Kirche sind. Als *Apostel* sind sie die bevoll-
mächtigten Gestanden und damit Repräsentanten
Jesus als Hirten und Priester; als *Propheten* dagegen
die authentischen Lehrer und Verkünder der von ihnen
empfangenen Offenbarung." (*Die Kirche als Bau*, Rome
(1960), 96.)
3. It also in a few instances translates *ro'eh* "seer"
and *hozeh* "seer".

4. Cf. L. Koehler—W. Baumgartner, *Lexicon in Veteris Testamenti Libros,* Leiden (1958), *s.v.*

5. Cf. W. F. Albright, *From the Stone Age to Christianity,* New York (1957), 303. Also Rendtoroff, *TWNT,* vol. 6, 796.

6. Cf. E. Mangenot, *Prophète, DBV,* 5, 709; A. Gelin, in *Introduction à la Bible,* vol. 1, ed. A. Robert and A. Feuillet, Paris (1959), 468.

7. Yahweh's question is to be understood as a direct summons. Cf. P. Beguerie, J. Leclercq, J. Steinmann, *Études sur les prophetes d'Israel,* Paris (1954), 30.

8. In view of the etymology accepted for *nabi',* it will not be out of place to remark Paul's insistence on the fact that he was *called* to his preaching ministry. (Rom. 1.1: 1 Cor. 1.1: Gal. 1.15: 1 Tim. 1.12.)

9. For the extra-New-Testament background we draw on the article of G. Friedrich in the *TWNT,* vol. 3, 683 ff., from which we take the references.

10. Cf. R. Taubenschlag, "The Herald in the Law of the Papyri", *Archives d'histoire du droit oriental,* 6 (1949), 189–94 (reprinted in *Opera Minora,* 2, 151–7), to whom we owe the papyrological references.

11. Fuad I, Univ. Pap., ed. Crawford (1949), no. 31; P. Petr. III, 125,9,13.

12. P. Hamb. 29,5; Copt. 135,B,6.

13. PSI X, 1162,8.

14. Cf. F. Preisigke and F. Filabel, *Sammelbuch griechischer Urkunden aus Aegypten,* 7336,5.

15. The closest parallel to the content of the Greek term in the Old Testament is the office of *mazkir.* The presence of this title in a number of very restricted lists of officials of the Israelite kingdom (2 Sam. 8.16–18 = 1 Chron. 18.15–17: 2 Sam. 20.23–6: 1 Kings 4.2–6) inclines one to doubt that its value is translated by such banal terms as "annalist" or "scribe". The only biblical evidence of the *mazkir's* function is to be found in the account of his mission (together with the other officers of the court) to meet the emissary of the King of Assyria (2 Kings 18.18–37). Following Begrich (*Zeit.*

morgentländische Gesellschaft, 84 (1933), *10), De Vaux emphasizes the root value of *zkr* in the *hifil* and clarifies the concept by a reference to the Egyptian *whm.w*, who is also "he who repeats, calls, announces" ("Titres et fonctionnaires Égyptiens à la cour de David et de Salomon", *RB*, 49 (1939), 394–7.) This official, over and above his ceremonial functions, had as his duty to report to the Pharaoh what concerned the people and the country and, inversely, to communicate to the people the orders of the king. Cf. R. de Vaux, *Les Institutions de l'Ancien Testament*, col. 1, 202–3. H. Reventlow has an entirely different concept of the functions of the *mazkir*. In his interpretation this official combines the offices of a modern Solicitor-General and Public Prosecutor ("Das Amt des Mazkir", *Theologische Zeitschrift*, 15 (1959), 161–75, esp. 171).

16. Especially since "apostle" occurs over seventy times and Herodotus had already used the two as synonyms. (*Hist.*, 1.21.)

17. Cf. *TWNT*, vol. 3, 695.

18. The bibliography on "apostle" is immense. That given by Rengstorf (*TWNT*, vol. 1, 406) should be completed by Rigaux's list (*Thess.*, 152, *n.* 1) to which three important recent studies should be added: H. Mosbech, "*Apostolos* in the New Testament", *Studia Theologica*, 2 (1948), 166–200; E. M. Kredel, "Der Apostelbegriff in der neueren Exegese", *ZKT*, 78 (1956), 169–93, 257–305; L. Cerfaux, "Pour l'Histoire du titre 'Apostolos' dans le Nouveau Testament", *RSR*, 48 (1960), 76–92. We are here concerned only with the Pauline use of the term and we leave the usage of the term in other New-Testament writings, together with the question of apostolic authority (in the modern sense), entirely out of account.

19. Cf. Rengstorf, *TWNT*, vol 1, 406–7, from whom the non-biblical references are taken.

20. This reading is supported only by A, for B lacks 1 Kings 14.1–20. Symmacus employs "apostle" to translate *çir* in Isa. 13.2.

21. No authority to preach is "from men", i.e., of human origin, in counter-distinction, for example, to the power of Caesar, which was considered to come from the people. (Cf. Lagrange, *Gal.*, 2.) Divine power may, however, be transmitted by a human intermediary.

22. Opinion is sharply divided (cf. Allo, *1 Cor.*, 397) on whether "apostles" here is coextensive with "the Twelve". The fact that Paul immediately afterwards (*vv.* 8–9) claims the title for himself, inclines us to think that the term is being used in the wider sense it has in Rom. 16.7 ("Andronicus and Junias . . . eminent among the apostles"), 1 Thess. 2.7 and 1 Cor. 4.9.

23 Even in Phil. 2.25 and 2 Cor. 8.23 there is a connection with the spread of the Gospel, although a rather tenuous one.

24. Cf. ch. 3.

25. The "slave" is contrasted with the "master" (1 Cor. 12.13: Gal. 3.28: Eph. 6.8: Col. 3.11) and the "freeman" (Eph. 6.5: Col. 3.22: 1 Tim. 6.1: Titus 2.9).

26. The difference between a slave and a freeman was so fundamental and so deeply ingrained in the Greek mentality that it was unthinkable for a Greek to describe his relationship to God in terms of slavery. The few instances that do exist are to be attributed to the influence of the Eastern mystery religions. (Cf. Rengstorf, *TWNT*, vol. 2, 264, 267.)

27. Cf. G. Sass, "Zur Bedeutung von *doulos* bei Paulus", *ZNW*, 40 (1941), 24–32.

28. One who entered the royal service ceased to be attached to the clan organization and became a "slave" of the king in a legal sense. Cf. W. F. Albright, "The Seal of Eliakim and the latest Preexilic History of Judah", *JBL*, 51 (1932), 80, *n.* 7.

29. Cf. R. de Vaux, *Les Institutions de l'Ancien Testament*, vol. 1, 125.

30. "He who was a slave at the time of his call is a freeman of the Lord, just as he who was free at the time of his call is a slave of Christ." (1 Cor. 7.22.) The point Paul is concerned to make in this context is

that each one should remain in the social state in which the call of God found him. Slaves, then, should not be anxious to better their condition for in a higher sense they are already free, just as those who are free are, in a mystical sense, slaves. Paul's use of "slave" here is in all probability due entirely to his love of paradoxical expression—for if a freeman is made a slave by his conversion so is a slave.

Eph. 6.5–6 falls into a slightly different category, though again addressed to those who are slaves in the physical sense: "Slaves, obey your earthly masters ... as serving Christ, not with eye-service to please men, but as *douloi Christou*, doing whole-heartedly the will of God." The context shows that *douloi Christou* is most accurately translated as "Christian slaves". Paul's Semitic background adequately explains the adjectival use of the genitive.

31. *Synonyms of the New Testament*, London (1894), 32.

32. *Synonyms*, 32. Paul only once gives Christ this title: *diakonos ... peritomēs*. (Rom. 15.8.) He is a *diakonos* in carrying out or bringing to fulfilment the promises implied in the Covenant, the seal of which was circumcision. (Lagrange, Sanday-Headlam.)

33. *Synonyms*, 34.

34. "In the language of the papyri, *hypēretēs* designates anyone at the service of another", H. Kupiszewski —J. Modrzejewski, "Hyperetai: Étude sur les fonctions et le rôle des hyperetes dans l'administration civile et judiciaire de l'Egypte gréco-romaine", *Journal of Juristic Papyrology*, 11–12 (1957–8), 142. Cf. B. Holmes, "Luke's Description of John Mark", *JBL*, 54 (1935), 63–72.

35. Cf. Plato, *Rep.* 8,7,522b.

36. Cf. W. Hobart, *The Medical Language of Saint Luke*, Dublin (1882), 88.

37. "Hyperetai etc", 161. The papyrological references which follow are taken from this study. With his customary perspicacity Trench notes that it is "the more

official character and functions of the *hypēretēs"* (his italics) which distinguish this term from the closely allied *diakonos*. (*Synonyms*, 34.)

38. Cf. BGU 1775, 1825; P. Princ. II, 16; P. Par. 15; P. Strasb. 5; P. Oxy. 2187.

39. Cf. P. Tebt. 434; BGU 226 (lines 24–5).

40. Cf. P. Lond. II, 214, PSI 448, 456.

41. Cf. P. Oxy. 51 (lines 5–13), 475, 476 (line 12); P. Oslo 95 (lines 9–13); BGU 647 (lines 5–17); PSI 455 (lines 3–12).

42. Cf. P. Fouad 22 (lines 17–19); BGU 581, 891 (verso line 19); and the study by J. Schwartz, "Un Formulaire de nomographe", *Journal of Juristic Papyrology*, 4 (1950), 209–14.

43. Cf. P. Oxy. 916 (lines 18–19); P. Flor. 312 (line 8); P. Rain. 14; P. Hamb. 3.

44. Cf. P. Flor. 2, 7; and the studies of U. Wilken, "Zu den Florintiner Papyri", *Arch. für Pap.* 4 (1908), 424–425, and R. Taubenschlag, "Les Publications officielles du stratège dans l'Égypte gréco-romaine", *Journal of Juristic Papyrology*, 5 (1951), 155 (=*Opera Minora*, 2, 130).

45. The *hypēretēs*, like all state functionaries in antiquity, had certain religious functions to perform, but the term was also applied explicitly to the servants of cult associations. The papyri contain many parallels to the *hypēretēs* of the synagogue of Luke 4.20 (cf. Moulton-Milligan, *Vocabulary of the Greek New Testament*, London (1949), s.v.). In one (P. Lond. 2710), containing the constitutions of a religious association in Egypt, an (unnamed) *hypēretēs*, together with a (named) president, are mentioned as the only officials; cf. C. Roberts, T. Skeat, A. D. Nock, "The Gild of Zeus Hypistos", *Harvard Theological Review*, 26 (1936), 40, 50, 79–80.

46. Cf. M. Zerwick, *Graecitas Biblica*, Rome (1955), n. 314i. A similar example is to be found in Gal. 4.2.

47. There is no reason to deny that Paul intended the legal overtones in a context where they are so per-

fectly in place. By New-Testament times Jewish theology had degenerated into a complicated form of jurisprudence. Consequently, if we cannot claim for Paul a detailed acquaintance with the Jewish law of his age, it is at least certain that at the feet of Gamaliel he absorbed something of the spirit and mentality of its practitioners. In the long-Hellenized city of Tarsus he would have acquired those elements of the science of law that formed part of the intellectual equipment of every gentleman. In fact, juridical allusions and formulae are found scattered throughout the Epistles; Gal. 3.15–18: 4.1–7: Rom. 7.1–6: 8.15ff.: Col. 2.14: Eph. 1.14: 2 Cor. 1.22: 5.5: 1 Tim. 6.20: 2 Tim. 1.14. Cf. C. Spicq, "Saint Paul et la loi des dépôts", *RB*, 40 (1931), 481–502; E. Heylen, "Les Métaphores et les métonymies dans les épîtres pauliniennes", *ETL*, 12 (1935), 267.

48. The inscriptional evidence for the use of this term, collected and studied by P. Landvogt, *Epigraphische Untersuchungen über den "oikonomos": ein Beitrag zum hellenistischen Beamtenwesen*, Diss. Strassburg., 1908, has been partially summarized by H. Cadbury, "Erastus of Corinth", *JBL*, 50 (1931), 47–51.

49. Cf. *A-G*, 562; Michel, *TWNT*, 151–2.

50. Cf. R. de Vaux, *Les Institutions de l'Ancien Testament*, vol. 1, 199–200.

51. Cf. H. Cadbury, "Erastus", 50.

52. Detailed evidence from Egypt and Asia Minor is to be found in J. Reumann, " 'Stewards of God'—Pre-Christian religious application of *oikonomos* in Greek", *JBL*, 77 (1958) 342–4.

53. Cf. J. Reumann, " 'Stewards of God' ", 345–8.

54. Cf. S. Belkin, " 'The Problem of Paul's Background", *JBL*, 54 (1935), 52–5.

55. Cerfaux (*L'Église*, 126, *n.* 2) criticizes Rengstorf's exaggeration of the "non-charismatic" character of the "teachers" of 1 Cor. 12.28. (*TWNT*, vol. 2, 160–61.) On the charism of "teaching" see Dupont, *Gnosis*, 213–16, and H. Greeven, "Propheten, Lehrer, Vorsteher bei Paulus", *ZNW*, 44 (1952–3), 17–30.

56. Twenty-four times in the Synoptic Gospels, of which nineteen are in the vocative case.

57. Cf. Lohse, *TWNT*, vol. 6, 962–3.

58. The whole structure of Judaism was based on instruction in the Law, and the role of the masters who taught it was exalted to the highest possible degree. "The merit of him who teaches the Law to the children of the people is so great that his prayers are sufficiently efficacious to modify the decrees of providence." (*B. Mecia*, 85a, quoted in Spicq, *Pastorales, DBS*, 7, 9.)

59. In the Hellenistic world it carried the same social connotation as did "governess" in Victorian England, cf. H. Marrou, *A History of Education in Antiquity*, London (1956), p. 267.

60. In strictly Greek usage *didaskalos* could be applied to anyone who had special competence in any field of knowledge and communicated that knowledge in a systematic way. "The essential thing is that systematic instruction be given: if this be the case, then *didaskalos* is perfectly in place, whatever be the area (of knowledge) in question; and it matters little if the term be employed in a real or a figurative sense." (Rengstorf, *TWNT*, vol. 2, 152.) It may be the connotation of systematization that explains the avoidance of the term by the Septuagint (Esther 6.1 and 2 Macc. 1.10 are the only instances of its use), whereas it is found in the papyri with the meaning "schoolmaster" and also in contracts of apprenticeship (cf. Moulton-Milligan, *Vocabulary of the Greek New Testament*, s.v.).

61. Cf. O. Glombiza, "Die Titel *didaskalos* und *epistatēs* für Jesus bei Lukas", *ZNW*, 49 (1958), 275–8.

62. The same phenomenon characterizes the usage of its correlative *mathētēs*, "disciple". Frequent in the Gospels and Acts, this term is never used by Paul, probably because of his awareness of its insufficiency to express adequately the status of a *follower* of Christ. Rengstorf puts it very well: "What is most characteristic of the *mathētēs* is not really the *manthanein* [learning] but much more the *akolouthein* [following] ... It is self-

evident that the *mathētēs* of Jesus in so far as he is an *akoluthōn* is also a *manthanōn* (cf. Matt. 11.29); but the *manthanein*—and here it differs from the *talmid* of the Rabbis—is not that which makes him a *mathētēs.*" (*TWNT*, vol. 4, 408.)

63. "You must not be called 'rabbi', for you have one 'teacher' and you are all brothers. Do not call any man on earth 'father', for you have one 'father' and he is in heaven." (Matt. 23.8–9.) Paul's rabbinic training would also have accustomed him to a non-Christological use of the term, cf. Rom. 2.20.

64. Cf. Spicq, *Pastorales,* lv.

65. Cf. *Sifre Deut.,* 6, 7, and also *Sanhed.,* 19b. "Rabbi Samuel and Rabbi Jonathan has said : 'If anyone teaches the Torah to the son of his neighbour the Scripture considers it as if he had begotten him'", quoted from Spicq, "Une Allusion au Docteur de Justice dans Matt. 23.10?", *RB*, 66 (1959), 389.

66. A. J. Festugière, *La Révélation d'Hermès Trismégiste* I, Paris (1944), 332–6; E. Bikermann, "La Chaîne de la tradition pharisienne", *RB*, 59 (1952), 44–54.

67. Rom. 1.7: 1 Cor. 1.3: 2 Cor. 1.2: Gal. 1.4: Eph. 1.2: Phil. 1.2: Col. 1.3.

68. 1 Thess. 2.11: 1 Cor. 4.15: 2 Cor. 6.13: Gal. 4.19: Phil. 2.22: 1 Tim. 1.2: 2 Tim. 1.2: Titus 1.4.

69. Westcott and Hort, Tischendorf, Von Soden, Merk.

70. L. Vaganay, *Initiation à la critique textuelle néotestamentaire,* Paris (1934), 171–3.

71. "Fellow-workers in God's Service", *JBL*, 80 (1961), 364–70.

72. *1 Cor.,* 58.

73. On this passage, cf. above, p. 91.

74. Robertson-Plummer, Godet, St Thomas.

75. In Rom. 5.4 *dokimē* is presented as a reality in the Christian produced through the endurance of suffering. In this text, as in 1 Cor. 9.27 and 2 Cor. 8.2, *dokimē* is a quality common to all true believers. 2 Cor. 10.18

evidences, though not as clearly as 1 Thess. 2.4, the existence of another type of *dokimē*, cf. A. Denis, "L'Apôtre Paul, 'prophète messianique' des Gentils", *ETL*, 32 (1957), 287–300.

76. Because, in a context referring to activity, this grace has not been *kenē*, "without result, without effect, without reaching its goal". Cf. 1 Thess. 2.1: 2 Cor. 12.9.

77. As Lyonnet translates in the *Bible de Jérusalem*.

78. *Energein* is not a verb compound with *en-*, but derives from *en ergō*, "effective", and means simply "to act, operate, work". To designate the place in which activity is exercised the preposition *en* is used, e.g., Gal. 3.5: 1 Cor. 12.6: Eph. 2.2 etc. Cf. T. Zahn, *Der Brief des Paulus an die Galater*, Leipzig (1922), 102, *n.* 29.

79. The perfect *pepisteumai* implies a permanent commission (Lightfoot) and references scattered throughout the Epistles manifest the *fact* of this permanence; 2 Cor. 4.7: 12.9: 13.4: Eph. 3.20: Col. 1.28–9: Phil. 4.13: 2 Tim. 4.17.

80. Lagrange, Zahn, Burton.

81. Paul certainly implies a cause-and-effect relationship between preaching and faith. (Rom. 10.17.) St Thomas understood this as a relationship of dispositive causality. (*In Epistola ad Romanos*, ch. 10, lect. 2.) A disposition essentially ordained to faith is itself a reality of the supernatural order and cannot be produced by merely natural activity. Hence a special grace (power) is necessary to enable any man to communicate his faith to others. This grace St Thomas terms *gratia sermonis* (II-II, q.177, a.2) or *gratia locutionis* (*III Contra Gentiles*, c.154).

82. Cf. above, p. 55.

83. This is the sole text in the Pastorals in which "charity" is mentioned without "faith". This suggestion that its object is the neighbour rather than God is confirmed by the association of this charity with power and prudence. Cf. Spicq. *Agapé*, vol. 3, 50.

84. "Him Christ do we proclaim, admonishing every man and teaching every man with all wisdom, that we

may present every man perfect in Christ. For this I labour and struggle, with the aid of that divine energy which works powerfully in me." (Col. 1.28–9.)

85. Cf. below, p. 203.

86. Cf. Spicq, *Pastorales*, 324.

87. Cf. above, *n*. 81.

88. Cf. D. Smolders, "L'Audace de l'apôtre selon saint Paul: le thème de la *parresia*", *Collectanea Mechliniensia*, 28 (1958), 16–30, 177–33.

89. E. B. Allo, "L'Évolution de l'évangile de Paul", *Vivre et Penser* [=*RB*, 50] (1941), 48.

90. This passage is analysed in ch. 4, p. 172.

91. Robertson-Plummer, *1 Cor*., 57.

92. This passage is notoriously difficult to translate. St Thomas mentions the difficulty of determining the predicate of *theos ēn*. Is it *en Christō*, thus giving the meaning, "God was in Christ, reconciling the world"? Or is it *kosmon katallassōn*, thus giving the meaning "God was, in Christ, reconciling the world"? Allo prefers the former because it explains the value of Christ's death. Cornely, Plummer and Spicq opt for the latter, which echoes the "through Christ" of *v*. 18. Plummer's comment on the final phrase is important: "The force of *hōs* with a genitive absolute is not always the same. The *hōs* always gives a subjective view of what is stated by the gen. absolute, but that subjective view may be shown by the context to be right or wrong. When it is given as right [as is the case here where "it is manifest that God's entreating is given as a fact"] *hōs* may be rendered 'seeing that'." Cf. also Allo and Spicq.

93. R. Asting goes too far in saying: "Natürlich is das Wort auch ein Wort *von* der Versöhnung; aber die Hauptsache ist, dass es die Versöhnung selbst *erzeugt*." (*Die Verkündigung des Wortes in Urchristentum*, Stuttgart, 1939, 142, his italics.) It is true that he modifies this slightly in the next sentence: "Werden die Menschen vor diese Tatsache gestellt: es fragt sich, ob sie sich

dieser Versöhnungstat Gottes in Christus beugen und
sie annehmen wollen", but still does not express Paul's
thought accurately. The word of God exercises real
causality but only in those in whom God is active; cf.
below, p. 236.

A PROLONGATION OF THE MINISTRY OF CHRIST

IN the last chapter we saw that Paul conceived the preacher as a man chosen by God for a specific task: the salvation of mankind. Special graces which effect the identification of his word with God's make him equal to the exigencies of that mission. The message he brings is a participation of the divine salvific power. Now, the text which brought out this point most clearly (2 Cor. 5.17–20) also suggested a relationship between the activity of the preacher and that of Christ—both are instruments in the reconciliation of humanity with God.[1] The present chapter determines more precisely how the Apostle understood this relationship. That he conceived it as a dynamic union, we might almost say identification, of the preacher and the saving Christ, emerges from the fact that Paul, while sharing the awareness of the Primitive Church that Christ was the Servant of Yahweh prophesied by the Deutero-Isaias, conceived his own function in terms of the office of that same Servant. An examination of the notions of Spirit and Light brings out other aspects of this relationship between Christ and the preacher. Christ the Light of the World is also the giver of the Spirit; preaching is a luminous radiation entirely penetrated by the power of that Spirit.

THE SERVANT OF YAHWEH

What the convictions of the Pharisee Saul of Tarsus concerning the Messias were, are not known. What is certain, however, is that his first efforts after his conversion were directed to convincing his erstwhile brethren that the messianic prophecies of the Old Testament were fulfilled in the person of Jesus of Nazareth. At Damascus, we are told by Luke, "he silenced the Jews, demonstrating that Jesus is the Christ" (Acts 9.22), and such an approach was employed constantly in his preaching to Jews:

> Following his usual practice Paul went to their meetings, and for the next three sabbaths argued with them, quoting texts of Scripture which he expounded and applied to show that the Christ had to suffer and arise from the dead. "And the Christ", he said, "is this Jesus whom I proclaim to you." [Acts 17.2–3; cf. 13.23–47: 18.5,28: 26.22–23]

This evidence provided by Luke indicates that it is extremely unlikely that Paul in using the

term "Christ" was ever unmindful of its resonance in Jewish ears, even when speaking to a
pagan audience, to whom it would in itself have
conveyed nothing. In other words the presumption must be that Paul intended it to be understood, not simply as a proper name devoid of
real significance, but as an appellative designating Jesus as Messias.[2]

This is important for an adequate understanding of Paul's conception of his function
in the plan of salvation. Although he became
an apostle in receiving the revelation of the
Son (Gal. 1.16), that is in seeing "Jesus, our
Lord" (1 Cor. 9.1), he never claims to be an
"apostle of Jesus" or an "apostle of the Son of
God" as we might perhaps have expected. In
accenting the fact of his commission he does
use "apostle" without any further qualification,[3] but when it is a question of a title expressing his function it is always "apostle of *Christ*
Jesus by the will of God",[4] or "apostle of Jesus
Christ". (Titus 1.1.) Only once does he employ
"slave of God" (Titus 1.1), and this usage is
explained by the Old Testament idea he wished
to evoke.[5] At all other times he prefers "slave
of *Christ* Jesus" (Rom. 1.1: Phil. 1.1) or simply
"slave of *Christ*". (Gal. 1.10.) The same striking
consistency is found in the terms he uses to
qualify his message. Naturally it can be described as "the word of God",[6] "the gospel of

God",[7] and "the witness of God" (1 Cor. 2.1),
because God is the source of this message and
its saving power. But it is also termed "the
gospel of *the Christ*",[8] "the witness of *Christ*"
(1 Cor. 1.6; cf. 1 Tim. 2.6), "the preaching of
Jesus *Christ*" (Rom. 16.25), "the mystery of
Christ". (Eph. 3.4: Col. 4.3.) This predilection
for the messianic title immediately suggests that
Paul conceived his preaching office as a messianic function. A number of passages will enable us to make this affirmation more precise.

Paul's conversion is described three times by
Luke in Acts (9.1ff.: 22.3ff.: 26.4ff.). He himself
alludes to it only once but in terms that are
very significant:

> But when he who *set me apart from my
> mother's womb and called me* by his grace
> was to reveal his Son in me that I might
> preach him among the Gentiles, at once with-
> out taking counsel with flesh and blood and
> without going up to Jerusalem to those who
> were apostles before me, I retired into
> Arabia . . . [Gal. 1.15–17]

The expression "from my mother's womb"
immediately captures our attention, since a
feature common to all the accounts of the event
on the Damascus Road is its totally unexpected
character. The call came suddenly without
warning or preparation. This suggests, then,

that "set apart from my mother's womb" is an allusion. But to what? In the Septuagint the expression occurs five times,[9] but only twice is it associated immediately with a divine choice, namely in the cases of Jeremias (Jer. 1.4–5) and the Servant of Yahweh. (Isa. 49.1–6.)[10] Rengstorf considers the allusion to be to the vocation of Jeremias,[11] and it is true that there is a marked parallel between the functions of the prophet and the preacher, and in particular between the vocation of Paul and the prophetic vocations of the Old Testament.[12] However, the fact that Paul views his office in a messianic perspective weighs the balance of probability in favour of the Servant Song[13]:

Isles hear me, attend peoples afar off! From the womb Yahweh called me, *from my mother's womb he called my name*. He made my mouth a sharp sword. . . . Now Yahweh has spoken who formed me from the womb to be his slave to bring back to him Jacob and gather together Israel . . . And he said, "It is a small thing that you should be my slave to raise up the tribes of Jacob and to bring back the survivors of Israel. I will make you a light of the nations to bear my salvation to the ends of the earth." [Isa. 49.1,2,5,6]

The last verse of this passage is moreover reported by Luke to have been used by Paul to justify his mission to the pagans,[14] and in Gal. 1.16 (above) the declared purpose of the revelation of the Son is that he may be preached by Paul among the Gentiles. In adding the notion of "setting apart" Paul modifies the text of Isaias slightly; it is possible that he does so deliberately with the intention of emphasizing again (Gal. 1.1) that even though he was "set apart", along with Barnabas, by the community at Antioch under the direction of the Spirit (Acts 13.2), his commission came directly from God.[15] The idea of "setting apart" is also found in Isa. 29.22 and 56.3 and in both instances the context is messianic. Paul moves in the same realm of ideas in Rom. 1.1, where he says that he was "set apart for the proclamation of the good news", because the use of "to proclaim good news" (*evangelizein*) as the verb *par excellence* to characterize Christian preaching is to be traced to its use in Isaias to signify the proclamation of messianic salvation. (Isa. 40.9: 41.27: 52.7: 60.6: 61.1.)[16]

It would be entirely foreign to Hebrew psychology to merely adopt a formula, to introduce an allusion without intending that a conclusion be drawn from it. If Paul applies to himself a phrase which the Deutero-Isaias applied to the Servant of Yahweh, it is because he saw himself in the role of the Servant, fulfilling the same function in these latter days as the prophet foretold for the Servant, namely, bearing salvation to the furthest corners of the earth.[17]

In the generally accepted exegesis of 2 Cor. 6.2 the quotation from Isa. 49.8, which it contains, is taken as referring to the Corinthians:

> Yea, [as God's] fellow-workers we exhort you not to receive the grace of God in vain. For he said, "In an acceptable time have I heard thee and in the day of salvation have I succoured thee." Behold ... now is the day of salvation. We give no offence in aught so the ministry be not blamed. But in everything we commend ourselves as ministers of God, in much patience, in tribulations, in hardships, in straits ... [2 Cor. 6.1–4]

Perceiving not only the interruption in the flow of thought, but the implicit contradiction with *v.* 1 which it is, on the contrary, intended to justify (*gar*), Cerfaux has proposed that the citation be considered an allusion to Paul and his associates.[18] Referred to the Corinthians, the quotation is completely out of harmony with *v.* 1 which implies the possibility of the refusal of grace. Understood as a reference to the preachers, it becomes a warning to the Corinthians that this may be their last chance—and the continuity of thought between *v.* 1 and *v.* 2 becomes immediately evident. The grace of God is present among the Corinthians, as offered concretely in the ministry of Paul and his collaborators. It is this which makes "now" the "day of salvation".[19] If rejected now the offer may not be made again. The Corinthians themselves would be all the more likely to apply the text of the prophecy to Paul, in that in drawing attention to the difficulties he has to cope with, he insinuates the similarity of his lot to that of the Servant who, though consti- tuted the bearer of salvation, was despised and abhorred. (Isa. 49.7: 50.5–7.)

A third allusion to the Servant is to be found, again under Cerfaux's guidance, in Rom. 15.21, where Paul speaks of the principle on which he bases his choice of mission territory:

> And I have been eager to evangelize, not where Christ has already been named, lest I might build on another's foundation, but rather according as it is written: "They shall see that have not been told of him and they that have not heard shall understand."

The passage obviously concerns the extension of the knowledge of the true Servant (Sanday- Headlam) and, just as clearly, Paul is aware that in spreading this knowledge he is bringing the prophecy of the Deutero-Isaias to fulfilment (Viard). The whole tenor of the passage, how- ever, suggests that this prophecy plays a deter- minant role in Paul's decision as to where he should preach; he must proclaim the good news where it has not been preached before—because it had been so foretold. Such care to conform his activity to the prophecy can only indicate that Paul again sees himself in the role of the Servant. And so his anxiety not to build on another's foundation appears not as a worry about a possible stain on his apostolic honour, but as a fear of failing to play the part providentially assigned to him in the execution of the plan of salvation.

There is also a real sense in which this text may be taken as an allusion to Christ (Lagrange), because what the Gentiles will see and understand (as in the prophecy) is Christ, not Paul. Here, then, the Apostle makes a double application of the theme of the Servant: to himself *and* to Christ. Paul could not have been unaware that the primitive Church interpreted the role of Jesus in function of the Servant of Yahweh, for J. Jeremias goes so far as to say that "... there is no area of the primitive Christian life of faith which was not stamped and moulded by the *'ebed* Christology."[20] That he gave his consent to this conception is the conclusion of a great number of commentators on the Christological hymn of Phil. 2.6–11. Apart from the presence of the term *doulos* and a number of minor indications (such as an explicit reference to Isa. 45.23), they appeal to the

identity of theme and movement of thought—
voluntary humiliation *resulting* in exaltation
by *God*—to demonstrate that this hymn was inspired by the fourth Servant Song and constructed on its model.[21]

For Paul, then, to apply the Servant prophecies to himself must mean that he had a
very clear concept of his mission as the prolongation of that of Christ. It is Christ who
acts in and through his ministers, so that in so
far as these latter are one with him the prophecies had them equally in view. This identification of the preacher with his Lord must be
understood in a dynamic, not a static, sense;
Paul identifies his activity, not his person, with
that of the Servant. Only such a profound im-
pregnation of the preacher's action by the
saving power of the risen Christ can explain
the absolute character of such expressions as
"to preach to the Gentiles in order that they be
saved" (1 Thess. 2.16) and especially, "I have
become all things to all men, that at all costs I
may save some". (1 Cor. 9.22.) This too appears
to be the meaning of "in Christ" as referred
specifically to preaching: "We speak in Christ
as sent from God and in his presence." (2 Cor.
2.17; cf. 12.19: 13.13.) His ministers are "in
Christ" in a special way in so far as by virtue
of their special union with him they enjoy the
power of re-creating other men "in Christ".

THE SPIRIT

We have just seen that Paul views preaching essentially in a messianic context; it is the prolongation of the activity of the Messias, the Servant "on whom Yahweh has sent his spirit". (Isa. 42.1; cf. 11.2.) This alone, particularly when we recall that the Prophets characterized the messianic age as the time of the fullest outpouring of the Spirit, is sufficient to establish a relationship between the Spirit and preaching. This relationship must now be examined more closely with a view especially to seeing what light it throws on the dynamic identification of preaching with the saving ministry of Christ.

O. Michel has well said that "charity" and "Spirit" are the essential characteristics both of the new era and of the individual Christian.[23] The key role played by preaching in the introduction of the individual into this new dimension should prepare us to find both "charity" and "the Spirit" associated with it, but to appreciate just how closely all three were linked in Paul's mind it is only necessary to juxtapose two passages from his letters.

The first, concerning *the Spirit and Charity*, is found in the middle of a section of Romans devoted to the idea that here and now we possess the seed of eternal glory. "Having been justified by faith" (5.1), we have been recon-

ciled with God. The immediate consequence of
the cessation of the state of enmity is peace, and
associated with it, the hope of definitive union
with God. The guarantee that this hope is not
a vain illusion is the fact that "the love of God
is poured forth in our hearts by the Holy Spirit
who is given to us". (Rom. 5.5.) The fundamental basis of Christian hope is the presence
of the Spirit communicated to us in baptism.
(Titus 3.5.) The use of the verb "to pour out"
(*ekcheō*) immediately evokes the famous messianic prophecy of Joel, cited by Peter at Pente-
cost:

> It shall come to pass in the last days, said the
> Lord, that I shall pour forth [of] my spirit on
> all flesh. [Joel 2.28 = Acts 2.17]

However, what is here given in plenitude is not
directly the Spirit but the love of God. The
genitive clearly indicates the divine origin of
this love, but whom is this love directed to, God
or man? Paul does not say and, indeed, the
point is not of importance for our purpose.
What must be noted is that this love is poured
out "by the Holy Spirit", who is himself a gift.
Further on in the same epistle, Paul speaks
again of love infused by the Spirit:

> I implore you by our Lord Jesus Christ and
> by the love that the Spirit inspires, be my
> allies in the fight. [Rom. 15.30]

And in yet another passage (Gal. 5.22) love is ranged among the "fruits" of the Spirit.

The second passage associates *Preaching and Charity*:

> The object of this command [*to de telos tēs parangelias*] is a love [flowing] from a clean heart, a good conscience and a sincere faith. [1 Tim. 1.5]

"Command" (*parangelia*) is here the charge laid by Paul on Timothy (1 Tim. 1.18), that is, the government of the Church at Ephesus. (1 Tim. 1.3.)[24] Elsewhere Paul has pointed out that the principal function of a "steward" in the House of God, which is the Church (Titus 1.7: 1 Tim. 3.15), is preaching—doctrinal, moral and apologetic. In the immediate context of the passage quoted, it is a question of impeding the propagation of erroneous doctrines "which tend to promote discussions rather than the plan of God through faith". (*v.* 4.) This plan, God's salvific design for humanity, is brought to fulfilment in being received in faith by those who hear it preached. Heterodox preaching does not contribute to this realization, because it gives more importance to "interminable myths and genealogies" (*v.* 4) than to the simple salvific fact: Christ crucified. (1 Cor. 1.23.) Its goal is the satisfaction of vain curiosity while, on the contrary, the end true preaching has in view is love.[25] And how could we really expect otherwise, since it is a factor in a plan conceived in love (Eph. 1.6), put into operation through an epiphany of love (Titus 3.4–5) and destined to ensure that men be "holy and immaculate in his [God's] sight in love". (Eph. 1.4.) The whole raison d'être of preaching is the engendering of love; and not just any sort of love (even though as in Rom. 5.5 its object is here unspecified), but the total dedication of an undivided self.

If we associate these two texts, the conclusion that the goal assigned to preaching—love—is achieved by the Holy Spirit is inescapable. Further texts, also when juxtaposed, reveal that what is true of charity is proportionately true of faith. Faith, we are told, "comes through hearing [the Gospel]" (Rom. 10.17), yet the reception of the Gospel is impossible without the activity of the Spirit (1 Cor. 2.14),[26] and no-one can express his faith unless moved by the Spirit: "No-one can say 'Jesus [is] Lord' except by the Holy Spirit." (1 Cor. 12.3.)[27] Furthermore, even though "the Spirit is our life" (Gal. 5.25), the Gospel is "the word of life". (Phil. 2.16.)

In a word, preaching appears as so penetrated with the power of the Spirit that its effects can be attributed to the Spirit. But now the question arises: How is this to be reconciled with our previous conclusion that preaching is the prolongation of the ministry of *Christ*? To answer requires an investigation of the relationship between Christ and the Spirit, not, however, in all its aspects but only in so far as it concerns man's sanctification.

At once we notice a curious fact. Not alone is the new life of the believer defined as the presence in him of Christ (Rom. 8.10: 2 Cor. 13.5) or of the Spirit (Rom. 8.9: 1 Cor. 3.16), but in every case where "in the spirit" definitely means the Holy Spirit, it can be replaced by "in Christ"—except when it is a question of *charismata*.[28] The believers, sanctified in Christ Jesus (1 Cor. 1.2) or in the Holy Spirit (1 Cor. 6.11), have been sealed in Christ (Eph. 4.30) or in the Spirit (Eph. 1.13), and constitute a holy temple in the Lord (Eph. 2.21) or in the Spirit (Eph. 2.22). If they have been accorded joy and peace in the Spirit (Rom. 14.17) these gifts are equally given in the Lord. (Rom. 5.1: Phil. 4.4.) Their justification has been in the Spirit (1 Cor. 6.11) or in the Lord. (Gal. 2.17.)

It would be going too far to say that in all these instances the preposition "in" merely indicates association or union,[29] but equally we cannot assert its causal value in every case, even though the union here considered must rest on the exercise of efficient causality. However, the idea of causality comes to the fore in another series of texts. The Holy Spirit is the dispenser of the charismata (1 Cor. 12.11), but they are given "according to the measure of the gift of Christ". (Eph. 4.7.) The life of the believer is that of the Spirit (Gal. 5.25: Col. 3.4) or that of Christ. (Phil. 1.21: 2 Cor. 4.10.) Through Jesus Christ we become sons of God (Gal. 4.5: Eph. 1.5), yet it is through the advent of the Spirit that we are made sons. (Rom. 8.15.)

This attribution of one and the same effect to two different agents has led some exegetes to conclude that the difference between these agents is only apparent, that Christ and the Spirit are but different names for a unique reality. Alan Richardson, for example, says: "The Holy Spirit is not a person existing independently of God; it is a way of speaking about God's personally acting in history, or of the risen Christ's personally acting in the life and witness of the Church."[30] This error is fundamentally one of logic, because a single effect when viewed under different aspects may be attributed to distinct causes, and this, as we shall see, is the case here. Both Christ and the Spirit are the source of our sanctification but in different ways. Paul's expressions suggest only the intimate association of Christ and the Spirit in the work of redemption. So complete is the union that in this action they seem to become identical. Though based on a false exegesis of the famous *ho de kurios to pneuma estin* (2 Cor.

3.17), Neill Hamilton's formula is perfect: "The identity here posited is not ontological, an identity of being, but dynamic, an identity which occurs in redemptive action."[31] A passage from Romans affords ample confirmation:

> You are not in the flesh but in the spirit, if it is true that the Spirit of God dwells in you. Now if anyone has not the Spirit of Christ he does not belong to him. But if Christ is in you, the body is dead because of sin, but your spirit is life because of justice. And if the Spirit of him who raised Jesus from the dead dwells within you . . . [8.9–11]

In this passage "Spirit of God", "Spirit of Christ" and "Christ" are used interchangeably (Sanday-Headlam)—but the expression "Spirit of Christ" opens the way to an understanding of this dynamic union. Together with formulae such as "the Spirit of his Son" (Gal. 4.6) and "the Spirit of Jesus Christ" (Phil. 1.19), it suggests that the Spirit pertains in some way to Christ, that his activity is conditioned in some way by that of Christ.

Although the earthly ministry of Christ as presented by the Synoptics appears as performed under the continuing movement of the Holy Spirit,[32] Paul displays little interest in it. It was for him the time of "his manifestation in the flesh" (1 Tim. 3.16), in which, though God, "he emptied himself taking the form of a slave"

(Phil. 2.7), and the only events he considers
worthy of note are the Incarnation and the Passion. After the Resurrection, however, all is different. Christ is then seen as "a life-giving
spirit" (1 Cor. 15.45), as "constituted Son of God
in power, according to [his] spirit of holiness"
(Rom. 1.4). He is full messianic *Lord*. As the
Son of God from all eternity Christ always possessed the fullness of the divine life, but in the
design of God's wisdom that life was not to be
communicated to men until Christ, having freely
submitted himself to the power of sin and its
instrument the Law, was "spiritualized", that is,
constituted the life-giving head of his body,
which is the Church. (Col. 1.18, 24.)[33] The giving
of this life to those who have been reconciled
with God through the blood of Christ (Col. 1.20:
Eph. 2.13) is effected by the Holy Spirit. Christ
as Lord plays a double role with regard to this
gift: his redemptive death and justifying resurrection (Rom. 4.25) condition its giving, and he
is also the source and term of what is given.

> God saved us, not in virtue of works of justice
> done by us, but out of his mercy by the bath
> of regeneration and renewal of the Holy Spirit,
> whom he poured out richly on us through
> Jesus Christ our Saviour, in order that justi-
> fied by his grace we might become in hope
> heirs of eternal life. [Titus 3.5–7]

In this magnificent synthesis we see that the initiative, as always, lies with God, that the wonderful regeneration effected in baptism is caused immediately by the Holy Spirit, and that this renewal is made possible by the saving act of Christ. It should be noted, however, that the term of the transformation is not the Spirit but Christ (Gal. 3.27: Eph. 3.17), into whose image we are changed (2 Cor. 3.18: Rom. 8.29), in whose death and resurrection we participate (Rom. 6.3–11), and into whose body we are incorporated. (1 Cor. 12.12–13.)

Now it is apparent that the influence of the Spirit in preaching, far from conflicting with the idea of preaching as the continuation of the ministry of Christ, is that which makes such a prolongation possible. Were preaching totally outside the area of influence of the Spirit, it might bear a superficial resemblance to the earthly preaching ministry of Christ, but it would not be the communication of the saving power of the risen Lord. True preaching is necessarily penetrated by the redemptive interaction of Christ and the Spirit. Consequently, the mission of the preacher is closely integrated with the temporal missions of the Son and the Holy Spirit:

When the fullness of time came, *God sent his Son*, born of a woman, born under the Law, to ransom the subjects of the Law, in order that we might attain the status of sons. And the proof that you are sons is that *God has sent the Spirit of his Son* into our hearts. [Gal. 4.4–6]

The preacher is always an "apostle of Christ by the will of God",[34] but texts such as 1 Tim. 4.14 and 2 Tim. 1.6, when read in the light of Acts 13.2 and 20.28, show that the Holy Spirit intervenes in a special way in his selection, and makes him capable of efficaciously exercising his office by conferring on him "a spirit of power, of charity and of prudence". (2 Tim. 1.7.) Hence the preacher's work is in a profound sense "a ministry of the Spirit" (2 Cor. 3.8), and the message he bears is proclaimed "not in word alone but with power and in the Holy Spirit". (1 Thess. 1.5.) A practically identical statement is found in 1 Cor. 2.4:

My discourse and my preaching were not in persuasive words of wisdom but in the form of a demonstration of [the] Spirit and power.

The best commentary on these declarations is provided by Paul himself:

I shall not venture to mention aught but what Christ has done through me unto the obedience of the Gentiles, by word and deed, by the force of miraculous signs, by the power of the Holy Spirit. [Rom. 15.18–19]

The Apostle is the chosen instrument of Christ to bring the Gentiles effectively into the "mystery" (Eph. 3.1–9) by winning their obedience to it, but the power he has at his disposition is that of the Spirit, whose presence is manifest in both the dynamism of his word and in the miracles which confirm it. Consequently any community converted by Paul could be truly termed "a letter of *Christ* drawn up by *us*, written with the *Spirit* of the living God". (2 Cor. 3.3.) Paul would fully concur with Luke's statement in Acts:

> The Church ... was being built up, walking in the fear of the Lord and was increasing in number by the pressing appeal of the Holy Spirit.[35] [9.31]

But besides the extensive increase in numbers there is also within the Church an intensive growth which is ensured by preaching and the Holy Spirit. All members of the Church have received the "Spirit which comes from God" (1 Cor. 2.12), and all may in consequence be termed "spirituals" (2.15). Paul, however, reserves this title to those who possess "the Spirit" in a superior degree, and who are "adults" (2.6) in the spiritual life, in contrast to the "infants" (3.1) in whom the activity of "the Spirit" is still fettered by the instincts of the flesh. It is the active presence of the Holy Spirit in the human spirit that enables the Christian to assimilate the doctrine preached to him. That capacity differs in "adults" and "children". The matter preached to both is basically the same, but to "adults" it is presented in such a way as to deepen their knowledge, stress being laid on those elements calculated to set ablaze an already purified heart. On this level of instruction Paul says: "We speak not in words learnt of human wisdom but in those learnt of the Spirit." (1 Cor. 2.13.) Just as the knowledge the preacher must communicate came through a revelation of the Spirit (cf. 2.10), so too that same Spirit aids him in expressing it both aptly and accurately.

The preacher's mission is related to the Incarnation in so far as it is the prolongation of the mission of the Word made flesh. Both are finalized by the same goal; the salvation of men. But the union is more profound than that effected by mere finality. The principle of the activity whereby this end is achieved is the same. Christ possesses the principle of new life within himself. In commissioning ministers and in communicating his Spirit to them he shares this power with them. It is because the preachers possess the Spirit of Christ in a special way that they can co-operate in the building of the Body of Christ, that they, like Christ (1 Cor. 3.11), can be termed its "foundations". (Eph. 2.20.) Their function is to engender faith (Rom. 10.17), and the participation of the Spirit in this action is the prerequisite to all his subsequent activity in both the Christian and the body of Christ.

LIGHT

The closeness of the bond between Christ and the preacher is seen under another aspect in Paul's use of the symbol of light. We have seen that Paul owes his understanding of his role in the realization of the plan of salvation to the Isaianic doctrine of the Servant, but his indebtedness to the prophet goes much further than that. In the tableau of the messianic age presented in the Book of Isaias light plays a very prominent part, and every aspect of its use there (to symbolize salvation and its advent, the agent of salvation, teaching etc.) is mirrored in Paul's letters, with the inevitable difference that he transposes it to describe, not the realities consequent on the *Parousia,* but the concrete situation of the preachers and of those who heed them.

The image of light in the Old Testament is not always, or even for the most part, eschatological. Its adaptability as a symbol is too obvious for it ever to have been restricted to any one sphere of thought. As dark characterizes the womb (Job. 3.16: Ps. 58.9) and the grave (Job 10.22), light is *par excellence* the symbol of life

(Job 3.20: 38.15: Ecclus. 22.10) and its absence
characterizes Sheol, the place of the dead. (Ps.
49.19: 88.11.) The coming of dawn puts an end
to the evil deeds done in darkness. (Job 24.13;
Prov. 2.13.) Light is, consequently, the symbol
of protection from evil (Job. 29.3: Ps. 27.1: Mic.
7.8), and of the joy (Esther 8.16), happiness and
prosperity (Job 22.28: Ps. 112.4) flowing from
this security. It would have been remarkable had
anyone familiar with this usage not perceived
the potentialities of light as a symbol for *messianic salvation.*[36] In the dark days (Isa. 5.30)
when Sennacherib menaced Jerusalem Isaias
concluded a prophecy of hope and encourage-
ment (couched in terms that carry its import far
beyond liberation from the present danger) with
these words:

> And the light of the moon shall be as the light
> of the sun and the light of the sun shall in-
> crease sevenfold—as the light of seven days—
> in the day when the Lord shall bind up the
> wound of his people and shall heal the stripe
> of their wound. [30.26; cf. 51.4: Zech 14.7]

The *advent of messianic salvation* appears as the
passage from darkness to light. The second
Emmanuel prophecy begins:

> The people that walked in darkness have seen
> a great light, to them that walked in the

region of the shadow of death, light is risen. [Isa. 9.2]

The pagans remain in obscurity, while the New Jerusalem[37] is bathed in the radiance of the glory of Yahweh:

Arise, behold, for behold thy light and the glory of Yahweh is risen upon thee, whereas darkness covers the earth and a mist the people. But Yahweh is risen upon thee and his glory shall be seen upon thee. The nations march towards thy light and kings towards thy dawning brightness. [Isa. 60.1–3: cf. 60.19–20][38]

The same sweeping symbolism is evident in Paul's antithetical questions contrasting man's state before and after redemption:

What has righteousness to do with wickedness? Can light consort with darkness? Can Christ agree with Belial? [2 Cor. 6.14–15]

As pagans the converts were "darkness", now as Christians they are "light" (Eph. 5.8) and must give thanks "to the Father who has made you fit to share the heritage of the saints in light. He rescued us from the domain of darkness and transferred us to the kingdom of his beloved Son." (Col. 1.12–13.)

In Isaias, the *agent of salvation* is the Servant who is made "a light of the nations" (42.6)[39] precisely in order that salvation may reach to the

ends of the earth. (43.6.) It is more than once
implied that he exercises his office by preaching:
"I have sent my spirit upon him that he bear to
the nations the judgement. He does not shout,
nor does he raise his voice" (42.1–2), and the
third song contains an exhortation "to hear the
voice" of the Servant. (50.10.) The prophecy
accentuates the instrumental character of the
Servant's function by showing him as receiving
daily the message he must preach. (50.4.) This
teaching is not described explicitly as light, but
the radiation of the glorious Jerusalem which
attracts nations and kings to its "dawning brightness", shines on them in the teaching of the
Law, "the light of Yahweh". (Isa. 2.2–5.)[40]

Paul's identification of both himself and
Christ with the Servant has already been noted.
For the formal affirmation of Christ as the Light
of the World we must wait for the Gospel of
John (1.9 etc.), but the Apostle quotes what
appears to be part of a primitive Christian
hymn[41] giving an equivalent sense:

Awake sleeper, rise from the dead,
And Christ will shine upon you. [Eph. 5.14]

Isa. 49.6 ("I will make you a light of the
nations") is applied to Paul in Acts 13.47, and in
a solemn declaration of the nature of his function
in the divine plan he says:

To me the very least of all the saints, there
was given this grace to announce among the

Gentiles the good tidings of the unfathomable riches of Christ, and to enlighten [*phōtisai*] all men as to what is the dispensation of the mystery. [Eph. 3.8–9]

It is entirely natural, then, to describe his activity in function of this symbol. His knowledge of Isaias adequately explains Paul's employment of the symbol in an eschatological context, but it is very probable that his predilection for its use sprang from the circumstances of his conversion, an event which made an indelible impression upon him. That moment of grace was everything for the Apostle: it was the source of his vocation and doctrine, the origin of his mission. One of the circumstances mentioned in all three accounts of it is that "a light from heaven enveloped him in brightness". (Acts 9.3; cf. 22.6: 26.13.) In that moment he became a "new creature". Since that moment Paul's preaching, when received with faith, produced the same effect. It is not surprising, then, to find him associating creation, light and preaching:

But if indeed our gospel is veiled, it is veiled in the case of those perishing, the unbelievers whose mind the god of this world has blinded, so that they see not the radiance of the gospel of the glory of Christ, who is the image of God. For we preach not ourselves but Jesus

> Christ as Lord, and ourselves merely as your
> slaves for Jesus' sake. For it is the God who
> said "Out of darkness shall shine light" that
> hath shone in our hearts, for the shining forth
> of the knowledge of the divine glory in the
> person of Jesus Christ. [2 Cor. 4.3–6]

Just as light was brought into darkness by the
creative word of God (Gen. 1.3), and as the divine
light was brought into the world by the radiant
Image of God, so now a new creation is effected
by a new light-word which is at once divine and
human. The key term in this passage is "glory"
(*doxa*), and the antithesis with Moses and his
ministry in the paragraph immediately preceding the one cited indicates that it must not be
understood as "honour, distinction" (as in
1 Thess. 2.20: Rom. 2.7,10) but as translating the
Hebrew *kabod*. As applied to God in the Old
Testament this term suggests the visible brightness of the divine presence, a manifestation of
God's being characterized by radiant splendour
and rendered accessible to human experience by
the accompanying action.[42] This luminous
phenomenon marks the Sacerdotal traditions of
the Pentateuch concerning the Law-giving and
the Tabernacle. In later times the vision of "the
glory" was reserved to the Prophets (Isa. 6.3:
Ezek. 8.4), but these foretold that the messianic
age would be characterized by the full unveiling

of the glory of Yahweh. (Isa. 60.1–3,19–20: 66.10,18: Ezek. 43.2.) They, however, could not have imagined the form that this unveiling would in fact take. For in virtue of their community of nature Christ is the perfect image of the Father, the incarnation of his glory: he is the "Lord of glory". (1 Cor. 2.8.)[43] With these phrases Paul evokes the amazing brightness and beauty brought by the Incarnation of the Son into a world darkened by sin. (Gal. 4.4.)

The Pastoral Epistles present the Incarnation as a glorious "epiphany", but it is not to be considered merely an illumination, because it is the embodiment in a person of God's love for men: "The grace of God has been manifested [*epephanē*] unto the salvation of all men." (Titus 2.11.) This Love Manifested is not so much a beacon dispelling the darkness of ignorance as an all-conquering, life-giving power:

God saved us and called us with a holy call, not in virtue of our works but in virtue of his own purpose and of the grace given us in Jesus Christ before time everlasting, but now manifested [*phanerōtheisan*] through the appearance of our Saviour Jesus Christ, who has abolished death and brought to light [*phōtistanos*] life and immortality through the Gospel, of which I have been appointed herald, apostle and teacher. [2 Tim. 1.9–11]

Since the preacher is to communicate this loving-light-power to men he himself must be the first to benefit. The divine illumination, the infusion of the "spirit of love" (2 Tim. 1.7), transforms his whole being. Consequently, his activity too participates in the qualities of this luminous love-force. As the revelation of Christ (1 Cor. 2.13) who is the "glory" of the Father, preaching participates in the splendour of his glory, so much so that Paul can speak of "the radiance [*phōtismos*] of the gospel of the glory of Christ". (2 Cor. 4.4: 1 Tim. 1.11.) In receiving the word of God, then, the Christians share Paul's experience on the Damascus Road. This for them is but the beginning of a profound metamorphosis. As it was with Moses, and with Paul himself, so it is with the believers. When Moses, the mediator of the Old Covenant, came down from the mountain after having heard the word of God and seen his glory, his face shone radiant. (2 Cor. 3.7.) The power of God had so enveloped him that its brilliance communicated itself even to his physical being. The ordinary believer is not granted such an immediate experience of God; his vision of the glory of the Lord is mediated to him by Christ and by the preachers. Nonetheless, the effect is the same: "We all reflect as in a mirror the glory of the Lord." (2 Cor. 3.18.) Christians are even superior to Moses, because whereas his reflection of the divine glory had been physical and transitory, theirs is spiritual and permanent, for they are transformed into the image of the glorious Christ (1 Cor. 15.49: Phil. 3.21: Rom. 8.29), an image which reproduces the resplendent qualities of the original. For others, then, it is a source of radiance whose intensity increases in proportion to its perfection—"from glory to glory". (2 Cor. 3.18.) In receiving the luminous revelation of Christ the believers become, as it were, a luminous living Gospel. Not only do they become "children of light" (1 Thess. 5.5), but "in the midst of a depraved and perverse generation" they shine "as lights, holding forth the word of life". (Phil. 2.15–16.)[44]

The pattern of thought thus outlined manifests how perfectly the salvation brought by Christ corresponds to the expectations of the Old Testament, and how closely the Pauline usage of the symbol of light is conformed to that of Isaias. In both the theme of "light" is closely associated with that of "glory", but Paul gives these themes a depth unsuspected by the Prophet by introducing the theme of "love". The point of union of all three themes is the person of Christ, where love has the radiance of glory, and glory is explained by love, for glory is the manifestation of the divine nature which is love. Christ is the tangible expression of the divine nature: he is Love Manifest. To those who sat

in darkness and the shadow of death this
"epiphany" was the "great light" promised by
Isaias, Luke 1.79 which, in the preaching of
Christ's ministers, sheds its warm radiance upon
the nations to kindle and foster in their souls the
bright flame of love. (1 Tim. 1.5.)

In this chapter we have tried to delineate
Paul's conception of his activity in function of
three ideas, the Servant, the Spirit, and Light,
all of which, as we saw, have their roots deep in
the Old Testament. These ideas, however, share
another characteristic. All carry a primarily
eschatological connotation. The Messias, the
Light of salvation, the outpouring of the Spirit,
were all blessings promised for the last days. But
now the Messias has come; the Spirit has been
given; the New Age has been inaugurated. (1
Cor. 10.11.) Yet there is still a future. (Phil 1.6.)
Christians live "looking for the blessed hope and
manifestation of the glory of our great God and
Saviour Christ Jesus". (Titus 2.13.) The present
age, therefore, is one of tension between the
"already" and the "not yet". This accords with
Paul's doctrine of the Spirit. There are many
passages in which he formally asserts the presence of the Spirit (e.g., Gal. 5.5: Rom. 8.9:
Eph. 2.22). Yet the Spirit now possessed is only
the "first fruits" (Rom. 8.23) "of the harvest
proper which will occur in the new creation of

the future age".[45] The life he communicates is
the same in kind as the life of the new age, but
as yet we have only the "pledge" or "earnest"
of the inheritance (Eph. 1.14: 2 Cor. 1.22: 5.5)
we shall one day receive in plenitude. For Paul,
then, the Spirit is still primarily an eschatological reality.[46] The close relationship of preaching to the Spirit places it too in this category,
but it acquires a more precise eschatological
significance in being evaluated as a *sign of the
end*—the end will come only when the Gospel
shall have been preached to all nations. This
idea, which Oscar Cullmann[47] develops with
force and clarity on the basis of two parallel
texts from the Synoptics—"And the Gospel
must first be preached to all the Gentiles" (Mark
13.10; cf. Matt. 24.14)—is not stated clearly by
Paul. However, his exposition of the plan of salvation in Rom. 9–11 (which Cullmann suggests is
really a commentary on Mark 13.10) shows that he
shared the convictions of the Evangelists. If the
criterion at the final judgement is to be man's
attitude *vis-à-vis* the Gospel (2 Thess. 1.7–10),
then all must be given an opportunity to hear
the word of God. And how are they to hear it
save by preaching? The message has been proclaimed to Israel. The pagans must now have
it preached to them "until the totality of the
Gentiles be entered in, and thus, when that
has happened, shall Israel also be saved". (Rom.

11.25–6.) Here the eschatological character of preaching as determined by its relation to the end is clear. The emphasis on the Gentiles is explained by the fact that Paul gives us no abstract theory of preaching, but a series of scattered statements which concern his own personal obligation. It is in this perspective too that we can better understand the compulsion under which the Apostle felt himself to labour (1 Cor. 9.16), for his activity appears as a factor on which God has made the definitive coming of his kingdom dependent.

NOTES

1. Compare "through Christ" (*v.* 18) and "through us" (*v.* 20).

2. Cf. Burton, "The Titles and Predicates of Jesus", *Gal.*, 396; Cerfaux, *Le Christ*, 364, 366.

3. Rom. 1.1: 1 Cor. 9.1: 15.9: 2 Tim. 1.11.

4. 1 Cor. 1.1: 2 Cor. 1.1: Eph. 1.1: Col. 1.1: 2 Tim. 1.1: "... by order of God", 1 Tim. 1.1.

5. Cf. above, p. 57.

6. 1 Cor. 14.36: 2 Cor. 2.17: 4.2: Phil. 1.14 etc.

7. Rom. 1.15,16: 2.16: 1 Cor. 2.6: 2 Cor. 11.7: 1 Thess. 2.8,9 etc.

8. 1 Thess. 3.2: Rom. 15.19: 1 Cor. 9.12: 2 Cor. 2.12: 9.13: 10.14: Gal. 1.7: Phil. 1.27.

9. Judges 16.17: Ps. 22.10–11: 71.6: Jer. 1.4–5: Isa. 49.1–6. Cf. Luke 1.15.

10. For the latest *status quaestionis* of the Servant Songs, cf. A. Gelin, in *Introduction à la Bible*, vol. 1, ed. A. Robert and A. Feuillet, Paris (1959), 555–60; J. van der Ploeg, "Serviteur de Jahvé (Chants)", *Dictionnaire Encyclopédique de la Bible*, Paris (1960), 1729–35.

11. *TWNT*, vol. 1, 440, *n*. 192.

12. Cf. J. Munch, "La Vocation de l'apôtre Paul", *Studia Theologica*, 1 (1947), 136–43.

13. Especially when we recall the prophetic traits of the Servant, cf. Lagrange, *Le Judaïsme avant Jésus-Christ*, Paris (1931), 378–80; V. de Leeuw, "Le Serviteur de Jahvé, figure royale ou prophétique?", in B. Rigaux et al., *L'Attente du Messie* (Rech. bibl., 1), Louvain (1953), 51–6.

14. "It was necessary that the word of God be declared to you first, but since you reject it and condemn yourselves as unworthy of eternal life we now turn to the Gentiles. For so the Lord commanded us saying: I have made you a light of the nations to bear salvation to the ends of the earth." (Acts 13.46–7.)

15. Cf. A. M. Denis, "L'Élection et la vocation de Paul, faveurs célestes", *RT*, 57 (1957), 421.

16. Lagrange, *Rom.*, 4; Sanday-Headlam, *Rom.*, 5; Cerfaux, *L'Église*, 134, *n*. 2; A. Richardson, *An Introduction to the Theology of the New Testament*, London (1958), 26.

17. It is entirely natural that a Jew who had received such an important task from God should seek in the Old Testament the passages that foreshadowed it, and perfectly in keeping with his mentality that he should convey his conclusions in such a discreet way. This allusive theology is especially clear in Luke's account of the Infancy (cf. R. Laurentin, *Structure et théologie de Luc I–II*, Paris (1957)), and Dupont has shown that he adopted the same allusive procedure to show that the evangelization of the Gentiles was the fulfilment of messianic prophecy, being part of the programme determined by God for the Messias ("Le salut des gentils et la signification théologique du livre des Actes", *NTS*, 6 (1959), 132–55).

18. "Saint Paul et le 'Serviteur de Dieu' d'Isaïe", *Recueil II*, 447–8.

19. Spicq notes the parallel to Luke 4.19, the scene in the synagogue at Nazareth when Jesus, after reading

the text of Isa. 61.1-2, announces the inauguration of the messianic era. The parallel is all the more striking if Paul applies Isa. 49.8 to the preachers, because their function is to introduce the individual to the blessings of that era.

20. W. Zimmerli and J. Jeremias, *The Servant of God* (Studies in Biblical Theology, no. 20), London (1957), 98. The description of Jesus' baptism (Matt. 3.13-17 and parallels) spontaneously recalls the inaugural visions of the Old-Testament prophets. F. Gils has shown that the divine proclamation (Matt. 3.17) implies a reference to a citation concerning not just any prophet but the Servant of Yahweh (*Jésus prophète d'après les évangiles synoptiques.* Louvain (1957), 65; cf. also A. Legault, "Le baptême de Jésus et la doctrine du Serviteur souffrant", *Sciences Ecclésiastiques, 13* (1961), 147-66). Such a suggestion in the thought of a Semite would mean a task to be carried out, and in fact Jesus' mission is synthesized in function of that of the Servant. Not alone does he realize the programme of the humble Servant (Matt. 8.17=Isa. 53.4: Matt. 12.18-25=Isa. 42. 1-2), but he is conscious of doing so. When the disciples of John the Baptist ask him if he is the Messias, his reply (Matt. 11.5-6) contains an allusion to Isa. 35.5-6 and 61.1, which latter text is to be compared with Isa. 42.1. Jesus' description of himself as meek and humble immediately evokes the characteristic traits of the Servant (Isa. 42.2-3). Gils is careful to point out that while the early parts of the Gospels allude to Christ as the Servant, there is no reference to his sufferings as recounted in Isa. 53. This element enters with the account of Christ's second prophetic vision, the Transfiguration, where the intervention of the Father is clearly and naturally seen as a sign of approval given to Christ on his full acceptance of the dolorous destiny of the Servant (*Jésus prophète,* 75-6). The Synoptics certainly saw Jesus' passion as the realization of the Servant prophecies, for they all highlight the three prophecies of the Passion (Matt. 16.21 and

par.; 17.22–3 and par.; 20.18–19 and par.), and all these pericopes show a marked dependence on Isa. 53 (*op. cit.*, 135). The discourses of Acts manifest the same understanding of the person and work of Jesus. Peter begins and concludes his second great speech with a reference to Jesus as the Servant. (3.13,26.) The prayer of the persecuted community contains a reference to "thy holy servant Jesus". (4.27; cf. 4.30.) Cf. J. Schmitt, "Le Christ Jésus dans la foi et la vie de la naissante Église apostolique", *Lumière et Vie*, no. 9 (1953), 34–7.

21. Cf. P. Henry, *Kénose*, DBS, 5, 45, who avows that he can add little to the study by L. Cerfaux, "L'Hymne au Christ-Serviteur de Dieu (Phil. 2.6–11 = Isa. 52.13–53:12)", *Recueil II*, 425–37. The most recent study is that of L. Krinetzki, "Der Influss von Isa. 52.13–53.12 Par auf Phil. 2.6–11", *Theologische Quartalschrift*, 139 (1959), 157–93, 291–336, who concludes that this hymn constitutes a synthesis of the New-Testament theology of the Servant. It is very probable also that Paul had Isa. 53.9–11 in mind in writing 2 Cor. 5.21. Cf. L. Sabourin, *Rédemption sacrificielle* (1961), 156–7; J. Hoad, "Some New Testament References to Isaiah 53", *Expository Times*, 68 (1957), 254.

22. Ezek. 11.19: 36.26: 37.14: Isa. 32.15: Zech. 12.10: Jer. 31.34: and esp. Joel 2.28.

23. *Der Brief an die Römer*, Gottingen (1955), 270, n. 2.

24. Cf. Spicq, *Agapé III*, 10.

25. "*To telos* does not signify 'term, end' in the chronological sense, but the end willed or the goal, that is to say, the completion of a process, the result of a gradual evolution, and consequently, the consummation and crowning." (Spicq, *Agapé III*, 12.)

26. Cf. below, ch. 5.

27. Cf. O. Cullmann, *The Earliest Christian Confessions*, London (1949), 58; Cerfaux, *Le Christ*, 269.

28. Cf. Prat, *Theol.*, vol. 2, 394. He admits that this almost always causes the loss of a very delicate shade of meaning, and notes that the substitution is impos-

sible in three cases: when it is a question (1) of God loving, choosing or predestinating us in Christ; (2) of Christ in his redemptive mediation; (3) of "in Christ" in the sense of "as a Christian".

29. As M. Zerwick seems to imply (*Graecitas Biblica*, Rome (1953), no. 87).

30. *An Introduction to the Theology of the New Testament*, London (1958), 120.

31. *The Holy Spirit and Eschatology in Saint Paul*, Edinburgh (1957), 6. Cf. St. Thomas, *In Epistola ad Ephesios*, ch. 2, lect. 5. "Christ is in us through his Spirit, whom he imparts to us and through whom he so acts within us that any divine effect operated in our souls by the Holy Spirit must be said to be operated in us also by Christ." (Encylical *Mystici Corporis Christi*, CTS trans., no. 76; official Latin version in *AAS*, 35 (1943), 212). See also Y. Congar, "Le Saint-Ésprit et le Corps Apostolique réalisateurs de l'œuvre du Christ", *RSPT*, 36 (1952), 618; 37 (1953), 32.

32. The Spirit is active in the circumstances of Christ's birth (Matt. 1.18,20: Luke 1.15 etc.) and descends on him at his baptism (Mark 1.10 and par.). By the descent of the Spirit, Christ is consecrated for his mission: in the synagogue at Nazareth he says, "The Spirit of the Lord is upon me because he has anointed me to bear the good news to the poor..." (Luke 4.18). The Spirit leads him into the desert (Matt. 4.1). "Filled with the Spirit" (Luke 4.1), he returns to Galilee "in the power of the Spirit" (Luke 4.14), and casts out demons "by the Spirit of God". (Matt. 12.28.)

33. This idea is expressed with perfect clarity by St John: "For the Spirit had not been given, seeing that Jesus had not yet been glorified." (7.39.) "It is expedient for you that I go. For if I do not go, the Paraclete will not come to you, but if I go, I will send him to you." (16.7.)

34. Cf. above, note 4.

35. Here we render *paraklēsis* by "pressing appeal". Others (*Bible de Jérusalem, A-G*, 623) prefer the mean-

ing "consolation". For these the increase is in the favours of the Holy Spirit, not in numbers. However, the use of the same verb (*plēthunomai*) in 6.1,7: 7.17: 12.24 in the undoubted sense of numerical increase, associated in 6.7 and 12.24 with the growth of the word of God, inclines us to prefer the idea of exhortation-appeal. The conclusion to Peter's speech provides an enlightening parallel: "With many other words he rendered testimony and exhorted [*parekalei*] them, saying, 'Save yourselves from this perverse generation'." (2.40.) *Paraklēsis* in this passage appears as one of the essential acts of the apostolic preaching, "the final decisive act, the direct appeal to the auditors whom he wishes to win to the Faith or to confirm in it". (A. Lemonnyer, "L'Esprit-Saint Paraclet", *RSPT*, 16 (1927), 304). This definition perfectly covers the Pauline usage in 1 Thess. 2.3 and especially in 2 Cor. 5.20. It is possible that in the use of this term we have an allusion to the *paraklēsis* that appears in the work of the Deutero-Isaias as one of the blessings of the messianic era (Isa. 40.1 etc.; cf. A. M. Denis, "L'Apôtre Paul, 'prophète messianique' des gentils", *ETL*, 33 (1957), 265–6).

36. The reverse of the picture is to be found in the description of the pre-exilic prophets of the Day of Yahweh. "What will the day of Yahweh be for you [sinners]? It will be darkness and not light." (Amos 5.18: cf. Soph. 1.15.)

37. Tournay draws attention to the parallelism between the exaltation of the Servant (Isa. 53.11–12) and that of the new Jerusalem (54.11ff.) which concludes with the words "such will be the lot of the servants of Yahweh". (*v.* 17.) ("Les Chants du Serviteur dans la seconde partie d'Isaïe", *RB*, 59 (1952), 501.)

38. The extremely important place this text occupied in later Jewish and rabbinical teaching is well brought out by S. Aalen, *Die Begriffe "Licht" und "Finsternis" im alten Testament, im Spätjudentum und im Rabbinismus*, Oslo (1951), 88.

39. Lagrange, Van der Ploeg, North etc. reject "light of the nations" as a gloss. Tournay, however, argues strongly for its authenticity on account of the general rhythm of the phrase, and because of the parallelism with "covenant of people"—provided that one gives "people" here the general collective meaning it has in verse 5d ("Les Chants", 369-70; cf. Aalen, *"Licht" und "Finsternis"*, 92).

40. The Law is consistently considered as a divine light illuminating the path of the just. "Thy word is a lamp for my feet, a light for my path." (Ps. 119.105.) "The commandment is a lamp, the teaching a light." (Prov. 6.23.) "They merited to be deprived of light and shut up· in darkness who held captive your children through whom the imperishable light of the Law was to be given to the world." (Wisd. 18.4.) On this theme in later Judaism, cf. S. Aalen, *"Licht" und "Finsternis"*, 183-92. The theme of light is basic in Qumran, but the symbol does not appear to have been explicitly applied to the Law. But it is almost certainly the idea of the Law which underlies such expressions as "to contemplate the ways of light" (1QS III, 6), "to walk in the ways of light" (1QS III, 20); cf. F. Notscher, "Voies divines et humaines à Qumrân", in J. van der Ploeg et al., *La secte de Qumrân et les origines du Christianisme* (Rech. Bibl., 4), Louvain (1960), 147; O. Betz, *Offenbarung und Schriftforschung in der Qumransekte*, Tübingen (1960), 111-14. At Qumran, the priest who explains the Law is "a [great] luminary [who radiates] knowledge for the world and who illuminates the face of the multitude [with the wisdom of life]". 1QSb IV, 27; cf. 1QS IV, 2; D. Barthelemy—J. Milik, *Discoveries in the Judean Desert I; Qumran Cave I*, Oxford (1955), 126.)

41. Cf. Schlier, *Eph.*, 240.

42. "Eine öffentliche Selbstkundgebung Gottes als einer Majestät zum Zweck einer Aktion", G. Caspari, *Die Bedeutung der Gottes Wortsippe 'Kabod' im Hebräischen*, 1908, 152, cited from S. Aalen, *"Licht"*

und "Finsternis", 86, note 7. For Paul "glory" is sometimes the synonym for salvific power: Christ is raised from the dead "by the glory of the Father" (Rom. 6.4); Christians are strengthened "with all power by the might of his glory". (Col. 1.11; cf. Eph. 1.19.) It is an active and luminous presence.

43. "The Pauline image is not merely a faithful reproduction but a visible copy, a radiant imprint or impression; it is by reason of these two qualities of refulgence and visibility that it is so close to the notion of glory." (Spicq, *Dieu*, 187.) Hence we find, "image and glory of God" (1 Cor. 11.7); "glory of the Lord . . . image . . . glory to glory". (2 Cor. 3.18.)

44. This idea is further developed in ch. 5.

45. N. Hamilton, *op. cit.*, 19.

46. This is also confirmed by the causal relationship which Paul posits between faith and preaching (Rom. 10.17), for what is faith if not the anticipated possession of the *bona eschatologica*? Cf. D. Deden, "Le 'Mystère' paulinien", *ETL*, 13 (1955), 422.

47. *Christ and Time*, trans. F. V. Filson, London (1950), 157–67.

4

THE POWER OF THE WORD

WE have seen that the preacher is but an instrument in the hand of God, and that his activity is a continuation of the salvific activity of Christ. His commission and its exercise are penetrated by the power of the Spirit. It will not be surprising then, to find that it participates in the divine power, that the words of the preacher are never "mere words" but dynamic realities integral to the plan of salvation.

More than once Paul attributes a real efficacy to his preaching. In Col. 1.6 the word of truth is said to "fructify and develop". Power and preaching are closely associated in 2 Cor. 6.7a, while in Rom. 1.16 Paul explicitly affirms that the Gospel is "a divine power for the salvation of every believer". This chapter endeavours to set these ideas in their correct perspective by showing their roots in the primitive Christian community, and by bringing to light their relation to the oriental conception of the power of the spoken word, especially as we find it expressed in the Old Testament.

OLD-TESTAMENT TIMES

In conceding to *logos* a real efficacy (Col. 1.6: 1 Thess. 2.13) Paul uses this term in a way completely foreign to Greek thought. *Logos* became the common term for "word" only after Homeric times,[1] and originally had nothing to do with the function of speech. It evoked only the meaning, the ordered and reasonable content of what was said.[2] The basic signification of its root *leg-* is "to gather, to put together according to a definite plan, to arrange" and its fundamental connotation is that of (mental) organization.[3] *Logos* is the end product of a mental effort aimed at capturing and expressing internally the intelligible content (*logos*) of the multiple real.[4] As such it connoted the mental function rated highest by the Greeks. For the Semites this connotation attached to the term *dabar*, but there the resemblance ceased. *Logos* and *dabar* are related as the static to the dynamic.[5]

For the peoples of the Orient, word is not merely the expression of thought or desire. It is not a transient sound that no longer exists when its vibrations cease. Like the breath that proffers it, it is invisible but real.[6] It is an externalization, a making real, of what is conceived in the heart[7]; not a reaction to but a domination and shaping of external reality. Through speech the Semite impresses his personality on the stream of events.

The word has permanence and power, especially when it reaches from the present into the future, as it does in blessings, curses and commands. Isaac could not take back the blessing he had given in mistake to Jacob. (Gen. 27.35–7.) Even though he had erred with regard to the identity of the recipient, an energy had been released that he could not recapture. The curse pronounced by Josue on whoever would rebuild Jericho (Jos. 6.26) became effective two centuries later. (1 Kings 16.34: Judges 9.20,49,56.) When Michas, in fear of his mother's curse, restored the money he had stolen, all she could do was attempt to neutralize the curse by means of a blessing. (Judges 17.1–2; cf. 2 Sam. 21.3: Ps. 109.28.) Because of the active power of Balaam's word, Yahweh at first did not permit him to pronounce a curse against Israel (Num. 22.12), and later because of his love for Israel changed his curse into a blessing. (Deut. 23.5; cf. Neh. 13.2.) The blessings and curses recounted in Deut. 28 are, to a certain extent, personified, or at least considered as subsistent forces acting upon the Israelites.

These examples illustrate well the dynamic character of the Israelite conception of word. But while they manifest the spoken word as endowed with vitality and power, and capable of bringing into existence the reality it expresses, they also imply that the word does not enjoy this power *of itself*. Its vitality is rooted in the dynamism of him who utters it; its effectiveness is proportioned to his power. Even though the Israelites conceived curses and blessings as necessarily producing their effects, they did not attribute this efficacy in the last instance to the words themselves, but to the power of Yahweh. (Gen. 12.3: Num. 23.8.)[8] Speech, which always implies some measure of self-revelation, is as it were, an extension of the speaker's personality, a participation and prolongation of his power.

THE DIVINE WORD IN THE ANCIENT NEAR EAST

Consequently, not alone in the Old Testament, but also in the religious literature of the two great cultures that bracketed Israel—Egypt and Mesopotamia—supreme efficacy was attributed to the divine word, which was conceived as a release of the divine personality whose unique omnipotence it shared.

There is clear evidence in Egyptian texts of a strong belief in the identification of a person with his name.[9] Naturally, then, creation was conceived as the pronouncing of a name.[10] No being could exist until it had been named, defined, distinguished from all other beings. What was nameless was unintelligible, and therefore unreal. Amon is presented as creating himself by forming his own name: "No God came into existence before him . . . there was no other God with him when he pronounced his form."[11] A text from Karnak presents creation by Amon in these terms: "He announced the things to come and they were immediately produced. He created that which was cried by his voice."[12] In a passage which Wilson, its translator, entitles "The Theology of Memphis", (*c*. 2700 B.C.) we find the outline of a methodical analysis of the efficacy of the creative word:

There came into being as the heart and there came into being as the tongue [something] in the form of Atum. The mighty great one is Ptah, who transmitted [life to all the gods] as well as [to] their *ka's*, through this heart, by which Horus became Ptah, and through this tongue, by which Thoth became Ptah. (Thus it happened that the heart and tongue gained control over every [other] member of the body, by teaching that he is in every body and in every mouth of all gods, all men, [all] cattle, all creeping things, and [everything] that lives, by thinking and commanding everything that he wishes.

His Ennead is before him [in the form of] teeth and lips. That is [the equivalent of] the

semen and hands of Atum. Whereas the
Ennead of Atum came into being by his
semen and his fingers, the Ennead [of Ptah],
however, is the teeth and lips in his mouth,
which pronounced the name of everything,
from which Shu and Tefnut came forth, and
which was the fashioned of the Ennead.

The sight of the eyes, the hearing of the
ears, and the smelling of the air by the nose,
they report to the heart. It is this which causes
every completed [concept] to come forth, and
it is the tongue which announces what the
heart thinks. Thus all the gods were formed
and his Ennead was completed. Indeed all the
divine order [literally "every word of god"]
really came into being through what the heart
thought and the tongue commanded.[13]

This is not the place for a detailed exegesis of
this passage. For our purpose it suffices to notice
that the god Ptah conceives the elements of the
universe with his mind ("heart") and brings
them into being through his commanding speech
("tongue").[14] All proportions guarded, a similar
efficacy is attributed to the king's or ruler's word,
no doubt because he was considered a divine
being.[15]

The idea of *creation* by means of a word is
absent from Mesopotamian texts, but there is
no dearth of evidence manifesting belief in the

sovereign efficacy of the divine word.[16] A hymn to the moon-god Sin will serve as an example:

> When thy word drifts along in heaven like the wind it makes rich the feeding and drinking of the land.
>
> When thy word settles down on the earth green vegetation is produced.
>
> Thy word makes fat the sheepfold and the stall: it makes living creatures widespread.
>
> Thy word causes truth and justice to be, so that the people speak the truth.
>
> Thy word which is far away in heaven, which is hidden in the earth, is something no-one sees.
>
> Who can comprehend thy word, who can equal it?[17]

In the creation epic *Enuma Elish*, Marduk, when invited to undertake the combat of the gods against Tiamat, demands the right to decree the fates (the equivalent of kingship over the entire universe). The deities demur but eventually, assembled together, consent and invest him with the word of Anu, or more accurately, make his word *to be* Anu (IV,4,6). Then, spreading a cloth before him in a dramatic test, they demand that he prove his word has the dynamic force of the person and word of Anu[18]:

> Say but to wreck or to create: it shall be.
> Open thy mouth! The cloth will vanish!

Speak again, and the cloth shall be whole!

At the word of his mouth the cloth vanished.

When the gods, his fathers, saw the fruit of
his word [literally "the outcome of his
mouth"]

Joyfully they did homage: Marduk is king! [19]

The Mesopotamian texts show the divine word laden with irresistible power: even the gods must bow before it, and for the land and for living creatures it is a principle of fertility. Again, all proportion guarded, a similar efficacy was considered to belong to a royal command, [20] and to an even greater extent, to magical formulae whose force was compelling. [21]

THE WORD OF YAHWEH

From many points of view the Israelite conception of the word of God and its power resembles those of Egypt and Mesopotamia outlined above. [22] Nonetheless the differences between them can hardly be overemphasized. The theology of the word presented in the Mesopotamian and Egyptian writings reflects the polytheistic milieu in which these had their origin, while the Old-Testament concept of the divine word draws its richness and clarity (unparalleled in other literatures) from the fact that Yahweh was conceived as unique, transcendent, all-powerful. Yahweh's word is always the function of a conscious, moral personality, and nothing permits its being understood either as a force of nature or as a divine emanation.[23]

In the Old Testament, creation is presented, without elaboration, as the work of the divine word: "God said: Let there be light. And light was." (Gen. 1.3; cf. Ps. 33.9: Isa. 48.13: Ecclus. 39.17: Wisd. 9.1.)[24] By his word Yahweh conserves and governs all nature:

> He counts the number of the stars, to all of them he gives names . . .
> He sends his utterance to the earth; his word runs very swiftly.
> He gives snow like wool; he scatters frost like ashes. He casts his ice like crumbs; who can withstand his cold?
> He sends his word and melts them; when he blows with his wind the waters flow. [Ps. 147.4,15–18; cf. Job 37.5–13: Ecclus. 39.21: 43.25]

The word of God is eternal (Isa. 40.8) and irrevocable (Isa. 45.23: Ps. 89.35: Rom. 11.29), infallibly efficacious. (Jos. 21.45: Isa. 55.11.)

However, the Old Testament is not so much concerned with the divine word considered in itself, as with the divine word as confided to a particular individual. The statistical survey of the occurrences of *dabar* as meaning "divine word" carried out by Oskar Grether[25] reveals that the phrase "word of Yahweh" is found 241 times, and that in 93% of these instances it designates the word of Yahweh as received or declared by a prophet. When the plural ("words of Yahweh") is employed—much more infrequently—over half the occurrences designate the prophetic word. The remaining instances of the usage of these expressions to a fair extent concern the Law.[26]

The charter of Israel was always considered by the Israelites to be the body of moral and cultural prescriptions given by Yahweh on Sinai. This primitive body of law underlies, not alone the legislative development but the whole life of the Chosen People, and was understood as a divine command, a "word" addressed by God to man:

> Yahweh said to Moses: Put in writing these words because they are the provisions of the covenant that I make with you and with Israel ... And he wrote on the tablets the words of the covenant—*the Ten Words*.[27] [Exod. 34.27–8]

These words were a pattern to be lived out in daily life. On Sinai Yahweh had made himself known to men, and in his intention, men were to express that knowledge not in verbal promises but in deeds, in fidelity to his will. (Os. 2.22: 6.2: Amos 5.21: Jer. 7.23.)

But the people failed him. Accordingly, Yahweh again sent his word to Israel in raising up
the Prophets, who were his mouth. (Jer. 15.19:
Os. 6.5: Amos 5.1.) Immediately with the advent of the writing prophets, the dynamism of
the *dabar Yahweh* comes strongly to the fore.
After exalting Yahweh's power over the nations
(ch. 1–2) and with his own vocation obviously
in mind, Amos asks rhetorically: "The Lord
Yahweh speaks; who would not prophesy!"
(3.8.) The divine word is a force acting on the
person of the prophet; his words are endowed
with similar power, as the parallelism in Os.
6.5 indicates:

> I have cut them in pieces by the prophets.
> I have put them to death by the words of my
> mouth.

It is through these messengers that "the Lord
has sent a word to Jacob, and it has fallen on
Israel". (Isa. 9.8.)[28] The continuation of this
latter passage ascribes to the word a latent energy
whose effects are manifested only gradually.[29]

This aspect of the *dabar Yahweh* receives its
most profound expression, as we might expect,
from one who felt its full power in his own
person: Jeremias. He had moments of exaltation
when the word of God was a delicious sweetness
(15.16), moments of sharp awareness when he
was vividly conscious of the honour of being the

mouth of Yahweh. (15.19.) But he had also his
hours of bitter doubt when he wished to re-
linquish his charge, to bottle up the word of
God and speak it no more (20.7). "But then", he
says, "it was in my heart as a burning fire, buried
deep in my bones. I wore myself out trying to
contain it. I could not support it." (20.9.) For his
soul's salvation the prophet had to give this
terrible energy release. The divine fire must
shine forth, else it consumes its bearer as fire
consumes straw, crushes him as a hammer shat-
ters a stone (23.29)—the word of God brings death
to those who, having received it, fail to satisfy
its exigencies. The burden it laid on the prophet
was to *preach* it; the demand it made on his
hearers was to *live* it.[30] Should they fail in this,
then: "I will make my words a fire in your
mouth and this people wood that this fire will
devour." (5.14; cf. 6.11.) The mission of the
prophet was to destroy and to ruin, to build up
and to plant. (1.9–10.) His power to carry it out
lay simply in the charism given him to utter the
prophetic word, whose intrinsic dynamism
brought into existence the reality it signified.
(25.13: 26.12: 51.60.)

This conception was later given vigorous expression by the Deutero-Isaias. The "Book of
Consolation" (Isa. 40–55), which opens with a
eulogy of the eternity of God's word (40.6–8),
closes with the sublime lines:

> For as the rain comes down and the snow from
> heaven,
> And does not return thither until it has
> watered the earth.
> And makes it give birth and sprout, and gives
> seed to the sower and bread to the eater.
> So it shall be, the word that proceeds from my
> mouth, it shall not return to me empty,
> Until it accomplishes what I will and does
> that for which I sent it. [Isa. 55.10–11]

To "return" for a word is for it to be inefficacious. Such cannot be the fate of the word of Yahweh (Isa. 45.23–4).[31] It is as infallible in its mission as the forces of nature which it brings into being. (Ps. 147.15–18.) The exiled prophet fans the flame of hope among his compatriots with the promise that the word will restore Jerusalem, the temple and the towns of Judea. (44.26–8.) Such will be the course of history because Yahweh has so decreed.[32] His word is the dynamic instrument whereby he rules his chosen people. On the lips of the Servant it is "a shearing sword". (49.2.)

Given the dynamism of the prophetic word and the complete identification of the word of God with the written *torah* (law) which was the prevalent conception at the time of Christ, it is tempting to envisage the development of the theology of the word as a steady shift of emphasis from the dynamic to the noetic whose stages would correspond to the chronological order of the writings of the Old Testament. This, however, would be a gross oversimplification. The change of emphasis can be discerned with clarity only when the process has terminated. In the intermediary stages the picture is often cloudy and the division between the two aspects very fluid.

The dynamic character of the word so clear in Jeremias and the Deutero-Isaias is also emphasized by Ecclesiasticus. Two long passages (39.12–35: 42.15–43.33) exalt the power of the divine word in the creation of the universe: "At his word all that he desires is accomplished." (39.18.) A third (chs. 45–8) manifests its efficacy in history through the mediation of the great servants of the word. But even here, in texts such as "By the word of Moses he made miracles to come to pass ... he gave him commandments for his people" (45.2–3), the dynamic and dianoetic elements are found side by side. (Ps. 33.4–9: 147.15–20.)

The *dabar* we find in Ezechiel is the prophetic word endowed by Yahweh (13.6) with a dynamism that infallibly brings into existence the events "said". (12.25,28: 24.14.) This undergoes a slight modification if we taken into account the prophet's inaugural vision for, whereas Jeremias simply received the word (Jer. 1.9), Ezechiel is given it under the form of a *book*. (Ezek. 2.9: 3.1,4.) The noetic value of the word is further accentuated after the fall of Jerusalem (decreed and realized by the word) through a certain stress on personal responsibility (33.10–20) with the word as a code of life to be put into practice (33.31) and not listened to passively.[33]

In Deuteronomy, while the word is essentially a revealed guide to human living (4.2: 30.14: 32.47)[34] it is not conceived as an abstract, impersonal imperative inscribed in a statute book. The word is immutable (4.2) and written (30.10) but it is not a dead letter. In keeping with the description of the very personal relationship between Yahweh and the people he has chosen in love (7.6: 8.5), this word is conceived as a personal, ever-actual invitation, a grace always proffered: "The word is very close to thee; it is in thy mouth and in thy heart, that thou mayst practise it." (30.14.) The accent is very definitely on the aspect of revelation, but it is a living revelation. The stress on the immediacy of the word is probably due to an effort to assimilate the vitality of the prophetic experience to the point of view proper to the Deuteronomic school.[35]

Because of its relationship to Wisdom which is there given such prominence, it is in the sapiential literature that we see the concept of word undergo its most profound transformation.[36] It might be true to say that in general Wisdom (here personified) is endowed with the dynamic qualities attributed to *dabar* by the prophetic tradition (Prov. 1–9), whereas *dabar* itself is equated with the teaching proposed by the sages, which is, ultimately the moral prescriptions of the Law and the Prophets.[37] The tentative character of this summing-up must be stressed. Moreover, it shares the coefficient of error common to all generalization, and which increases with its extension. A number of passages modify slightly our general picture. In the Book of Ecclesiasticus, where we already noted the equal play given the two aspects of word, Wisdom, who existed before the Law, declares: "I came forth *from the mouth* of the Most High" (24.5), after the manner of a word, or perhaps better, a breath. The parallelism of the Book of Wisdom is also significant: "God of the fathers . . . you who made all things by your word and who established man by your wisdom." (9.1–2.) But most important of all is its hypostatization of the Word in 18.14–16:

> For when the gentle silence enveloped everything,
> And night was midway in her swift course,
> Your all-powerful word leaped from heaven, from the royal throne,
> A stern warrior, into the midst of the doomed land

Carrying for a sharp sword your undisguised
  command,
And stood still, and filled all things with death
And touched heaven but walked on earth.

The poetic vigour of this presentation is
unique,[38] but it does not seem on closer examination to be a significant development of the
concept of word. McKenzie, following Bousset-
Gressmann,[39] is probably correct in including
this passage "among instances of the hypostatization of divine attributes as a substitute for God
and the divine name which is characteristic of
later Judaism".[40] The reverence of the Jews of
this period took the form of avoidance of all
direct reference to God. And so where Exodus
spoke of Yahweh (12.29) or of Yahweh and the
"destroyer" (12.23), the Alexandrian writer
speaks of his "word", as other writers of the
period speak of the "name" or the "angel".[41]
This is confirmed by the indication that the instrument of the Word is itself a word.

Coming to Esdras and Nehemias, the word of
God *par excellence* is the written word of the
Torah (law), whose authority is indisputable.
(Ezek. 3.4: Neh. 8.15: 10.35–37.) The rare
references to the divine word in the books of
the Maccabees designate the sacred writings (1
Macc. 7.16: Macc. 7.6). This conception pre-
vailed until the Christian era, and is well

summed-up by R. H. Charles: "In the third century B.C. the Law had come to be conceived as the final and supreme revelation of God. When once this idea of an inspired Law—adequate, infallible and valid for all time—had become an accepted dogma of Judaism, as it became in the post-Exilic period, there was no longer room for independent representatives of God appearing before men, such as the pre-Exilic prophets. God had, according to the official teachers of the Church, spoken his last and final word through the Law."[42]

New-Testament times

In the epistles of St Paul, as we noted briefly, there is a reversion to the conception of the word of God as a dynamic force endowed with power to give life and salvation. This is fully in keeping with his understanding of the messianic and prophetic character of his function, but it would be a mistake to consider it an exclusively Pauline development. The break with the current Jewish conception of the word had been made by the ministry of Jesus, and Paul only articulated clearly the semi-conscious impressions engendered in the minds of the early Christians by that ministry.

THE SYNOPTIC GOSPELS AND THE ACTS OF THE
APOSTLES

The Synoptic Gospels are in the main the record of the public life of our Lord. Much attention is naturally devoted to his preaching. It is carefully noted by Matthew that his audiences were astounded at the authority with which he taught (7.28), but it can hardly be doubted that the greatest source of wonder for his hearers was the supreme power of his unembellished word. At a single word of command the demons were driven from the two possessed (Matt. 8.32 and parallels); the wind and the sea obeyed his voice (Mark 4.39 and parallels). Cures were effected through the medium of a simple expression: "I do so will. Be thou cured!" (Matt. 8.3); "Ephphatha (Be thou opened)!" (Mark 7.34); "Young man! I command thee. Rise up!" (Luke 7.14.) His words of forgiveness sufficed to blot out the sins of the paralytic. (Mark 2.10–11: Matt. 9.6.) When he sent the Twelve to preach, he fortified them for the task ahead by communicating to their words the power "to cure the sick, raise the dead, purify the leprous, drive out demons"—and all this by a simple imperative. (Matt. 10.8: Luke 10.9.)

For a reflective Jew these events must have brought to mind many passages of the prophetic books. As presented in the Synoptics the

prophetic character of Jesus' ministry is very
marked, especially in the accounts of the Baptism and Transfiguration,[43] but for the absence
of any introductory formula such as accompanies
many inaugural visions in the Old Testament
—"The word of Yahweh came to . . ." (e.g., Jer.
1.4). Kittel is probably correct in considering
this an indication that the sacred writers were,
at least in a vague way, aware that Jesus did not
receive the word of God, because he *was* the
Word.[44] This would also explain their sparing
use of the phrase "to speak the word" with Jesus
as subject,[45] and also the fact that only once does
Jesus himself speak of the message he brought
as a "word".[46] The semi-conscious character of
such a perception, however, must be emphasized.
Many thoughtful years would have to elapse
before the Prologue to the Fourth Gospel could
be written. In fact, at first the theology of the
word in the primitive community did not develop along these lines at all.

"The word of God" or simply "the word" (*ho
logos*) is found so constantly in the Acts of the
Apostles as a synonym for the Good News
preached by the Apostles that it must have been
generally accepted as a technical term for the
Gospel which had as its object the person of
Jesus. (Acts 2.14–39.)[47] It is, then, a question of
a word concerning Jesus, a message. The dianoetic aspect is to the fore. To speak the word

is to propagate the revelation brought by Christ. Nonetheless, some passages so qualify the "word" as to enable us to detect, in its initial stages, a reversion to the prophetic emphasis on the dynamic aspect.

In three of the little summaries with which he likes to round off sections of Acts, Luke presents the word as "growing":

The word of God was growing. [6.7]
The word of the Lord was growing and being multiplied. [12.24]
Mightily was the word of the Lord increasing and growing strong [*ischuen*]. [19.20][48]

The use of the imperfect tense in all three instances draws attention to the progressive, continuing character of the action. The contexts of both 6.7 and 12.24 make it clear that "growth" or "increase" is to be understood extensively because it is explained by the multiplication of believers. *Ischuō* in 19.20 adds a new idea but is more difficult to interpret. Basically this verb means "to be strong, powerful".[49] A few verses previously to this one, Luke employs it to describe the driving power of a man possessed by an evil spirit (19.16), and indeed it is always used to designate an intrinsic capacity to do something.[50] Hence, it would seem that the meaning intended in 19.20 is that the word is a power capable of producing a real effect on those who hear it, and that this efficacy is the explanation of the extensive growth. (Acts 2.41: 4.4.)

Real power is also attributed to the word in the account of Paul's farewell to the Elders of Ephesus:

> And now I commend you to the Lord and to the word of his grace which has the power to build up and to give the inheritance among all the sanctified. [20.32]

Grammatically, "power" in this verse should qualify "word", the nearest antecedent, but some authors refer it to "Lord".[51] The difference of opinion, however, is of slight importance and, indeed, serves to throw into relief an important characteristic of the dynamism of the word of God. If the word enjoys real effectiveness it is only because it participates in the salvific power of the risen Lord.

SAINT PAUL

The theology of the word that emerges from a study of Paul's own letters is a step forward by comparison with the doctrine of Acts. Like Luke, Paul frequently uses "the word of the Lord", "the word of God" and "the word" as the equivalent of "the Gospel",[52] but his emphasis on the dynamic character of the message is much more marked.

In the second letter to the Thessalonians the word appears as personified: "I pray that the word may run and be glorified even as among you." (3.1.) Paul elsewhere employs the image of an athlete in reference to his own spiritual life, which is necessarily bound up with the exigencies of his vocation (Phil. 3.12) and in reference to the new lives of those who have received his preaching. (Gal. 5.7: 1 Cor. 9.24–6.) Here this figure is used to describe the reality that relates the hearers to the speaker, namely, the word. Just as the athlete is glorified in finishing his course successfully, so too the word is glorified in winning entrance to men's hearts. (1 Thess. 1.6.) The image suggests vividly the energy and vitality of a word whose activity is not impeded even by the imprisonment of its ministers. (2 Tim. 2.9.)

This line of thought is continued and amplified in the Epistle to the Colossians. After the introductory salutation, Paul thanks God for their faith and charity which are rooted in the hope laid up for them in heaven:

That hope of which you have heard through the word of the truth of the Gospel which reached you, and indeed in the whole world that Gospel is bearing fruit and growing [*karpophoroumenon kai auxanomenon*] as it is among you, for the day you first came to hear

and recognize the grace of God in truth.
[1.5–6]

To find not one but two genitives qualifying
"word" is a little unusual. The fact, however,
that in the Greek the participle "reached" agrees
with "Gospel" and not with "truth" indicates
that "Gospel" is the principal notion, a genitive
of apposition that explains "the word of truth".
(Eph. 1.13: Gal. 2.5,14.)[53] The sequence of the
phrase can be understood in various ways de-
pending on one's estimation of the precise point
of comparison. The majority of commentators,
however, take this to be fruitfulness of the
Gospel—a dynamic force conquering the world
as it has conquered the hearts of the Colossians.[54]
This passage is the sole known instance of the
use of the middle voice *karpophoreisthai* which,
according to Bauer, means "to bear fruit *of
itself*".[55] Lightfoot, followed by Abbott, contrasts
the use of the middle voice here with that of the
indicative of the same verb in *v.* 10 of the same
chapter, where it is again associated with "growing". In *v.* 10 Paul prays that the Colossians will
come to a more profound awareness of the
exigencies of the message they have received and
so lead a life fully worthy of the Lord, "bearing
fruit in all kinds of good deeds and growing in
the knowledge of God". The nuance differen-
tiating the middle and active voices would be

that "the middle is *intensive*, the active *extensive*. The middle denotes the inherent energy, the active the external diffusion." (Lightfoot.) However, it is probably going a little too far to dissociate these two aspects so radically. In the present context the image suggested is a growing thing, a tree or plant, and the idea evoked is power in action. It is not a simple affirmation of the intrinsic dynamism of the Gospel. The use of the verb "to be" with a present participle ("is bearing fruit and growing") emphasizes the continuity of present action. The power of the Gospel is known and appreciated in the change its advent is bringing about in the community at Colossae. I use the phrase "is bringing about" advisedly because this passage strongly suggests that the spoken word does not lose its vitality when received. It would be difficult to find an image more apt to convey the dynamism and the inevitable progression of the word of truth. Not alone does it grow in virtue of its intrinsic energy, but it has the power to communicate that life to others who will in turn grow and bear fruit.

Later in the same letter Paul comes back to the idea of the word as a power operative within the Christian when he prays: "May the word of Christ dwell in you [*enoikeitō en humin*] in rich abundance." (3.16.)[56] The qualification "word *of Christ*" is unique but there is no reason to

suspect that it is not authentic, because its appearance here is perfectly in keeping with the
emphasis on the dignity of Christ characteristic
of this epistle. The phrase signifies the message
which has Christ for its subject-matter (Col.
1.28: Phil. 1.15: 2 Cor. 1.19), and which has its
origin in him. (Eph. 4.20–21.)[57] The problem is
to determine the force of *enoikeitō en humin*.
Enoikeō means "to live, dwell [in]". Its usage
in the New Testament is exclusively Pauline
and, with the exception of 2 Cor. 6.16 (a quotation from Leviticus referring to God's dwelling
among the Chosen People, but intended by Paul
to support his claim, "We are the temples of the
living God"), all the texts have reference to
spiritual things that take up their abode in
men.[58] This usage favours the rendering "*in* you"
rather than "*among* you", i.e., the word is intrinsic to the individual and not merely to the
community. In any case it is difficult to envisage
how the word could be present in the community were it not received individually by
each of its members. This indwelling of the
word is qualified by a rather peculiar adverb,
"in rich abundance" (*plousiōs*)—peculiar, because as found elsewhere in the New Testament
this adverb is a qualification of divine *giving*.
(Titus 3.6: 1 Tim. 6.17: 2 Pet. 1.11.) Associated
with "indwelling", *plousiōs* would suggest a
dynamic energy-filled presence that manifests

itself in obedience to Paul's counsels and directives.

That this is the Apostle's mind is evidenced by 1 Thess. 2.13:

> And for this reason, we too as well as you thank God continually, namely, because when you had received from us the word which you heard, God's word [*logos akoēs par' hēmōn tou theou*], you welcomed it, not as a human word but, as it really is, a word of God which also is made operative in you who believe [*logon theou, hos kai energeitai humin tois pisteuousin*].

The conciseness of the phrase *logos akoēs par' hēmōn tou theou* makes it almost impossible to translate. In fact, it is a combination of two expressions, *logos akoēs*, "word heard", and *logos theou*, "word of God", that Paul has run together because of his vivid consciousness of the divine nature of his message.[59] Though spoken by men, it is not a human word: it is still God's word. That word has been received and welcomed by the Thessalonians. Those who have received it are the believers, and in them the word is "operative".[60] The verb *energeirai* is passive.[61] In the active voice it means "to work, to operate, to be effective", and J. A. Robinson, after a careful study of both the classical and New-Testament usage of these verbs, concludes that "in actual meaning *energein* and *energeis-thai* come nearly to the same thing. Only the passive serves to remind us that the operation is not self-originated. (Cf. Phil. 2.13.) The powers 'work' indeed, but they 'are made to work'."[62] Since the word of God, which is also Paul's, produces determined visible effects among the Thessalonians, it must be a dynamic force as were the words of the Prophets. (1 Thess. 2.14 ff.) It is perfectly in keeping with Paul's conception of his function that he should here, by the use of a passive, underline both the real power of the word and its instrumental character. The spoken word is God's instrument in bringing the plan of salvation to perfection, and in view of this end is endowed with the salvific power of Christ, the messianic Saviour.

The thought expressed in the above passage invites us to see something more than a merely accidental juxtaposition of "word" and "power of God" in Paul's character-sketch of a true "servant of God". After recounting his own sufferings and labours in the cause of the Gospel, the Apostle points out that the evidence that he and his collaborators are God's ministers may be seen:

In innocence of life and in knowledge of the truth
in patient long-suffering and in kindliness of heart,

> in a spirit that is holy, and in love that is
> unfeigned.
>
> in teaching that is true and in power that is
> divine. [2 Cor. 6.6–7]

This translation by A. Plummer conveys something of the rhythm of the Greek and has the
further advantage of bringing out clearly the
pairing of the virtues. The association of "innocence" and "knowledge" does not seem to be
more than accidental; but this cannot be said of
the other pairings. In each case there is evidence
from other Pauline epistles that the virtues in
question were linked in Paul's mind almost
habitually. This suggests that even though the
power of God is the reality that underlies the
preacher's whole existence (2 Cor. 4.7: Eph.
3.20: Col. 1.29) it is especially associated with
his words.

From the idea of power-laden word, the transition to the image of offensive and defensive
arms in the succeeding verse (2 Cor. 6.7b) is easy
and natural. In fact, in the Epistle to the Ephesians, where there is an explicit description of
the spiritual armoury of the Christian, we find
"the word of God" (*rhēma theou*) listed as the
explanation and equivalent of "the sword of the
Spirit". (6.17.) Paul's enumeration of the pieces
of armour contains definite allusions to passages
from the Book of Isaias (Isa. 11.4–5: 34.3–9:

52.7: 59.17), among which is found, in an evocation of the qualities of the messianic king, the following description of the dynamism of his word: "His word is a baton that strikes the violent: the breath of his lips slays the wicked." (11.4.) Words that in turn recall a verse of the Second Servant Song: "He has made my mouth a sharp sword." (49.2.) It may be doubted, however, whether these texts provide a real parallel to the passage in Ephesians, because they refer to an individual with a definite authoritative mission, whereas the epistle has in view *all* Christians. This latter point, when taken in conjunction with Masson's observation that wherever the Septuagint employs *rhēma theou* (both in the singular and plural) it always signifies particular words of God, might incline one to understand "the word of God" here as prayer. The meaning, then, would be that the believer, in moments of temptation, is urged in imitation of Christ (Matt. 4.4–10) to use the sword of the word of God, pronouncing in each case the word suggested by the Spirit (Matt. 10.19–20) who prays in him. (Rom. 8.15,26.) On the other hand, in view of the fact that *vv.* 18–20 are devoted to an exhortation to continual prayer, it does not seem likely that such a veiled reference to prayer is intended here. It is difficult also to see the force of Masson's argument from Septuagint usage. It is true that in the prophetic books the

Septuagint invariably uses *logos* in its translation
of the phrase "the word of the Lord came . . .",
but in the historical books *rhēma* and *logos* are
used indiscriminately to render the same phrase
(e.g., 1 Sam. 8.10: 9.27: 2 Sam. 7.4: 1 Kings
12.24). Absolutely speaking, then, *rhēma theou*
could designate divine revelation. There is no
evidence that the phrase was ever used of words
addressed *to* God. Rather, Paul's own use of
rhēma introduces us into the preaching-faith
context of Rom. 10,[63] and Schlier rightly considers that the *rhēma theou* of Eph. 6.17 is to be
understood in the light of Rom. 10.8: "The
word [*rhēma*] is close to thee in thy lips and in
thy heart, that is the word [*rhēma*] of faith that
we preach."[64] "Word of faith" in this verse is
not "the Faith" i.e., the Gospel message as an
objective reality whose subject matter is salvation through faith alone; it is rather the word
which, when preached, gives rise to faith. The
believers possess this word, and in them it re-
tains its vitality and energy. (1 Thess. 2.13.)[65]
This brings us back to the context of Ephesians,
where the whole point of the detailed enumeration of the spiritual arms of the Christian is to
emphasize and explain the initial exhortation:
"Find your strength in the Lord, in his mighty
power." (6.10.) It is not so much a question of
acquiring new virtues as of becoming really conscious of the spiritual realities already possessed.

In receiving the "word of God" Christians have received the "sword of the Spirit". The genitive is one of quality and of authorship. The Spirit is active both in the word as preached and in the word as received in faith. Perhaps the best commentary on the verse under consideration is another passage from the same epistle:

I kneel in prayer to the Father . . . that out of the treasures of his glory he may strengthen you with power through his Spirit, in the interior man, that through faith Christ may dwell in your hearts in love. [Eph. 3.14–7; cf. Rom. 8.10: Gal. 2.20]

Note the association power-Spirit-faith. Faith is the acceptance of the word of God, the opening of the heart to Christ. The indwelling of Christ is the strengthening of the interior man through faith and the Spirit. In 6.10 the source of power is "the Lord", i.e., Christ, the messianic saviour who sends the Spirit. (1 Cor. 15.45: Rom. 1.4: 8.11.) Equipped with the sword of the Spirit, that is, the power of the Spirit operative in the word of God received in faith, the Christian has nothing to fear from Principalities and Powers (6.12).

It is, however, at the beginning of the Epistle to the Romans that we find the clearest expression of Paul's theology of the word. He states simply:

> I am not ashamed of the Gospel since it is a
> divine power for the salvation of every be-
> liever. [1.16]

He could not be more explicit. The efficacy of
the Gospel is not due to the personality of the
preacher or to the manner in which it is presented (1 Cor. 1.17); it *is* the saving power of
God. "Gospel" here is to be understood as com-
prising both the content and the actual preaching of the Good News, as in the parallel 1 Cor.
1.18:

> The word of the Cross is sheer folly to those on
> their way to ruin, but to those who are on the
> way to salvation, to us, it is the power of God.

The Gospel is not an inert body of doctrines but
a vital reality capable of communicating its life
to those who come into real contact with it.

Hence when Paul says, "We announce Christ"
(Col. 1.28; cf. Phil. 1.18) the meaning is not
simply that he explains the fact and implications
of Christ's passion and resurrection. In his words
Christ is rendered present (Eph. 3.16) together
with the redemptive power acquired at his resurrection. (1 Cor. 15.45: Rom. 1.4.) Similarly, the
genitives with which Paul qualifies "the word",
or "the Gospel", signify the content of his message, but in indicating that object render it
present.[66] In "the word of the Cross" (1 Cor. 1.18)

it is the Cross that speaks; in "the Gospel of your salvation" (Eph. 1.13) salvation is conferred on him who hears it. "The word of life" (Phil. 2.16) really communicates the new life of grace. By "the word of reconciliation" (2 Cor. 5.19) men are reconciled with God.[67]

The mere fact of the existence of Paul's epistles is clear evidence of his awareness of the dianoetic value of the word of God. In these letters he shows the word to be a message conveying an understanding of definite historical realities. (1 Tim. 1.15.) Every word is a revelation and, to a greater or less degree, a self-revelation; conversely, every revelation can be interpreted as a word. The "word of God" is the revelation of God's definitive intervention in history. The instrument of that intervention, which was the manifestation of a superabundant love, was Christ, He was in his person, as distinct altogether from his words, the revelation of God's love, and even though Paul explicitly admits him to be such (Titus 3.4–6) he never affirms as clearly and as unequivocally as St John does that Christ is the *Word* of God. Two texts, however, show his thought to have been moving in that direction. Both are from letters written in the very last years of his life and had he lived longer it is not impossible that he might have anticipated the Prologue.

The first is:

He manifested his word in due season by the preaching which was entrusted to me. [Titus 1.3]

If the beginning of this verse, particularly because of the use of the aorist with its connotation of a precise historical moment and of the phrase "in due season" (Gal. 4.4: Eph. 1.10: Titus 3.4–6), immediately evokes the Johannine equation Christ = the Word, the sequence makes it clear that the manifestation in question is effected not by birth but by preaching. Far from being a title of the Redeemer, "Word" here signifies the whole plan of redemption as conceived by God and already put into execution. It is not, then, a question of a personal (static) identification of Christ as the Word such as John teaches. But, if both Paul's conception of his mission as the continuation of Christ's and his insistence on the word as a power-laden revelation at work in history are kept in mind, it seems permissible to see underlying this text an identification of the word with Christ actually exercising his salvific function. If for John, Christ is the Word, for Paul the word is *Christ saving*.

This is, perhaps, more explicit in the second passage:

Such indeed is the commission of God [*oikonomia tou theou*] given me in your regard, to fulfil *the word of God [plērōsai ton logon tou theou]*, *the mystery* hidden from former generations and ages, but now disclosed to his saints, to whom God has willed to make known what is the wealth of the glory of *this mystery* among the Gentiles, *which is Christ* among you, your hope of glory. [Col. 1.25–7]

To consider the italicized words alone it would seem that we have a perfect set of equations: "the word of God" = "the mystery" and "this mystery" = "Christ". The context, however, which is concerned with preaching, urges caution. Paul, a few verses previously, has reminded the Colossians that he is suffering and for the sake of Christ's body, "which is the Church, of which I became the servant according to the *oikonomia tou theou*". (1.24–5.) In the New Testament *oikonomia* can have two meanings: (1) The divine plan of salvation (Eph. 1.10), and (2) the charge confided to certain men by God in view of its realization. (1 Cor. 9.17: Eph. 3.2.) The continuation of the verse —"given me in your regard"—indicates that the second sense is the one immediately applicable here. This, however, is not to exclude the first and even the most rigorous would find it difficult to quarrel with Masson's paraphrase, "according to God's plan, whose execution, inso-

far as it concerns you, has been entrusted to me."
The embarrassment of translators when forced
with the succeeding phrase *plērōsai ton logon
tou theou* is evident in the variety of their
renderings:

   to complete the preaching of God (Knox)
   to fulfil the word of God (Douay Version, AV,
      RSV)
   to fully declare God's word (Spencer, also
      Phillips, Moule, Osty)
   to deliver his message in full (New English
      Bible).

The differences, it is apparent, are more than
verbal. The uncertainty is due to the rather
unusual association of verb and noun, and interpretation is not made any easier by the fact
that there is only one other instance of this
verb in a similar context, namely, *peplērōkenai
to euangelion.* (Rom. 15.19.)[68] *Plēroō* means "(i)
to make full, to fill (full); (ii) to bring something
to completion, to finish; (iii) to fulfil by deeds a
prophecy, an obligation etc."[69] It is impossible
to see what sense the first meaning could have
in the present context, and how the translations
of Phillips etc. and the New English Bible could
be reconciled with any of the meanings of *plēroō.*
In view of the fact that it is a question of Paul's
duty and since his stress on the power of the
word has already been noted, it seems likely that

the *two* remaining meanings are intended here.
This involves attributing a rather fluid, but
nonetheless unified, meaning to "the word of
God".[70] In the first place it is the *oikonomia*
entrusted to Paul; by declaring the mystery
(Col. 2.2) he is fulfilling the exigencies of his
vocation. (Acts 9.15: Col. 4.17: 2 Tim. 4.5.) But
it is also possible that the "word of God" should
be the divine *oikonomia* that is progressively fulfilled by Paul as, by his words, he makes the
mystery actual.[71] The mystery is indeed Christ
(Col. 2.2), not a static divine being, but a
dynamic messianic saviour. In virtue of his commission Paul's preaching makes Christ present,
in his salvific power, among the Gentiles. Kittel
is correct in saying that Christ is the word
spoken by God to his saints[72]—if we add *through
Paul*. This is brought out with his customary
adroitness by Benoit in the *Bible de Jérusalem*;
he paraphrases, " de réaliser chez vous l'avène-
ment de sa Parole". The advent of the Word is
effected by Paul. If this rendering has a defect it
is that it obscures the relationship between
preaching and the plan of salvation, which, as
noted *à propos* of Titus 1.3, is also termed a
"word". The disclosure of the mystery is its
realization, its fulfilment. The preacher's words
do not merely expose "the great love wherewith
God loved us" made manifest in Christ (Eph.
2.4); they make that love actually present. The

Gospel proclaims "You are saved", and those who receive this assurance with faith really are —and by that fact alone. (Eph. 1.13.)[73]

The same idea of preaching as a double fulfilment recurred again to Paul at the very end of his life. Referring to one of his terms of imprisonment he says:

> But the Lord stood by me and strengthened me, in order that through me the preaching might be brought to completion [*to kērugma plēropherēthē*] and that all the nations might hear. [2 Tim. 4.17]

The significance of this passage is entirely lost in Spencer's version of the key-phrase: ". . . that through me the Word might be fully proclaimed". Apart altogether from the totally unwarranted introduction of the capital letter, it is impossible to see how he (and Phillips and the *Bible de Jérusalem*) could justify "proclaim" as a translation of *plerophoreō*, for this verb means "to fulfil perfectly, to complete, to bring to perfection". In *v.* 5 of this same chapter Paul employs it in his admonition to Timothy: "Do the work of an evangelist; *fully discharge* your ministry." In the present instance it is again a question of the fulfilment of Paul's own duty, but the expression (*to kērugma*) seems rather too strong to be taken literally and it is easy to see why Spicq should consider it "manifestly hyperbolical", and also to appreciate the translators' difficulty. This difficulty, however, disappears, or is at any rate greatly attenuated, if we do not limit the idea of fulfilment to Paul's discharge of his duty. In exercising his ministry the preacher fulfils the role assigned to him by God, but at the same time, in virtue of that activity, God's plan for humanity is fulfilled in the sense that it is put into execution with tangible results. Within the limits of his charge, then, Paul can say with full truth that *the* mystery (for *kērugma* can mean "preaching" in the sense of "that which is preached") has been brought to completion.

Paul gives the prophetic conception of the word of God a new dimension. The divine power in the prophetic word directed history according to a divine plan which was only dimly perceived by its executants. (Rom. 16.26.) In Christ, however, history has in a sense reached its term. (Eph. 2.5: Titus 3.5.) But from another point of view the goal is still to be achieved (1 Cor. 15.2: 2 Tim. 1.10), and the instrument of its realization is the word. (1 Thess. 2.16.) Christ, when he came, was the living embodiment of the Father's love for men (Titus 3.4–6), and of his will to save them. (1 Tim. 2.4.) The full revelation of the divine plan of salvation was a Person; an *event* in history. The revelation effected by the spoken word is still *that event*. In preaching, the revelation that is Christ is made present (Col. 1.28), and rendered accessible to those who never knew him. This presence of Christ in the word is not a presence in the flesh but a presence in power. As Christ is "the power of God" (1 Cor. 1.23–4), so is the Gospel "the power of God" (1 Cor. 1.18), "a divine power for salvation". (Rom. 1.16.) The intrinsic dynamism of this word impregnated with the saving force of Christ is clearly brought out when he compares it both to an athlete (2 Thess. 3.1) and to a growing tree. (Col. 1.6.) The word is a directed, controlled force aimed at the hearts of men. Received in faith, its latent energy causes it to grow and bear fruit. (1 Thess. 2.13.) Through faith the word of Christ dwells in the heart of man (Col. 3.16), communicating to it the riches of salvation he has won by his passion and resurrection. (Eph. 3.16–17.) In accepting the word as addressed personally to him by God (1 Thess. 2.13) man is brought into contact with the power of the Cross (1 Cor. 1.18), participates the new life of grace (Phil. 2.16), and in his unending contest with the forces of evil has at his disposition the sword of the Spirit. (Eph. 6.17.) Through the word he is absorbed into the mystery. Heard by the nations only because formulated and proclaimed by the preachers, the divine plan for the salvation of humanity is gradually brought to the full perfection it will attain only at the moment of the "epiphany of glory" (Titus 2.13), the Second Coming.

NOTES

1. Previous to Homer the terms used were *epos* and *mythos*. According to H. Fournier, *epos* signified the thought-content of speech and *mythos* the material expression. In post-Homeric times, however, after being superseded by *logos*, *epos* retained the meaning "word" only in poetry, and the general acceptation of *mythos* was "fairytale, legend, fable etc." (H. Fournier, *Les Verbes "dire" en Grec ancien*, Paris (1946), 215–16). The synonyms of *logos* current in later Greek do not require serious attention. *Lalia* signified disordered utterance, mere prattle, whereas *rhēma* designated formulae, expressions, and turns of phrase with a well-determined form. (Cf. Fournier, 224.)

2. Cf. T. Boman, *Hebrew Thought compared with Greek*, London (1960), 67.

3. Cf. H. Fournier, *Les Verbes*, 53–4; also *TWNT*, vol. 4, 71–2. This explains the very varied acceptations of *logos*. It is used to mean (a) expression, language, phrase, word, history; (b) principle, law, fundament, explanation; (c) proportion, relation, connection; (d) faculty of thought (synonym of *nous*), human spirit and thought [from second half of fifth century]. (*TWNT*, vol. 4, 76–7.)

4. Greek philosophical (*logos* as the principle of intelligibility of being) and religious (*logos* as revelation, sacred teaching) speculation are personified and drawn together in Hermes (and others), the god of reason, order, number and science, who as *angelos* and *kērux* announces to men the will of the gods and even plays a certain soteriological role. Kleinknecht concludes: "Hence, in Greek mysticism, *logos* is essentially a

cosmic-creative power, the guide to and the bearer of knowledge—which gradually becomes more and more a religious doctrine of salvation—the revealer of hidden things." (*TWNT*, vol. 4, 86.) Evidently *logos* was never considered as having a dynamic quality until it was identified with a divine being, who was the medium of revelation and knowledge.

5. The etymology of *dabar* is still disputed. Procksch holds that it must be sought, not from the verb, but from the noun, and on the basis of its relationship to *debir*, concludes that its basic meaning is "reverse" (*Ruckseite*) "background" (*Hintergrund*). "One must seek in *dabar* the background of a thing...each thing has a *dabar*, that is to say, its background and meaning." (*TWNT*, vol. 4, 90.) His analysis of its usage shows that, together with its dianoetic content, *dabar* has a dynamic value. Boman refers *dabar* to the verb *dabar* normally used in the *Pi'el*, whose basic meaning is "'to be behind and drive forward', hence 'to let words follow one another' or even better 'to drive forward that which is behind'." (*Hebrew Thought compared with Greek*, London (1960), 65.) Thus understood the verb portrays somehow the function of speech. *Dabar* can also mean "thing" or "deed" (e.g., Gen. 24.66), but given the basic signification of the root it is clear that these are not different meanings; "the 'deed' is the consequence of the basic meaning inherent in *dabar*". (Boman, p. 65.) A. Robert, on the other hand, thinks it more prudent to assume two parallel roots "to be behind" and "to speak" (*DBS*. 5, 442), and this is the supposition underlying Koehler's classification. (Cf. L. Koehler—W. Baumgartner, *Lexicon in V.T. Libros*, Leiden (1958), 199.)

6. This is probably why *dabar* is often found in parallel with *ruah*, e.g., Ps. 35.4: Isa. 34.16: Prov. 1.23: Job 15.13: Judith 16.17.

7. The word exteriorizes what man has already said in his heart (Gen. 17.17: Ps. 14.1: Ecclus. 2.15), or that which rises up in his heart (Jer. 3.16: Isa. 65.7), or in

his spirit (Ezek. 11.5). The close relationship between word (*dabar*), heart (*leb*) and spirit (*ruah*), is stressed in Isa. 32.6: Ps. 39.4: 44.2. The "heart" in Semitic anthropology is the source of intellectual and volitional activity. On the Hebrew psychology of the word, cf. C. Larcher, "La Parole de Dieu en tant que révélation dans l'Ancien Testament", in *La Parole de Dieu en Jésus-Christ* (Cahiers de l'actualité religieuse, 15) Tournai (1961), 36–40; F. J. Leenhardt, "La Signification de la notion de parole dans la pensée chrétienne", *RHPR*, 35 (1955), 263–73.

8. That is why both curses and blessings are often presented as an appeal to Yahweh (Judges 17.2). There is no indication in the Old Testament that the Israelites considered words as an incantation, a formula endowed with magical efficacy. Note David's words: "Let him curse, if Yahweh has commanded him. Perhaps Yahweh will look on my misery and grant me good fortune in place of misfortune." (2 Sam. 16.11–12.) Ezechiel scoffs sarcastically at the false prophets who foolishly expect *their* words to produce an effect. (Ezek. 13.6.)

9. Cf. A. Barucq, "Logos, dans la littérature égyptienne", *DBS*, 5, 435.

10. "Who is he? He is Re who created the names of the parts of his body. That is how the gods who follow him came into being"; translation by J. A. Wilson, in J. B. Pritchard, *ANET*, 4.

11. Translated from the French version in A. Barucq, "Logos", 436.

12. Translated from the French version in A. Barucq, "Logos", 438.

13. Translation by J. A. Wilson, in J. B. Pritchard, *ANET*, 5.

14. Even in this passage mention is made of creation by other means, and while thus it seems impossible to state that the intellectual way in which creation is here described ever entirely dominated the field, there is evidence that its success was more enduring than more

imaginative, earthy theories, cf. A. Barucq, "Logos", 440.

15. Cf. A. Barucq, "Logos", 438, 440.

16. Cf. L. Durr, *Die Wertung des göttlichen Wortes im AT und in AO*, Leipzig (1938), 32, as quoted by C. Larcher, "La Parole", 42.

17. Translation by F. J. Stephens, in J. B. Pritchard, *ANET*, 386.

18. Cf. R. Follet, "Les Aspects du divin et des dieux dans la Mesopotamie antique", *RSR*, 38 (1951), 206.

19. Translation by E. A. Speiser, in J. B. Pritchard, *ANET*. 66.

20. Cf. R. Tournay, "Logos, dans la littérature babylonienne", *DBS*, 5, 431.

21. Cf. R. Tournay, "Logos", 426. Larcher ("La Parole", 44) introduces some texts from Ras Shamra-Ugarit, but their interpretation is not at all sure.

22. Larcher notes that these resemblances occur most frequently in the poetic passages of the Old Testament, where it is question of God's action on nature. They are much less striking in the case of the prophetic word, and non-existent when the "word" is understood as a precise divine law. ("La Parole", 45.)

23. Cf. T. Boman, *Hebrew Thought*, 60.

24. The idea of the *creative* word of Yahweh was a comparatively late phenomenon in Israelite literature, appearing first in all probability in the writings of the Deutero-Isaias; cf. J. L. McKenzie, "The Word of God in the Old Testament", *TS*, 21 (1960), 201. The texts from Gen. cited here all pertain to the Priestly account of creation. The Yahwist narrative makes no mention of "word"; creatures are simply *made* by God. (Gen. 2.4.)

25. *Name und Wort Gottes im Alten Testament*, Giessen (1934).

26. These conclusions are quoted as presented in A. Robert, "Logos, parole divine dans l'Ancien Testament", *DBS*, 5, 443, and J. L. McKenzie, "The Word of God", 191.

27. The Decalogue is the "word" of Yahweh in the most basic sense and the starting point of the Israelite theology of the word; cf. A. Robert, "Logos", 443; J. L. McKenzie, "The Word of God", 203. Procksch does not agree and considers the roots of the theological development of the idea of word to lie in prophecy. (*TWNT*, vol. 4, 92.) It is to be noted, however, that even on Sinai it was a question of one individual receiving the word of God for transmission to the whole people. And Israelite tradition saw Moses not just as the Legislator but also as the greatest of the Prophets. (Deut. 34.10: Num. 12.6–8.) Cf. A. Gelin, "Moïse dans l'Ancien Testament", in *Moïse, l'homme de l'Alliance* (Cahiers Sioniens), Paris (1955), 45, 138 *n.* 127.

28. The dianoetic aspect of word is not absent in Isaias: "Hear the word [*dabar*] of Yahweh, chiefs of Sodom; hear the command [*torah*] of our God, people of Gomorrah." (1.10.) *Torah* here, as in 2.3, indicates the moral code promulgated by Yahweh, cf. 30.9–12.

29. Note the repeated refrain in 9.11,16,20: 10.4. Compare Col. 1.16: 1 Thess. 2.13.

30. It is to be noted that while Jeremias distinguishes the functions of the priest and the prophet, attributing to the first *torah* and to the second *dabar* (18.18, compare Mal. 2.7), he twice equates the two (6.19: 8.8–9). The promises of chastisement uttered by the prophets suppose a refusal to accept a view of reality revealed by Yahweh, the original revelation being clarified and applied to concrete situations by the preaching of the prophets. That the *dabar Yahweh* implied communication of knowledge is evident from its use at the beginning of books (e.g. Os. 1.1: Mic. 1.1: Isa. 2.1) and at the start of a new train of thought (e.g. Isa. 1.10: 9.8: Ezek. 3.16: 6.1).

31. For Jeremias there is one infallible criterion of the authenticity of a prophet's word: Was it fulfilled? "When the word of the prophet shall come to pass, then shall the prophet be known, that the Lord hath truly sent him." (28.9.) Compare Judges 13.12,17: Ps. 105.19.

32. For a presentation of Old-Testament history as a chain of events linked by, and dependent on, divine words, cf. J. L. McKenzie, "The Word of God", 199. The finality of history is clearly evident in texts such as Isa. 41.4: 44.6: 48.12. History is intelligible because it unrolls according to a plan that the *dabar Yahweh* both reveals and puts into effect, cf. 1 Kings 15.29: 16.12,34: 2 Kings 1.17: 7.16: 9.26,36.

33. Cf. A. Robert, "Logos", 451.

34. The prophetic word is true only if in harmony with the Law, cf. Deut. 13.1–5. New revelations are in principle possible but will be in dependence on the Law, cf. Deut. 18.

35. It will not be out of place to underline the contacts between the writings of Jeremias and those of the Deuteronomic school. Cazelles, for example, is of the opinion that the editor of Jeremias made use of Deuteronomy, and that the second edition of Deuteronomy shows a marked dependence on the images and thought of the prophet. ("Jérémie et le Deutéronome", *RSR*, 38 (1951), 36.) Cf. also, C. Larcher, "La Parole de Dieu", 60.

36. Cf. C. Larcher, "La Parole de Dieu", 65, 66.

37. Cf. A. Robert, "Logos", 457.

38. Passages such as Ps. 107.20: 119.89: 147.4,15–18: Isa. 55.11: Zech. 9.1, can be satisfactorily interpreted as vivid poetic expression of the idea of instrumentality, cf. Isa. 44.25–26.

39. *Die Religion des Judentums in späthellenistischen Zeitalter*, Tübingen (1926), 437.

40. "The Word of God", 198, *n.* 2.

41. The Aramaic *memra*, "word", occurs frequently in the Targums of the Old Testament in a divine context. The choice of this term may have been influenced by the texts cited in note 38 above, but is only a rabbinic device for avoiding the name of God. We have here a literary devotional usage, not a significant development in the theology of the word; cf. M. Lagrange, *Le Judaïsme avant Jesus Christ*, Paris (1931),

352–6; J. Starcky, "Logos, la parole divine à l'époque néotestamentaire", *DBS*, 5, 466–72.

42. R. H. Charles, *The Apocrypha and Pseudepigrapha of the Old Testament II*, Oxford (1913), viii. The term *torah*, "law", in its widest meaning was used as a collective designation for the whole of the authoritative tradition, not merely that codified in sacred Scripture but also that which was carried forward orally. The whole of the oral tradition did not originate as Scripture interpretation, but that did not prevent the rabbis from seeing—in principle—the oral *torah* as the interpretation of the written *torah*, cf. B. Gerhardsson, *Memory and Manuscript, Oral Tradition and Written Transmission in Rabbinic Judaism and Early Christianity*, Uppsala (1961), 19–21, 82.

43. Cf. F. Gils, *Jésus prophète d'après les évangiles synoptiques*, Louvain (1957), 49–77.

44. Cf. *TWNT*, vol. 4, 114, 126.

45. In fact it only occurs four times, Mark 2.2: 4.33: 8.32: Luke 5.1: cf. Kittel, *TWNT*, vol. 4, 122.

46. Kittel is most likely correct in considering the presence of "word" in Luke 8.21 as redactional, because in the parallels we find "the will of God" (Mark 3.35) and "the will of my Father". (Matt. 12.50.) Its presence in 11.28 could then be explained by the influence of the former passage. His attempt to deal with the Parable of the Sower is not at all so convincing, cf. *TWNT*, vol. 4, 123.

47. Acts 4.4: 6.7: 8.4: 10.44: 11.19: 12.24 etc. If *logos* had indeed become a technical term for the Christian gospel, it would explain why Luke uses *rhēma* rather than *logos* (which would have been more appropriate in view of the consistent usage of the Septuagint) in the phrase "the word of the Lord came to John" (3.2), cf. A. Richardson, *An Introduction to the Theology of the New Testament*, London (1958), 160, *n*. 1.

48. Absolutely speaking, another translation is possible: "According to the power of the Lord the word was increasing and growing strong." So M. Zerwick,

Analysis Philologica N. T. Greece, Rome (1953), but cf.
Kittel, *TWNT*, vol. 4, 119, *n*. 198.

49. Cf. *A-G*, 384.

50. To season (of salt) (Matt. 5.13): to stay awake
(Mark 14.37: Matt. 26.40): to pass, or to control, a possessed person (Mark 5.4: Matt. 8.28): to expel demons
(Mark 9.17): to knock down a building (Luke 6.48): to
cure a sick person (Luke 8.43).

51. Cf. E. Jacquier, *Les Actes des Apôtres*, Paris (1926),
618.

52. 1 Thess. 1.6,8: 2.13: 2 Thess. 3.1: 1 Cor. 2.4,7:
14.36: 2 Cor. 4.2: Phil. 1.14: Col. 1.25: 3.16: 4.3: Eph.
1.13: 6.19: Gal. 6.6.

53. Abbott, Masson, Lightfoot, Ewald.

54. Abbott, Masson, Dibelius, Lightfoot, Ewald.

55. Cf. *A-G*, 406.

56. There is some uncertainty as to whether "with
all wisdom" is to be joined to what precedes or to what
follows. Lightfoot links it with the preceding phrase in
the light of parallels such as Eph. 5.18–19. Masson does
likewise because, following Lohmeyer, he considers that
the principle phrase, "May the word of Christ . . . in all
wisdom", is amplified and explained by the two succeeding parallel phrases both beginning with a participle,
(1) *didaskontes* . . . (2) *adontes* . . . To support this view
he offers no argument. On the other hand *plousiōs* has
a definitive terminative effect (Abbott). Consequently,
with Abbott, Benoit, Dibelius, Ewald, Scott, it seems
preferable to associate it with what follows.

57. Paul regularly writes "the Gospel of Christ". (1
Thess 3.2: Gal. 1.7: Rom. 15.19: 1 Cor. 9.12: 2 Cor. 2.12:
Phil. 1.27.)

58. Spirit (Rom. 8.11: 2 Tim. 1.14): sin (Rom. 7.17):
faith (2 Tim. 1.5).

59. Dibelius, Rigaux.

60. Since *logos* receives the emphasis, *hos* refers to it
and not to *theou*. So Frame, Stabb, Wohlenberg, Steinmann. The only dissenter is Dibelius, but how then

explain the passive verb? How can God be said to be made operative?

61. Many authors have accepted Lightfoot's dictum that *energeisthai* is always middle voice and never passive in St Paul (on Gal. 5.6). J. A. Robinson's reaction against this absolutism ("On *Energein* and its Cognates", in his *Saint Paul's Epistle to the Ephesians,* London (1928), 241–7) has found confirmation in K. W. Clark's study, "The Meaning of *energeō* and *katergeō* in the New Testament", *JBL,* 54 (1935), 93–101, and in Rigaux's commentary (on 2 Thess. 2.7). They have shown that the passive was the current Greek usage and that all the New-Testament passages can legitimately be understood as passives.

62. J. A. Robinson, *Ephesians,* 247.

63. This chapter contains half the Pauline instances of its use, *vv.* 8, 17, 18. The three other occurrences are in 2 Cor. 12.4: Eph. 5.26: 6.17.

64. *Die Brief an die Epheser,* Düsseldorf (1957), 298.

65. Note the force of the exposition of the author of Hebrews: "The word of God is alive and active. It cuts more keenly than any two-edged sword, piercing as far as the place where life and spirit, joints and marrow, divide. It sifts the thoughts of the heart." (4.12.)

66. Cf. G. Kittel, *TWNT,* vol. 4, 119–20: H. Schlier, "La Notion paulinienne de la parole de Dieu", in A. Descamps et al., *Littérature et théologie pauliniennes* (Rech. Bibl., 5), Louvain (1960), 135.

67. Cf. above, p. 91–2.

68. The translations of this verse vary as much as those of Col. 1.25:

"I have fully preached the Gospel of Christ" (RV, Spencer, Phillips)

"I have replenished the Gospel of Christ" (Douay Version)

"My own work has been to complete the preaching of Christ's Gospel in a wide sweep from Jerusalem as far as Illyria" (Knox)

"'Accomplir (la mission) de la bonne nouvelle' ou bien 'remplir (de) la bonne nouvelle'" (Cerfaux, *L'Église*, 244).

69. *A-G*, 676.

70. Since we know from Acts and Thessalonians that *logos* had already become a technical term for the Gospel, it would be surprising to find Paul explain it here did he not do so with the object of introducing a new shade of meaning.

71. Cf. C. F. D. Moule, *The Epistles of Saint Paul the Apostle to the Colossians and to Philemon*, Cambridge (1957), 80.

72. *TWNT*, vol. 4, 127; cf. S. Lyonnet, "Hellénisme et Christianisme", *Biblica* 26 (1945), 127.

73. All that has been said is equally valid for Rom. 15.19, which Lyonnet translates as, "J'ai procuré l'accomplissement de l'évangile du Christ." (*Bible de Jérusalem*.) This is perfectly in keeping with the context, which is concerned, not so much with the perfection of preaching (as Lagrange and Sanday-Headlam imply), as with its fruit (Cornely).

5

THE PREACHER AND HIS AUDIENCE

IN describing the word of God as "bearing fruit and growing" (Col. 1.6), Paul ascribes to it the latent dynamism of a living thing. It is possible, even probable, that this image was suggested to him by Christ's parable of the Sower (Mark 4.1–9 and parallels)[1] in which Christ depicts the word of God as a seed scattered broadcast by the preacher and whose proper soil is the heart of man. In essence the parable concerns the interaction of the seed and its environment. If, however, we read the Gospel accounts closely, it soon becomes apparent that the explanation (Mark 4.13–20 and parallels) does not exactly fit the parable. In the original parable attention is focused on the vitality of the seed, whereas the explanation is a challenge to all who have heard the Gospel to examine themselves and to weigh up their reactions. Canfield highlights the change of emphasis by entitling the parable-explained, "The Parable of the Various Soils". The explanation—at least in the form in which the Evangelists transmit it to us —is almost certainly a product of the primitive Church. To what extent, however, we cannot really say, but it is difficult to think that the fact that all three Evangelists attribute it to Jesus is without significance. It is reasonable to assume that he did sometimes explain his parables, and what we have in the present Gospel text is most likely a retouched version of his commentary on this parable. Whether Paul was also aware of the new slant given the parable of the Sower by the Church is not of great consequence here. What is of interest is the perfect frame of reference the parable itself provides for an appreciation of the Apostle's thought on the difficult question of the reception of the Gospel. The general import of the parable is easily grasped: the growth of a seed is conditioned by the soil on which it falls. The seed has life within itself yet the fruit of which it is capable may never come to be. In a similar way do the dispositions of those who hear the word of God qualify the exercise of its saving power. Only in the generous-hearted can it produce its full effect. The explanation of the parable distinguishes four types of hearers; three groups in which the word is operative with varying degrees of effectiveness, and one group on which it has no influence at all. Paul is satisfied with two broad categories; those who reject the word completely and those who receive it in faith. These he terms respectively, "those perishing" and "those being saved." (1 Cor. 1.18: 2 Cor. 2.15.)

The function of the present chapter is to endeavour to isolate and examine the complex factors determining the constitution of these two groups. Stated as Paul himself might put it, the problem is: Why is the word of God to some folly and a stumbling-block and to others the power and wisdom of God (1 Cor. 1.23–4)? Why have not *all* obeyed the Gospel (Rom. 10.16)? The failure involved cannot be laid to the charge of the word of God itself, for the last chapter has amply demonstrated its inherent power and dynamism. Only two possibilities, then, remain. Responsibility must lie either with the preacher or with his audience. Consequently, in the first part of this chapter we examine the influence the manner of presentation has on the word's reception. The second part, after an examination of the passages in which Paul speaks of the audience's reaction to preaching, considers in turn the three factors (God, Satan, human dispositions) whose interplay is seen to condition acceptance or refusal.

THE PROPOSAL OF THE WORD

THE PREACHER

One key idea in Paul's thought is that of Christianity as essentially a heavenly gift to which man has not alone no claim (Rom. 1.18ff.), but whose giving can only be "explained" in terms of an inexpressible love. (Eph. 2.4.) The mystery of God, hidden from untold ages, has been realized on earth in the presence of a person who is Christ among us, the hope of glory. (Col. 1.26–7.) To communicate this mystery to men is to impart to them the wisdom of God (Col. 1.28: 1 Cor. 2.7), yet it is achieved by human means, the faltering words of men. These preachers have no right over the message. For it is a precious deposit with which they have been entrusted, not to make their own but to share with all others, while jealously guarding its integrity. (1 Tim. 6.20: 2 Tim. 1.12.) The message could have been entrusted to others or to no human intermediary at all. Indeed, at times the word almost appears as an independent agent acting in virtue of its own intrinsic dynamism. (2 Thess. 3.1: Col. 1.5–6.)[2] Yet Paul can and does speak of this message as "*my* gospel" (Rom. 2.16); "ours" (1 Thess. 1.5: 2 Thess. 2.14). While the Gospel is essentially *God's* speaking to men in Christ (1 Thess. 2.13: Titus 3.4), by God's design it reaches men through the medium of other men, and in the concrete can no more be dissociated from them than a song from the voice of the singer. The truth of the Gospel is unique and invariable, but in its transmission it is personalized, "incarnated, so to speak, in the preacher's own Christian faith".[3] In being communicated by an individual the message inevitably acquires characteristic modalities which cannot fail to have an influence on its reception.

Now, the fundamental characteristic of the Christian message is that it is not a merely intellectual system and, therefore, cannot be presented or accepted as such. In order to communicate it the preacher must first have received it himself. This reception, as we shall see in the second part of this chapter, is more than a detached recognition of truth. For Paul it is an obedience, a deeply personal commitment of one's whole being to Truth. The preacher, then, cannot be a witness who stands aside and points. Because of the very nature of the message he conveys, he must be vitally involved in that to which he bears testimony.[4] The truth he presents must be *une vérité vécue*. If he points, it must be to himself.

And this is just what Paul does. Although he naturally places most emphasis upon the methodical and painstaking instruction that takes place in his oral delivery, it is clear that he considers his life and actions as a form of communication:

> You may have thousands of guides in Christianity. You have not a plurality of fathers, since, as regards your unity with Christ, it was I who fathered you through the Gospel. Consequently, I beg you *become imitators of me*. It was for this purpose I sent you Timothy,

my beloved child and faithful Christian, *to help you keep in mind my Christian way of life* according to my teaching everywhere in each community. [1 Cor. 4.15–17]

And further on in the same epistle:

Whatever you do, do everything for God's glory. Strive not to be an obstacle to Jews or Greeks or God's Church, just as I for my part render service to all in everything. I seek not what benefits myself, but what benefits everyone else, so that they may be saved. *Become imitators of me, just as I am an imitator of Christ.* [10.31–11.1]

That Paul should feel free to command the Corinthians to imitate not just Christ but himself is very significant. It shows that he did not conceive his function as being simply that of an easily-dispensed-with mouthpiece. Rather, he recognized that in the divine plan his place was a necessary one and that not only what he said but how he said it,[5] and what he was, had a part in its realization. (1 Tim. 1.16.) The basic obligation of a son of God is to live in imitation of his Father. In an effort to bring this fundamental point within the comprehension of his audience Paul elsewhere points out that in order to do this it is not necessary to have seen God, but only to love as Christ loved. (Eph. 5.1–2.) Here it is made even more concrete; Christ is perceptible in the preacher.[6] Not alone does he speak in the person of Christ (2 Cor. 2.17), he *is* "another Christ". (Gal. 4.14.)

Only a man of extraordinary sincerity could make such a claim—or a totally unscrupulous cynic. Paul's ringing declaration, "I have become all things to all men, that at all costs I may save some" (1 Cor. 9.22), could, absolutely speaking, be interpreted as an affirmation that the end justified the means, that he was not so much concerned about the "truth" of what he said as with "saving" his hearers. That such an accusation was, in fact, levelled against the Apostle, there can be no doubt.[7] The impassioned character of his defence in 2 Cor. 1.13–23 indicates that he was sensitive to this charge precisely because, though falsified by exaggeration, there was in it an element of truth.[8] The truth was that Paul did vary in his treatment of communities and individuals, but not to the extent—or with the motives—imputed to him by his opponents. He did not and could not repeat his message by rote. The word of God is not a cry launched out into the void, but an invitation directed to individuals. (1 Cor. 1.9.) Consequently, it is incumbent on the preacher to ensure that his message is always actual, that it is so integrated with the needs and capacities of his audience as to be a really vital appeal.[9]

This necessary adaptation underlines the in-

evitability of the personalization of the message
in its presentation. It is this close interpenetra-
tion of the divine and the human in the concrete
structure of the word of God that advises caution
in attributing an *ex-opere-operato* efficacy to
preaching. Certainly, for Paul, the effectiveness
of preaching is bound up with the preacher's
personal qualities. While the Apostle's stress on
the dynamism of the word would make one
hesitate to affirm that he makes the efficacy of
preaching completely dependent on the minister,
it is undeniable that it is, to a certain extent,
conditioned by the virtuous character of his life.
(1 Cor. 9.12.)[10]

The extent to which his preaching is *God's*
word depends on the apostle. There is always
the possibility of "falsifying" the word of God
(2 Cor. 2.17: 4.2), for though an instrument, he
is a free one. He is not a master but a "steward",
from whom fidelity and loyalty can only be
expected.[11] Through motives of human respect
(Gal. 1.10: 1 Thess. 2.4) or through a false sense
of shame (2 Cor. 4.2), he can distort the message
confided to his charge. (1 Thess. 2.4.) He may
preach himself or his pet interests and not Christ
(2 Cor. 3.1: 4.5). To present as the word of God
what is not, is to act with duplicity, treacherously
(1 Thess. 2.3), to build with "wood, hay and
straw" instead of "gold, silver and fine stone".
(1 Cor. 3.12.) This falsification of the word of

God is one of the major problems tackled by
Paul in the Pastoral Epistles and to express it he
coined the verb *heterodidaskaleō*. (1 Tim. 1.3:
6.3.)[12] This type of teaching was not necessarily
contrary to the Gospel. It was not so much a
question of doctrinal deviations as of the introduction of profane matters (1 Tim. 6.20: 2 Tim.
2.16), such as foolish useless speculations on
matters which contribute nothing to the spiritual
lives of those who hear them. (Titus 3.9: 2 Tim.
3.16–17.) To adulterate the word of God in this
way is to rob it of its dynamism, to make it
mataios, "inactive, powerless". (Titus 3.9; cf.
Acts 14.15.) The preacher may be motivated in
these changes by vainglory or even cupidity (1
Thess. 2.5), instead of keeping before his mind
the one motive that should be the mainspring of
all his service: the honour and glory of God. (2
Cor. 1.12: 1 Thess. 2.4.)

That he be not an obstacle but a perfect
mediator between God and man, the preacher's
life must be "religious, upright, irreproachable".
(1 Thess. 2.10.)[13] This implies, not alone the
avoidance of sin (2 Cor. 10.3: 1 Tim. 6.9), but of
everything, no matter how legitimate in itself,[14]
that might compromise his mission: "We give
no offence in aught that the ministry be not
blamed." (2 Cor. 6.3.) Such self-abnegation is
balanced on the positive side by a total dedication to the apostolate. Paul's enthusiasm is palp-

able in the phrase: "Now we really live, if you
but stand fast in the Lord." (1 Thess. 3.8.) The
whole being of the preacher is, as it were, *ad
alium*, totally other-centred. (Eph. 3.2,13: Col.
1.25.) Not only is he "God's slave" (Rom. 1.1
etc.), but "the slave of all" (1 Cor. 9.19), "the
servant of the Church". (Col. 1.25.)

The inspiration of such perfect dedication
must be "charity unfeigned". (2 Cor. 6.6.) Paul,
as we have already noted, images it in terms of a
father's love for his children, but this should
not lead us to conceive it as a mawkish paternal-
ism. What its true quality was as far as Paul
himself was concerned is apparent from the way
he acted. A particularly striking example is the
episode of the "letter written in tears". Our
knowledge of this letter which no longer exists
is pieced together from allusions in 2 Cor. It
was a harsh letter "written out of much affliction
and anguish of heart, with many tears" (2 Cor.
2.4) and once sent to Corinth Paul trembled for
its effect. When he heard that the culprits had
reformed he burst out: "I never meant to cause
you pain. I only wanted you to know the superabundant love I have for you." (2 Cor. 2.4.) Yet
he did not really regret having been so severe.
The sincerity of his love bred in him a special
affinity with truth (2 Cor. 13.8), forcing him
to discern the realities of the situation, and he
admitted candidly that in similar circumstances

he would act again in just the same way. (2 Cor. 13.10.) This love, expressed by absence and wounding words, is certainly not mere human affection but divine charity in the fullest sense: disinterested, spiritual, uncompromising, prepared to cause pain in order to procure the ultimate good of the beloved. The principal quality Paul looked for in his assistants was a "genuine interest" in the things which concerned his hearers, which he identified with true ambition for the things of Jesus Christ. (Phil. 2.20.)

One has only to read the bald statements of the tribulations he suffered (2 Cor. 4.17: 7.5: 11.22–8) in order to realize how fully the apostle is expected to concretize in his flesh the apostolic charity of Christ (Eph. 5.2):

> Wherever we go we carry always in our body the dying of Jesus, that the life of Jesus may be manifested in our body. For continually while still alive, we are being surrendered into the hands of death, for Jesus' sake, so that the life of Jesus can be revealed in this mortal body of ours. [2 Cor. 4.10–11; cf. Col. 1.25]

The reason for such self-sacrifice, for such complete immersion of self in the word, is also plain. It is the generosity of his acceptance and the zeal with which he carries out the duty imposed upon him, that permits the word of God active within the preacher to shine through the confines of the "vessel of clay". (2 Cor. 4.7.) Only when the preacher's whole existence is modelled on Christ (1 Cor. 11.1) will he be for his hearers a "road to Christ". (1 Cor. 4.17.) Then, and then alone, will "the word that he announces be, as it were, reinforced by another word, i.e., by the very existence of the Apostle offered to the word of Christ, an existence likewise penetrated and formed by the word of Christ".[15] Without this "existential" reinforcement the word cannot exercise to the full its latent power.[16]

"HEARERS AND DOERS OF THE WORD"

Paul's preoccupation with the good opinion pagans should have of his converts is a rather striking feature of his letters right from the first letter to the Thessalonians, through Corinthians and Colossians, to the Pastorals. In a mild reprimand to those Thessalonians who had ceased to work and were therefore a burden to the community, Paul admonishes them to work with their hands "as we charged you, so that you walk honourably with an eye to them that are without". (1 Thess. 4.11.) Almost exactly the same phrase recurs in Col. 4.5: "Walk wisely in your dealings with them that are without, using the present opportunity to the full." Christians are continually in contact with non-believers (1 Cor. 5.9–10) and it is their duty to show wisdom in every aspect of their behaviour.

This insistence on "taking thought for what is good in the sight of all men" (Rom. 12.17; cf. 1 Tim. 3.7)[17] will seem a little strange only if we recall Paul's repeated affirmation that he himself acts to please God and not men (1 Thess. 2.4: Gal. 1.10) and do not advert to the difference in context. On the other hand it will seem the most natural thing in the world if we remember his allusion to the repercussions that the example of the Chosen People of the Old Dispensation had:

> While you take pride in the Law you dishonour God by breaking it. For, as Scripture says, "Because of you the name of God is dishonoured among the Gentiles." [Rom. 2.23–4]

A whole religion and way of life was brought into disrepute through the evident contradiction between the principles and the practice of its adherents. Paul does not intend to permit that to become the fate of the New Israel, and puts it bluntly to the Corinthians, whose lives could hardly be described as exemplary: "Strive not to be an obstacle to Jews or Greeks or God's Church." (1 Cor. 10.32.)

No man is an island. No-one is totally immune to the external influences that are included under the general term "environment". Of these the most important for good or ill is probably the example of others. The behaviour of a group (or of individuals associated with it) can inspire a non-member with such feelings of disgust and antipathy as to prejudice him irremediably against it, or it can create in him a sympathetic attitude towards its aims and doctrines, a state of mind conditioned to give a warm reception to the formal proposal of its ideals. Paul was well aware of this elementary psychological fact, as his above admonitions show, but it is characteristic of his inspired originality that he should deliberately turn it into an apostolic weapon. The measure of the importance he attached to the full Christian life as a factor in the creation of an atmosphere favourable to the formal proposition of the word of God can be gauged from the fact that he presents it as a form of preaching:

Do all things without murmuring or criticizing, that you may prove yourselves blameless and sincere [*amemptoi, akeraioi*] "children of God, faultless [*amōma*] in the midst of a warped and crooked generation" in which you shine as lights in the world, holding forth the word of life [*logon zōēs epechontes*]. [Phil. 2.14–6]

In this passage, which demands close examination, the light motif makes its appearance again. We have already remarked Paul's adaptation of a common Jewish theme to express conversion in terms of a passage from darkness to light (1 Thess. 5.4–6: Eph. 5.6–9), effected initially by the proclamation and reception of the preaching, itself a radiant participation in the splendour of the "glory" of Christ. (2 Cor. 4.4.) Here, however, we have something new; the source of light is no longer the preacher but those who have received his word. Their activity, which concerns the word of life, is not characterized by any of the verbs used by Paul to describe his own preaching (*kērussō, laleō, euangelizomai* etc.) but by *epechō*, whose use in this context is highly unusual.[18] Moulton and Milligan admit that the papyri fail to provide any enlightening parallel.[19] Bauer claims to find one in the New Testament in a passage from Saint Luke's Gospel (4.42),[20] and thereby imputes to *epechō* in Philippians the meaning "*holding fast* the word of life". That this sense is implied in the passage there can be no doubt. It is precisely because the Philippians have received and are holding fast the luminous word that they exist as light-sources. But the context is an exhortation to virtuous activity, and as our Lord himself made clear, light shines forth only in activity: "Let your light shine before men in order that they may see your works and glorify your Father who is in heaven." (Matt. 5.16.) Consequently, the great majority of exegetes prefer the more active sense of this verb, "hold towards, hold forth", as better suited to the context.[21]

The Philippians, in a world of darkness, proffer the word of life to a "depraved and perverse" generation. The quotation used to characterize those who have not received the word of God is from the Canticle of Moses, and in its original context opposes to Yahweh, "a God faithful and without iniquity, just and upright", the crooked and degenerate Israelites. The contrast here is no longer between the qualities of Yahweh and those of his faithless people, but between the true children of God and the rest of humanity. Bonnard is of the opinion that the text insists not so much on the moral qualities of Christians as on their vocation as witnesses to humanity. It is, however, more accurate to say that they are witnesses precisely *in virtue of* their moral qualities, which are summed up by Paul in three adjectives, all very generic in meaning: *amemptos, akeraios and amōmos.*

Of the three *amōmos* is the most absolute and is explained by the other two. It affirms a complete lack of fault or blemish.[22] *Amemptos* also means "blameless or faultless", but New-Testament usage would suggest that it carries the connotation of a state resulting from the fulfilment of an obligation.[23] And it is precisely this that is in question in the context: "Work out your salvation" (2.12); "Do all things without mur-

muring or criticizing." (2.14.) Only by fulfilling
the obligations assumed at their baptism can the
Philippians show themselves blameless. *Akeraios*
is normally translated by "innocent", but the
fundamental idea is the absence of foreign
admixture.[24] A thing is said to be *akeraios* when
it is in its true and natural condition.[25] This connotation perfectly fits a context that has reference to good works, for such works are the
normal condition of the children of God: "We
are his handiwork, created in Christ Jesus for
good works." (Eph. 2.10.) The difference between the state of unredeemed man and the
state of one who is "in Christ" is so tremendous
that Paul conceives the passage from one to
the other as a transformation (2 Cor. 3.18) so
complete as to be a new creation (2 Cor. 5.17).
The "old man" (Rom. 6.6), having put on
Christ (Col. 3.10) is become a "new man". (Eph.
4.24.) The activity proportioned to this new state
is no longer the "sterile works of darkness" (Eph.
5.11) but the works of light (Eph. 5.9). If "falsehood" was the distinctive trait of the old man
(Eph. 4.25: Rom. 3.4) so is "truth" the dominant
characteristic of him whose entry into the
mystery of salvation was inaugurated by the
reception in faith of the "word of truth". (Eph.
1.13.) Paul's genius for turning a phrase was
never more evident than in his definition of the
Christian life as "living the truth in love"

(*alētheuontes en agapē*). (Eph. 4.15.)[26] Although
the addition of "in love" adds a specifically
Christian nuance, "living the truth" evokes an
Old-Testament theme, that is also found in the
Qumran texts. The just man who does the will
of God in fulfilling all the moral and religious
obligations of the Law is said "to walk in truth"
(1 Kings 2.4: 3.6: 2 Kings 20.3: Isa. 38.3: 1 QH
16,7), or "to do the truth". (2 Chron. 31.20: 1 QS
I,5: V,3: VIII,2.) It is hoped that it will not be
taken as an infringement of philosopher's rights
to claim that the Old Testament subscribed to
a correspondence theory of truth.[27] The ideal was
the standard against which the truth of things
was measured. A being failing to manifest the
qualities one had a right to expect of it was not
true. The vine that produced only bitter grapes
when all had been done to ensure its fruitfulness
was not considered a true vine. (Isa. 5.1–7.) Precisely the same conception was shared by Paul.
The believer who does not produce works in
perfect harmony with his new being is not a *true*
Christian (1 Tim. 5.8),[28] and could not be
described as *akeraios*. It is in virtue of this
activity, the natural flowering of the new life
they have received, that the Philippians "hold
forth the word of life" to an unbelieving world.

The immediate context of the above passage
does not permit us to go beyond this in determining the *how* of the "holding forth". Here,

however, the Pastorals come to our aid. These epistles use the adjective *kalos* to characterize the activity proper to a Christian whose life is informed by a vivid faith and an ardent charity to such an extent that *kala erga* must be considered a quasi-technical term.[29] It is normally translated "*good* works", but while it is true that the meanings of *kalos* and *agathos* overlap to a certain extent,[30] *kalos* carries a distinctive nuance that is very important. "Applied to a man it signifies handsome, noble, honourable, glorious... whence the nuances of perfect, complete", but its use by the Septuagint to translate the Hebrew *yāpeh* (Gen. 12.14: Deut. 21.11: Amos. 8.13 etc.) shows that it can also suggest the idea of "beautiful in outward appearance". For a Greek it implied harmonious completeness, the balance and proportion of all parts of a being one with the other.[31] It could thus be applied not merely to physical appearance but to moral perfection. To describe the virtuous life as *kalos* was to evoke its balance, dignity and nobility.[32]

Paul employs the expression only with reference to the external manifestations of virtue, and he deliberately does so in order to arouse his readers to an awareness of the power of attraction of the Christian life fully lived: "Good works are evident, or even if they are not, they cannot be concealed for ever." (1 Tim. 5.25; cf. 3.7: 5.10: 6.12.) The life of grace in its perfect manifestations is endowed with a quality of radiant beauty which cannot fail to have an effect on those beholding it. Such conduct adds lustre to the word of God; it is the setting that enhances the appeal of its brilliance:

> Tell slaves to respect their master's authority in everything and to comply with their demands without answering back; not to pilfer, but to show themselves strictly honest and trustworthy; for in all such ways they will add lustre (*kosmeō*) to the doctrine of God our Saviour. [Titus 2.9–10]

It is this text that gives us the key to the understanding of "holding forth the word of life". Obedience to the word expresses the respect and reverence in which it is held; the power it displays in the lives of those who have received it in faith manifests it as worthy of attention and study. To say that slaves accepted a doctrine was poor recommendation, if not a veritable condemnation. But to be able to point to this teaching as the source of an almost miraculous change in the habits of a slave was a very different matter. In conforming his life to the word the Christian unconsciously and without saying anything becomes a preacher, at least in so far as he provokes among those who are not of the Faith the question: What makes him different? Should the Christian fail to fulfil his obligations, it is to his personal detriment, but over and above that it creates a situation in which the word of God is in danger of being treated with cynical indifference. (Titus 2.5,8.)

RECEPTION AND REFUSAL

THE TEXTS

Paul speaks often and in very different contexts of the reception and/or rejection of the word of God. To study these passages in function of the verbs used has a double advantage; it provides a summary classification and at the same time enables us to perceive more accurately the exact value of the key-term in each passage.

"Hearing" (akouō)

The verb "to hear" is used seven times by Paul in the context of the reception of revelation; it is demanded by his presentation of revelation not as a vision but as the *word* of God. In harmony with the prophetic usage (Isa. 53.1) "what is heard" (akoē) is found as a technical term for the Gospel as early as 1 Thessalonians,[33] but, contrary to what might be expected, it is rather unusual to find Paul describing the full reception of the Gospel as "hearing". The one absolutely certain instance is 1 Tim. 4.16, where "hearing", since it is that whereby Timothy's auditors are saved, is the equivalent of "be-lieving". (Cf. Col. 1.23.)[34]

It is much more difficult to determine the precise value to be given to "to hear him" in Eph. 4.20–21:

> You have not so learnt Christ, provided that you heard him and were instructed in him, as [he] is truth in Jesus.

It is very probable that this aside is a barbed allusion to some who were upsetting the faith of Paul's converts by preaching a gnostic Christ to whom the historical Jesus was completely irrele-vant.[35] To them the Apostle opposes the state-ment: Christ is true only in Jesus; and appears to break down the process of "learning Christ"[36] into two stages, "hearing him" and "being taught in him". If the two are in fact distinct stages, and if it is correct to understand "in him" not of the subject matter of instruction, but of the situation of the Christians instructed (who, because they heard, believed and were baptised, are "in Christ"—Eph. 1.13),[37] "hearing him" would be the perfect co-relative of "we preach Christ" (1 Cor. 1.23), that is, the full acceptance of the Gospel with complete awareness of its implications.

The couple hearing-believing occurs in Eph. 1.13 and Rom. 10.14–18. In both passages "hear-ing" is distinct from "belief" but, nonetheless,

closely bound up with it. Just what their relationship is, Ephesians does not specify. The
passage in Romans, on the other hand, affords
a number of extremely important clarifications:

> How can they invoke him in whom they have
> not believed? And how can they believe him
> whom they have not heard? And how can they
> hear without a preacher? And how can they
> preach unless they be sent? As it is written:
>> How beautiful the feet of those
>> who bring glad tidings of good.
> Yet not all did not obey the Gospel. For Isaias
> says:
>> Lord, who has believed our preaching
>> [akoē]?
> Thus, faith comes through hearing [the Gos-
> pel] and hearing [is] through the instrumen-
> tality of the words of Christ.[38] But I ask, did
> they not hear? Yes, indeed:
>> Their voice has gone out into all the earth,
>> And their words to the end of the world.

Faith depends on the spoken word of an authorized preacher, i.e., on the word as heard. Yet
hearing alone is not faith; it is a reception of the
word but only in a material sense. The Jews, for
example, heard but did not obey.[39] Hearing is a
prerequisite to faith, but faith is not the inevitable consequence of hearing. It is in this connection that Paul introduced the notion of

understanding. The quotations from the Old Testament introduced in *vv.* 19–20 seem intended to prove (i) that the Gospel was not difficult to understand—because a "foolish people" would receive it (Deut. 32.21), and (ii) that the message was not difficult to discover—since it would be found by those who never sought it. (Isa. 65.1.) The citation from Isa. 65.2 with which the section concludes (*v.* 21), when taken in conjunction with the "being ignorant" of *v.* 3, indicates that though the message was understandable and was in fact heard, no real comprehension was possible for the Jews because of the rigidity of their preconceptions and the hardness of their hearts.[40] Because of their predispositions hearing could not lead to true religious knowledge, which implies full submission to the message and to its author. Hearing, therefore, in this context never rises above the level of aural sensation. In those who are better disposed, however, it is the preliminary acceptance of the word leading to full adhesion to the person of Christ in faith.

This distinction between what we may term "mere-hearing" and "faith-hearing" is probably what the Apostle intended to convey by his use of *akoē* in the rather cryptic phrase *ek akoēs pisteōs* in Gal. 3.2: "Did you receive the Spirit in virtue of works of the Law or in virtue of a hearing of faith?" The passive sense of *akoē*,

"preaching, message",[41] must be rejected because
it would exclude the idea of human co-operation
which is demanded by the balance of the phrase.
"Faith" could be interpreted in an objective
sense, but this is ruled out by the "just as"
(*kathōs*) introducing the reference to the faith
of Abraham in *v.* 6, which imposes the subjective
meaning. Consequently, opposed to the "works
of the Law" we have, not the "preaching of the
Gospel", but a "hearing of faith". In the light of
statements such as, "Man is justified by faith,
quite apart from the works of the Law" (Rom.
3.28), the term "hearing" would be entirely
superfluous were it not intended to point up a
distinction between mere aural sensation and
the hearing that leads to, or is accompanied by,
faith.[42] The Spirit is given to those who really
hear the word of God and not to those who
present only a façade of attention.

In Rom. 10 hearing, unaccompanied by understanding, terminates in a refusal to submit. In
Colossians on the other hand, hearing and understanding are coupled with a very different result:

In the whole world the Gospel is bearing fruit
and growing, as it is among you from the day
you first came to hear and recognize (*epegnōte*)
the grace of God in truth. [1.5–6]

This "recognition" (*epignōsis*) is certainly full
practical submission both to the intellectual and

to the moral demands of the Gospel, that is, full religious knowledge in the Old-Testament sense. This adds to the plausibility of Dupont's suggestion that the formula *epignōsis alētheias* underlies this phrase.[43] If this suggestion be correct it implies that the hearing of the word of truth (*v.* 5) is accompanied by dispositions which, under the fructifying power of the word, flower into faith.

To sum up:

(1) Paul distinguishes "mere-hearing" and "faith-hearing".

(2) "Mere-hearing", because of dispositions reducible to proud obstinacy, remains outside the religious sphere on the material level of aural sensation.

(3) "Faith-hearing" is accompanied by genuine religious knowledge and is so closely bound up with faith as to be practically identifiable with it.

"Receiving" (*dechomai*)

If we except 2 Cor. 11.4 as an ironical aside, this verb occurs in only three contexts concerned with the acceptance of the Gospel, and it is noteworthy that two of them contain an allusion to the Spirit.

Dechomai is used twice with reference to the same event in 1 Thess. In 1.6 the context demands the translation "welcome". The fact that the acceptance of the word is accompanied by joy of the Spirit despite persecution makes it clear that there is a question here of something more than mere "reception". The whole stress of the passage, conditioned by the idea of imitation "of ourselves and of the Lord", is on the manner of reception, that is, on the courage and joy of soul manifested in spite of determined opposition. The warmth of the welcome accorded the word of God is explained by the activity of the Holy Spirit; its quality is tested in tribulation.

In 1 Thess. 2.13 *dechomai* is used together with *paralambanō*:

> Having received [*paralambanō*] the word of God preached by us, you welcomed [*dechomai*] it not as a human word . . .

Since the two verbs are to all intents and purposes synonymous it is impossible to grasp the precise nuance of the gradation presumed by many commentators. The use of the second verb may simply have been occasioned by a recollection of its use at the beginning of the letter. If, however, there is a gradation Rigaux must be correct in considering *dechomai* as reiterating, and thereby emphasizing, an idea already adequately conveyed by *paralambanō*.

Much more revealing is the use of this verb in 1 Cor. 2.14–15:

The natural man [*psychikos*] does not receive the things of the Spirit of God; for him it is folly and he has not the power to understand because it is appreciated spiritually. The spiritual man [*pneumatikos*] appreciates all things.

The use of the verb "to understand" indicates that the "things of the Spirit" are to be understood of spiritual truths, and their qualification as "folly" inevitably inclines one to identify them with the "word of the Cross", three times so characterized in ch. 1 of this epistle. To the natural man the preaching is folly because he is radically incapable of understanding it. Whence this insufficiency? The answer must be sought in the difference between the natural man and the spiritual man. The natural man, to begin with, enjoys only the resources of his own soul. This is much clearer in the Greek because the term we translate as "natural man" is *psychikos*, which is the adjective constructed from the word for "soul", *psyche*. Bauer admits the difficulty of drawing hard and fast boundaries between the multiple meanings of this latter term, but is satisfied that in the Pauline corpus it never signifies more than natural (as opposed to supernatural) life, either in its principle or its manifestations. (*A-G*, p. 901.) The activity of the natural man, then, is entirely on the natural level, and the only knowledge he seeks is that which can be acquired by the unaided power of his reason. The spiritual man, on the other hand, is enlightened by the Holy Spirit (2.12) who infuses into him a new spirit of a higher order[44] which is the faculty of the divine in man.[45] All believers possess this spirit (2.12), though in varying degrees. The mature Christian, for example, is capable of assimilating spiritual truth more perfectly than the beginner because in him the activity of the Spirit is less fettered by the instincts of the flesh. But between these two the difference is only one of degree, and minimal when compared with the gulf separating them from the natural man, to whom the word of the Cross is folly, because he does not possess in any degree the spirit proportioned to it.

We may therefore conclude:

(1) Without the activity of the Holy Spirit infusing a new spirit proportioned to the object, reception of the word of God is impossible. "No-one can say 'Jesus is Lord' except by the Holy Spirit." (1 Cor. 12.3.)

(2) When the Spirit is actively present the word is received with joy whatever the difficulty.

"Accepting" (paralambanō)

Apart from one text containing an allusion to the reception of an office, all the instances of the use of this verb in the Epistles refer to the reception of the word of God. Paul employs it to describe his own acceptance of the Gospel (1 Cor. 11.23: 15.3: Gal. 1.12) as well as that of those to whom he transmitted it. He commands the latter to keep apart from members of the community who "do not walk according to the tradition received from us". (2 Thess. 3.6.)[46] This idea finds positive expression in Phil. 4.9 ("What you have learnt, and received, and heard and seen in me: put that into practice") and especially in Col. 2.6–7:

> As therefore, you have accepted Christ Jesus the Lord, so walk in him, rooted and built up in him and established in the faith according as you were taught.

"Accepting Christ" here is parallel to the "learning Christ" of Eph. 4.20 and is equivalent to faith, that is, a vital acceptance not only of Jesus as Christ and Lord, but also of the practical duties involved in this acceptance. In fulfilling these obligations, now that they are "in Christ" (cf. Eph. 4.21), the Colossians deepen and perfect their original acceptance. (1 Thess. 2.13.) The necessity of prolonging the attitude with which the Gospel was first received is stressed in 1 Cor. 1.5, for it is in preserving this attitude, characterized as "believing" that the Corinthians will be saved. (Cf. Gal. 1.9.)

"Learning" (manthanō)

The use of this verb in Eph. 4.20–21 has already been noted. There "to learn Christ" appears (in all probability) as a combination of two processes, namely, "hearing him" and "being instructed in him", whose global object is the entire salvation-event described in 1.13–14 and in 2. In consequence, "learning" includes much more than the initial reception of the word of God.

This is also evident in two warnings:

> I exhort you, brethren, to note and avoid those who cause the dissentions and difficulties contrary to the teaching you learnt. [Rom. 16.17] But, for your part, stand by the things you have learnt and of which you are certain. [2 Tim. 3.14]

In the latter instance, the context makes it evident that for Timothy it is not a question of first reception, but of assimilation over a long period, first from his Jewish mother and grandmother and later through continuous contact with Paul (*parakoloutheō*, 3.10; cf. 1 Tim. 4.6). In both passages Paul fears the contamination of the word of God. This accentuates slightly the intellectual character of the learning, but as the tone of the admonitions indicates, what the Apostle really desires is constancy in the generous initial attitude of reception.

It is the initial act alone that is designated by "learning" in Colossians. The "as you learnt" of Col. 1.7 must be referred to the "you first heard" mentioned two verses previously, and so signifies the full reception of the "word of truth of the Gospel". It is thus the equivalent of "you recognized" (v. 6), whose active, practical character it shares.[47]

"Obeying" (hupakouō)

The supreme realization of the notion of obedience is, for Paul, the obedience of Christ:

> And after he had appeared in outward form as man, he humbled himself becoming obedient unto death, even unto death on a cross. [Phil. 2.7–8]

It is his obedience that makes ours possible:

> As through the disobedience of one man the many were constituted sinners, so also through the obedience of the one the many shall be constituted just. [Rom. 5.19]

Thus creating the necessity of Paul's mission "to win all nations unto the obedience of faith". (Rom. 1.5.)[48] Accused of weakness in the exercise of this charge, he sums up his activity in a military metaphor:

> Though walking in the flesh we do not war according to the flesh, for the weapons of our

warfare are not of the flesh but divinely powerful to demolish strongholds; we demolish
sophistries and all that rears its proud head
against knowledge of God, we compel every
human thought to surrender in obedience to
Christ. [2 Cor. 10.4–5]

To destroy the pride that renders knowledge of
God impossible is to reduce human reason to
obedience. Consequently, in this text "knowledge of God" corresponds to "obedience to
Christ", but this latter expression brings out
more clearly that this submission is as much an
affair of the will as it is of the intellect. It is an
intellectual assent translated into action through
an accompanying surrender of the will. This
pairing knowledge-obedience is found in all the
contexts that refer to obedience to the word of
God.

In Rom. 6.17 this is brought out by the designation of the object of obedience as a "form of
teaching" (*typos didachēs*):

You obeyed from the heart the form of teaching to which you were delivered.[49]

In all this section of the epistle (6.15–23), Paul
presents conversion in terms of a change of
masters. Unredeemed man was, willingly or un-
willingly, the slave of Sin (*v.* 16), Impurity, and
Lawlessness (*v.* 19). Dead and risen with Christ
in baptism (3–4), the Christian is freed from

that master only to be delivered into the hands
of another, variously characterized as Obedience
(v. 16), Form of Teaching (v. 17), Justice (v. 19)
and finally God. (v. 22.) Paul's reversal of the
normal mode of expression (i.e., in saying that
a person is delivered over to a doctrine rather
than vice versa) can only be to emphasize the
properties of this "form of teaching". In presenting it as a living thing he again draws attention
to the Gospel[50] as a divine power for the salvation
of all who believe. (1.16.) In receiving this word,
in opening his heart to its power, the believer is
justified. This submission to the preaching is
depicted as a new slavery, "a slavery to
Obedience". (v. 16.) But all slavery of its nature
implies obedience. In the state of unredemption
man obeyed the desires and longings of the flesh
(v. 12), because through the sin of one man Sin
held dominion over all (5.12,21). But now, because of the obedience of one man, humanity is
free. The entire context stresses man's present
freedom. The sun has set on the empire of Sin:
it can no longer force men to yield to its influence. Nonetheless, man can voluntarily surrender himself again to its service (v. 13) and as
Paul knew from his experience at Corinth, many
had in fact done so. Similarly, man's choice of
Obedience, his acceptance of the Gospel, is fully
voluntary. The submission of the believer is
"from the heart". Perfectly in accord with the

Old Testament, the Apostle envisages the "heart" as the most intimate part of man, the focal point of his entire moral personality, intelligent and free.[51] To obey "from the heart", therefore, is to submit oneself totally to Christ present in his salvific power in the words of his ministers. (Rom. 10.14–15.) This submission is made consciously and in perfect freedom,[52] and the Christian life is only the prolongation into act of the generous dispositions with which the word was received.[53]

"Obeying" is the perfect verb to express the full, vital acceptance of preaching. The basic meaning of the Greek *hupakouō* is "to listen to",[54] but, as its technical use to describe the function of a door-keeper indicates,[55] it means "to listen in an effective way", to listen and do. In other words, it is a listening that forms an indivisible unity with the appropriate response to the claim made. (2 Thess. 3.14.)

The claim made by the ministers of the Gospel, namely, "to confess with the lips that Jesus is Lord and to believe with the heart that God raised him from the dead" (Rom. 10.9), the Jews refused. All heard (10.18), but their proud hearts did not know it for what it was, and led them instead into disobedience. (10.3.) The penalty to be meted out for such lack of submission is described in 2 Thess. 1.7–8:

When our Lord Jesus is revealed from heaven
with his mighty angels in blazing fire, then
will he do justice on those who do not know
God and on those who do not obey the Gospel
of our Lord Jesus Christ. They will suffer the
punishment of eternal ruin.

The promise of retribution serves to emphasize
strongly the reality of human responsibility for
failure to obey the Gospel.[56] A few verses later
it is specified that obedience to the word of God
is faith. (v. 10.)

To sum up:

(1) Obedience is the perfect reception of the
word of God. It is faith.

(2) This submission involves an intellectual
assent but is essentially an attitude of the
entire personality.

(3) Lack of obedience is traceable to bad dispositions.

(4) Man is responsible for his lack of submission.

THE FACTORS CONDITIONING RECEPTION
OR REFUSAL

Two points emerge with great clarity from
the above analysis of the contexts in which Paul
speaks of the reception of the word of God: (1)
The impossibility of such reception without
divine assistance; (2) Man's freedom in accept-

ance and his responsibility for refusal. Our purpose now is to see what further light the Epistles can shed on these points.

It is not easy to analyse with precision St Paul's thought in this matter. Difficulty arises, not so much from the unsystematic nature of his treatment of the interaction of divine and human causality, as from the fact that he isolates different aspects of the question and considers them absolutely, without troubling himself about possible misunderstandings or false interpretations.[57] Paradoxically, in the present instance the difficulty is diminished by the introduction of a third personage, Satan.

In the Second Letter to the Thessalonians, occasioned by the prevalence of erroneous ideas concerning the date of the *parousia*, Paul protests vehemently that no-one has the right to claim his authority for saying that the *parousia* is imminent. (2.2.) The Thessalonians should remember, he points out, that this glorious event must be preceded by another, infinitely sorrowful but no less striking, the great apostasy. In the few graphic sentences he devotes to this event Paul accurately delineates the roles played by the three actors, God, Man and Satan, in the fundamental drama of the conflict between truth and falsehood. This synthetic view will permit a surer interpretation of the passages which mention but one aspect of the problem.

> But that other's [Antichrist's] coming is,
> through Satan's working, attended by every
> kind of feat and sign and lying wonder and
> by every seduction to evil for those that are
> perishing, because they have not received the
> love of truth unto their salvation. And, there-
> fore, God sends them a working of error, that
> they should believe that lie, in order that all
> may be judged that have not believed the
> truth but have resolved upon unrighteous-
> ness. [2 Thess. 2.9–11]

The diabolic energy of Satan, exerted here
through the lying signs and wonders of Antichrist, has as its sole object the winning of men
to the banner of error and evil. But his display
has its desired effect only in those in whom God
has placed a "working of error", which bears
them on to belief in the lie.[58] These are "those
perishing". Why are they abandoned by God to
the seductive power of evil? *Because (anth'hōn)*[59]
they did not accept the "love of truth". Man is
not the prey of forces beyond his control; his
destiny is decided by his own free act. "Those
perishing" are those who have freely and
deliberately refused to receive the "love of
truth".[60] The question now is: What is this grace
and when is it given? There is little doubt that
a reference to the Gospel is intended in the term
"truth". But it would seem (*contra* Rigaux)

that it is indirect rather than immediate. "Truth" here includes the "word of truth" but only as a particular manifestation and is not limited to it. The general context of Paul's thought—the exact phrase is unparalleled in the entire Greek Bible—suggests that "love of truth" is best understood as an active openness to speculative-practical truth, a fundamental vital orientation towards the moral good. (2 Tim. 2.25.)[61] To one lacking this basic harmony with truth, the Gospel appears as "folly" (1 Cor. 1.18) and submission to it in faith as inconceivable stupidity. But in one who has permitted himself to be moulded by this love, the "word of the Cross" immediately strikes an answering chord.[62] It appears as the wisdom and power of God (1 Cor. 1.24) and submission to it is a joy. (1 Thess. 1.6.)

The use of the aorist "they have not received" refers the refusal of the love of truth to a definite moment in the past, and it seems reasonable to suppose that Paul had in mind the occasion of his preaching at Thessalonica. This would imply that the grace is given on the occasion of, or concomitantly with, the formal proposal of the word of truth.[63] To say, then, that man's destiny is determined by his attitude to the love of truth or by his attitude to the Gospel (2 Thess. 1.7–10), comes in effect to the same thing.

Divine Activity

The passage just examined was explicitly concerned only with "those perishing". Elsewhere
Paul opposes to these another class "those being
saved". (1 Cor. 1.18: 2 Cor. 2.15.) But, whereas
in the case of the former the element of human
responsibility is emphasized, in the case of the
latter the stress is entirely on the divine initiative. It is God who saves (2 Tim. 1.9), not in
virtue of our works (Titus 3.5), but motivated
solely by his love for us in Christ Jesus. (Eph.
1.4.) "It is by this grace you are saved, through
the medium of faith." (Eph. 2.8.) And faith, our
response to God's favour, is itself a gift: "To you
it has been granted as a favour on Christ's behalf, not only to believe in him, but also to
suffer for him." (Phil. 1.29.) But since faith is
nothing more or less than obedience to the word,
it is by full effective submission to the will of
Christ preached that man is saved. If, then, the
complete gratuity of salvation is to be preserved,
divine causality must be operative in the reception of the word. And this is precisely what Paul
more than once affirms.

Although the Gospel is a call (2 Thess. 2.14),
and as such is heard by all men, it is heeded
only by those who are called: "To those called,
Jews as well as Greeks, it is Christ, the power of
God and the wisdom of God." (1 Cor. 1.24.)

Consequently, in these alone does it exercise its power (Rom. 1.16)—in virtue of which they are "being saved" (1 Cor. 15.2)—and its reception can be seen by Paul as an infallible sign of election by God. (1 Thess. 1.4–5.) Reception of the Gospel is, therefore, linked with a choice whose motivation is hidden in the "unsearchable judgements and the untraceable ways" (Rom. 11.33) of "he who calls" (1 Thess. 5.24), but which becomes effective in a mysterious interior call. "The external word of the speaker is not sufficient to cause faith", says St Thomas, "unless man's heart is drawn by the interior call of God."[64]

This interior call is variously described by Paul. Two designations have already been noted: "love of truth" (2 Thess. 2.10),[65] and "new spirit". (1 Cor. 2.14.)[66] Two further passages remain yet to be examined.

The first refers directly to the preachers whose mission it is to spread the Gospel, but its import need not be restricted to them:

It is the Lord who said "Let light shine in the darkness" that has shone in our hearts to enlighten us for the revealing of the knowledge of the divine glory in the person of Christ. [2 Cor. 4.6]

There can be little doubt that the description is strongly influenced by the circumstances of

Paul's conversion (Acts 9.6), and were it a question of Paul alone the validity of any extension of its meaning could legitimately be questioned. But since with himself he associates others who certainly did not benefit by the same type of revelation, we may be permitted to understand that all who receive the revelation of Christ benefit by this interior illumination (Eph. 1.18), which permits them to see in the Christ presented by the preachers the glory of God.

The second passage is explicitly concerned with the recipients of the word and forms part of Paul's advice to Timothy, his assistant, regarding the exercise of his ministry:

> A servant of the Lord must ... be gentle towards all, a capable teacher, patient of evil, correcting opponents with meekness in case God should grant them repentance unto knowledge of truth [*metanoian eis epignōsin alētheias*]. [2 Tim. 2.24–5]

Paul doesn't say that the adversaries will be refuted or convinced by the preacher. They will be converted. But this will be by divine grace, to which the preacher must not prove an obstacle; his function is to propose the word, God's to make the heart apt to receive it, Again St Thomas: "For faith two things are necessary; one is the inclination of the heart to believe, and this comes not from hearing but from the grace

of God, the other is the specification of that
which is to be believed and that comes from
hearing."[67] Paul invariably uses *epignōsis* to
mean religious knowledge.[68] It is true that in
some cases *epignōsis* carries the same shade of
meaning as *gnōsis* (compare Rom. 1.28 and 1.21:
3.20 and 7.7), but this does not permit us to say,
as Bultmann does so absolutely, that "it is impossible to say that there is any difference between
gnōsis and *epignōsis* either in the New Testament or the Septuagint".[69] A comparison between
Phil. 1.9 and 1 Cor. 1.5 shows that a distinction
is possible,[70] and the careful use of the phrase
epignōsis alētheias in the Pastoral Epistles indicates that Paul attaches a very definite signification to it. Absolutely speaking, *aletheia* (truth)
could designate merely the object known, since
it was from the beginning an accepted synonym
for the Gospel, particularly as opposed to
erroneous teaching.[71] However, in view of the
dominant emphasis of the Pastorals on the
preservation of the truth despite heterodox
opposition, it is most probable that the genitive
also carries the force of the Hebrew adjectival
genitive. *Epignōsis alētheias* is then, "the exact
knowledge of the true religion",[72] or, in other
words, faith. (Titus 1.1: 2 Tim. 4.3.) The effective dimension of this knowledge is brought out
by the fact that it is assimilated only in virtue of
a "change of heart" (*metanoia*), a reorientation

of the entire personality. It is to be noted
that, in the Pastorals, a preposition of movement
—*eis* (1 Tim. 2.4: 2 Tim. 2.25: 3.7) or *kata*
(Titus 1.1)—is always found in conjunction with
the phrase *epignōsis alētheias*, indicating that
the reception of truth is the term of a movement
of the human spirit, of a free vital act. The
present text stresses that this act in which the
"change of heart" consists, is made possible only
by the infusion of divine grace.[73]

This teaching reveals Paul's fidelity to the
prophetic tradition of the Old Testament. The
Prophets recognized the necessity of the action
of God within their hearers if their words were
to be really assimilated and obeyed. The burden
of their mission was that Israel should "turn
again" to God. If some (e.g., Mic. 6.8) presented
this conversion as within man's unaided power,
others, more realistically, saw that, in order to
turn to God, man must first be turned by him:
"Turn me and I shall be turned." (Jer. 31.18:
Lam. 5.21: Ps. 80.4.) When the expected spiritual
renaissance did not materialize after the return
from the Exile, the eschatological character of
this turning to God became more and more
marked; it would come with the pouring out of
the Spirit at the inception of the messianic age,
when God would give Israel a new heart and a
new spirit. (Jer. 31.31–4: Ezek. 37.14,26: Ps.

51.10.) Only then would Israel really know God. (Isa. 11.9: 33.6 etc.)

For Paul, too, true religious knowledge of God, which is acquired and expressed in obedience to the word of God preached by his authorized ministers, is a divine gift:

> Now, having known God, or rather having been known by God, how can you turn back to the mean and beggarly spirits of the elements? [Gal. 4.9]

Conversion is not considered primarily as an accession to knowledge on the part of man but as an effect of the divine knowledge, which is here obviously much more than a speculative regard. It can only be explained in function of the Old Testament notion of knowledge as a dynamic orientation of the whole person, implying the activity not alone of the intelligence but also of the will. To know a thing, in the Old-Testament sense, is to make it in some way one's own, to take possession of it.[74] For man *to know God* is to make his revealed will his own. (Os. 4.1–6: Jer. 9.2–5: 22.15–16 etc.) *To be known by God* is to become the special object of his benevolent solicitude. Such condescension is a privilege and, consequently, sets its recipient in a special relationship with God. In certain instances in the Old Testament—Moses (Exod. 33.12,17) and Jeremias (Jer. 1.5)—and in the present text, divine knowledge is concretely equivalent to election,[75] since it implies the concomitant communication of power to really know God, that is, to believe.

But not all receive this grace. Among his own people Paul saw that only a very few submitted themselves to the Gospel. (Rom. 10.16.) The majority of the nation was stubborn in its unbelief:

> What Israel sought, Israel has not achieved, but the selected few have achieved it. The rest were made blind, exactly as it is written: "God brought upon them a numbness of spirit; he gave them blind eyes and deaf ears, and so it is still." [Rom. 11.7–8]

Those who saw and heard did so because they were chosen. Those who failed to see and hear did so because they were blinded. It seems to be that grace is denied to some quite arbitrarily and that, in consequence, they are eternally condemned for failing to realize a potentiality they never possessed. (2 Thess. 1.8.)

To try to envisage this problem as Paul saw it, it must be remembered, first of all, that the compatibility of human responsibility with divine omnipotence is an indisputable presupposition of all the New-Testament writers, Paul included.[76] They never raise the question formally but to magnify either man's freedom or

God's power at the expense of the other would be to do extreme violence to their thought. For example, in ch. 9. of the Epistle to the Romans, Paul affirms the absolute priority of the divine initiative in the matter of salvation so strongly as to appear to allow no part to human effort, yet in the succeeding chapter he lays just as much emphasis on the reality of man's culpability, if he is in fact not saved.

A second point to be noted is that Paul considers foreknowledge, election, call etc., only on the *social* level.[77] He lays no emphasis on the call of the individual; *klētos*, for example, is never found in the singular except when applied to Paul's own vocation to the apostolate of the Gentiles. (Rom. 1.1: 1 Cor. 1.1.) Furthermore, that salvation which is the object of call and election is not definitive, eschatological salvation, but constitution in a state pleasing to God.[78] It is perfectly true that the chosen ones, if they persevere, will be saved also in the world to come (1 Tim. 4.16)—but the mere existence of the Epistles shows that the possibility of falling away is very real indeed.[79] As Alan Richardson puts it, "In the New Testament, as in the Old Testament, election is a matter of service, not of privilege."[80] Election refers to the execution of God's purpose in time in this world, and the same must be said of his action in hardening hearts. This latter never appears in an eternal context, but is always presented as an instrument in the realization of the present stage of God's over-all plan for humanity. For example, Pharaoh's heart was hardened in order that the divine power might be manifested (Rom. 9.17) in the liberation of the Chosen People. Also, the hardening of the hearts of Jesus' contemporaries was essential to the plan of salvation, for God had planned to save the world by the death of his Son, a purpose which would not have been realized had the nation accepted him as the Messias. (1 Cor. 2.8.) Paul, faithful to this tradition, sees the blindness of the Jews of his day as ordered to the salvation of the Gentiles. (Rom. 11.11.)

These considerations permit a certain comprehension of the Apostle's thought. It is quite clear that those who persist in their rejection of the Gospel will suffer eternal damnation. (2 Thess. 1.8.) These do not see because God has put a "working of error" in their hearts. (2 Thess. 2.10.) This may be merely a further example of the Semitic penchant for attributing immediately to God what are in reality the effects of secondary causes,[81] but in view of the fact that this blindness is presented as the merited punishment of a voluntary fault, it is difficult to deny the phrase its literal value. One grace is refused and in consequence further graces are denied.[82] But who is to say that this denial will be perpetual? Even for those most violently opposed to the Gospel and its expansion Paul holds out the possibility of a God-given conversion and accession to the truth (2 Tim. 2.25: 1 Cor. 5.5). To the question, why is this grace given now and not at another time, why to one person and not to another, Paul will only answer with the Old-Testament words: "I will have mercy on whom I will have mercy." (Exod. 33.19 = Rom. 9.15.)

Even though his love for all his own wayward people is so great as to make him wish to be anathema from Christ for their sake (Rom. 9.3), Paul is fully conscious that his ministry is only for the elect. He offers the sufferings of his imprisonment "for the sake of the elect in order that they may also obtain the salvation which is in Christ Jesus". (2 Tim. 2.10.) His sufferings play a part in procuring the eternal salvation only of those who have been called and are already on the way to salvation. (1 Tim. 4.10.) He has been made an "apostle of Jesus Christ *for the faith of the elect of God*". (Titus 1.1.) The preachers speak to all the world, but their words are a real summons only for those whom God calls interiorly with that efficacious grace which moves them to receive the Gospel.[83] Faith is exclusively in the divine giving, and the preachers have no power to extend the number of its recipients.

Satanic Influence

For Paul the Christian life has two facets. (Rom. 13.13.) On the positive side, the believer must grow in Christ, while on the negative side, he must resist the allurement of evil. (Col. 3.5 etc.) These aspects are distinct only in the abstract, for in the concrete situation, resistance to temptation necessarily involves the positive exercize of virtue and, in consequence, progress in union with Christ. Paul however, in his frequent references to Satan and the powers of evil,[84] chooses to highlight the combative dimension of the life of faith.[85]

Baptism releases man from the state of subjection to the demons into which he was born as a son of Adam (Rom. 5.12), but doesn't remove him entirely from their sphere of influence. In the sacrament he has received the pledge of the Spirit (Eph. 1.13) and lives in the firm hope that death will be no more than a transition to eternal existence in Christ (Rom. 5.1–11), but he is not assured of his salvation. It is possible to have received the grace of God in vain. (2 Cor. 6.1.) God will indeed guard man from the Evil One (2 Thess. 3.3), but only to the extent of not permitting him to be tempted beyond his strength. (1 Cor. 10.13.) Thus a wide area of personal responsibility remains, and through failure to exercise the power within him

(Eph. 6.13ff.), man may stumble into the "snare of the devil". (2 Tim. 2.26; cf. 3.7.) Unfortunately Satan's power is not less real because it is not apparent. "To seem not to appear is part of his essence."[86] And Paul has to warn the Ephesians not to underrate the opposition:

> Our fight is not against human foes, but against the principalities and against the powers, against the world-rulers of this darkness, against the spirits of wickedness in regions above. [Eph. 6.12; cf. 2 Cor. 2.11][87]

The new life of the Christian is the life of faith:

> The life that I now live in the flesh, I live in the faith of the Son of God, who loved me and gave himself up for me. [Gal. 2.20; cf. Col. 2.6]

and the basic weapon in his spiritual armoury is the shield of faith:

> In all things taking up the shield of faith, wherewith you may be able to extinguish all the fiery darts of the Wicked One. [Eph. 6.16.]

Faith is the strongest bulwark against the attacks of the demons because it recognizes that, in triumphing over them, the Cross has made a contemptible exhibition of all principalities and powers. (Col. 2.15.)[88] They engineered this "triumph" (1 Cor. 2.8) which, however, in God's

hidden wisdom, meant the end of their reign.
Now they have no other expectation save the
final, public manifestation of their broken power
(1 Cor. 15.24) and eternal damnation. Thus faith
reveals the feebleness of their claims and the
illusory character of what they offer. (2 Thess.
2.9.) The only power still enjoyed by the devil
is that given him by unbelief:

> Ye also were dead in your transgressions and
> your sins, wherein sometime you walked after
> the fashion of this world under the prince of
> the power of the air, the spirit which now
> works in the children of disobedience. [Eph.
> 2.1–2]

A passage occurring later in this same epistle
(5.6) shows the "children of disobedience" to be
Christians who lost the faith and/or pagans who
did not avail themselves of the opportunity to
receive the Gospel. For if the Christian fortress
is breached by the sin of anger,[89] the sin of
apostasy razes it to the ground. (Col. 1.23.) Consequently, the devil's most consistent attacks are
directed against the virtue of faith. For Paul,
false apostles are but Satan's ministers (2 Cor.
11.14–15), and although in 1 Tim. he uses the
phrase "in the last times", the context shows that
the danger is present and actual, because the
"spirits of error" are already at work inspiring
the heretical doctrines that cause shipwreck in

the faith (2 Tim. 2.18): "The Spirit expressly says that in the last times some shall depart from the faith, giving heed to spirits of error and doctrine of devils." (1 Tim. 4.1 : cf. 2 Tim. 2.26.)

Naturally, then, the powers of evil strive vigorously to prevent the genesis of faith. But, in fact, Paul only once alludes explicitly to the influence of the devil on his missionary activity (1 Thess. 2.18). Yet there is a clear reference to the part he plays in the rejection of the Gospel:

> But if indeed our gospel is veiled, it is veiled in the case of those perishing, the unbelievers whose mind the god of this age has blinded so that they see not the radiance of the gospel of the glory of Christ. [2 Cor. 4.3–4; cf. Luke 8.12]

The context contrasts the ministry of death and the Spirit in terms of glory. The transitory character of the radiance communicated to Moses becomes significant of the true proportions of his ministry when compared with the lasting "overwhelming glory" of Paul's apostolate. With the mention of the veil a new motif is introduced. The image fluctuates when applied to Moses and the Jews: the veil is now on the face of Moses (2 Cor. 3.13) that the Jews might not see the glory; now on the hearts of the Jews (3.15), explaining their lack of under-

standing. The difference between the veiling of
the glory of Moses and the veiling of the Gospel
is that, whereas the glory of Moses was veiled to
all, the glory of the Gospel is veiled only to a
certain class, and as in 2 Thess. 2.10, these are
characterized as "those perishing". This veiling
is not an obstacle intrinsic to the message, nor
is it due to the manner of its presentation. (4.5.)
It is caused by the "god of this age" who has
blinded their minds precisely in order that they
may not be fixed on the Gospel. At this stage the
question arises, Does the passage contain the
reason why his interference is permitted? Some
commentators think so and translate: "In their
case, the god of this age has blinded their *unbelieving minds*." This would make the "unbelievers" exactly coextensive with "those
perishing", both terms designating the same
group.[90] A little thought, however, reveals that
this opinion involves a contradiction: *actual* unbelief is postulated as both the cause and the
effect of Satan's activity. Furthermore, as Cornely
points out, "unbeliever" (*apistos*) is never used
by Paul to signify one who has culpably refused
to obey the Gospel preached to him.[91] Consequently, it is preferable to consider this phrase
as explicative, not of the action of Satan, but of
the constitution of the category of "those perishing". This group is made up of unbelievers
whom Satan has blinded.[91a] For the reason

why some are blinded and others are not, recourse can be had to only one passage in the whole Pauline corpus, 2 Thess. 2.9–12 (cf. p. 234).

Human Dispositions

Beyond implying that a generous submission of the entire personality is involved (Rom. 6.17), Paul says nothing of the natural dispositions accompanying the *acceptance* of the Gospel. Similarly on the supernatural level he only notes that it is received with "joy of the Spirit". (1 Thess. 1.6.) This rather disconcerting silence on an extremely important aspect of the Christian life becomes a little more comprehensible, however, if we recall his teaching on the priority of the divine initiative, and his consequent stress on the necessity of grace for the reception of the word of God.

Paul is slightly less reticent concerning the dispositions underlying *rejection* of the Gospel. But even here, we have to be content with general observations on the group level, though these dispositions only really exist in the individual and differ in kind, combination and importance for each person.

In the case of the *Jews* these dispositions can be summed up as proud obstinacy. Paul conceded that the Jews were zealous. (Rom. 10.2.) The driving force behind the resistance to

Antiochus Epiphanes and Paul's own persecution
of the Church (Phil. 3.6), this zeal for the Law
was in itself no obstacle to conversion (1 Tim.
1.13), but in Romans, Paul characterizes it as
"not according to knowledge". (10.2.) It was the
boast of the Jews that in the Law they possessed
the "expression of knowledge and truth". (Rom.
2.20.) To say, then, that their zeal was unen-
lightened can only mean that their learning was
inspired not by a sincere desire to discern the
will of God, but rather by an attachment to
some personal advantage.[92] Such preoccupation
so coloured their study of the Law that they
failed to recognize (Rom. 10.3) in it the theme
of justification through faith. In regard to these
Jews Paul uses the term *agnoountes* (Rom. 10.3),
which can be interpreted as simple ignorance (as
in 1 Tim. 1.3). However, in presenting a series
of texts aimed at showing that this essential
point (salvation through faith) was easily (Rom.
10.19) discernible in the Law, Paul shows that
he considered their ignorance culpable. "Seek-
ing their own justice" (Rom. 10.3), a justice
arising from their works which would establish
a claim against God (Rom. 9.20), the Jews failed
to recognize for what it was, the revelation
brought by the preachers. They sought signs,
but only of their own choosing (1 Cor. 1.22), and
as a result, the crucified Christ, whom Paul
preached, was to them a "scandal". (1 Cor. 1.23.)

This rather generic description can be made slightly more precise with the aid of the Pastorals. In these letters, the defence of the Faith appears as one of the major obligations incumbent on Timothy and Titus. The nature of the errors against which they had to battle[93] suggests that their adversaries were of Jewish origin (Titus 1.10), men whose assent to the Gospel was at best superficial, and not at all the "obedience of the heart" (Rom. 6.17) which is the only true reception. These adversaries really knew nothing of the Gospel because they had been unwilling to expend their energy in the necessary patient effort of assimilation.[94] In 1 Tim. 6.3–5 Paul dissects this attitude and locates its roots in pride. Such conceit is essentially an exaltation of self at the expense of the divine order and, in reference to revelation, manifests itself by a refusal to admit what has not been discovered by oneself. It accordingly dissipates the energies of the intellect in futile endless speculation—the mental gymnastics so beloved by the doctors of the Law. (1 Tim. 1.7.) This vain curiosity eventually so corrodes[95] the mind as to deprive it of truth. Deprived, therefore, of the "love of truth" these adversaries are characterized as those "who turn their backs on the truth". (Titus 1.14.)

To discover the dispositions that motivated the refusal of the Gospel among *pagans* is a

much more difficult—not to say impossible—
task. The picture Paul paints of the moral de-
pravity of the pagan world—and he lays stress
on its culpability—is very black. His condemnation of its philosophy is no less absolute. What
must be kept in mind, however, is that these
judgements are essentially theological. Paul's
view of the pagan world is conditioned by his
vivid awareness of the change wrought by the
redemptive death of Christ. When contrasted
with "life in Christ", "life in the flesh" must
appear infinitely worthy of condemnation. (Titus
2.12–14.) Paul's judgement on the pagan world
is a judgement on unredeemed man as such, and
although it is true as a generalization, the
Apostle could not fail to recognize that, despite
the overall darkness, flickers of light became
apparent when reality was considered more concretely. He condemns the wisdom of this world
(pagan philosophy) for having failed to lead the
human spirit to God and having instead led
man into idolatry, the root cause of his moral
decadence. (Eph. 4.17ff.) But if Paul tells us that
human philosophy was capable of knowing God,
is it not because some had actually attained this
knowledge through contemplation of the wisdom and goodness displayed in the material
creation (Rom. 1.20)? Were we to assume that
the vices he catalogues[96] were the personal habits
of each and every pagan the conclusion that

none received the Gospel would be almost inevitable. The absurdity of this counsels prudence, and so we restrict ourselves to noting the one explicit allusion to an attitude incompatible with reception of the word of God, namely, intellectual arrogance. (1 Cor. 1.25.) The fantastic contradiction implied in a doctrine that taught the divinity of a man who died as an executed criminal made it totally unacceptable to minds which found their supreme satisfaction in the coherence of their intellectual synthesis. To such, a crucified Christ could only appear as "folly".

Preaching is the continuation of God's word to man in Christ. And just as the Eternal Word became incarnate in the person of Jesus Christ, so now is the word of God incarnated in the person of its bearer. In this profound sense is the preacher another Christ, *alter Christus*. If his witness is merely verbal and not existential, if his whole existence is not a living manifestation of the power of the word of God, he does not fulfil the role assigned to him by God in the scheme of salvation. His role is to be a bearer of salvation, another Christ. He does not fulfil it merely by proffering the words of Christ. If these words are not his own, they will not be the vibrant appeal to which men respond. And they will not be his unless Christ, operative in them by his salvific power, has been permitted to transform his minister to his own image. Only when the preacher's life has been modelled on Christ's will his words enjoy the power of Christ. Discrepancy between his doctrine and his life, spells failure for his ministry.

The comportment of the preacher and of those who have already obeyed his message are the normal channels whereby divine grace touches men's dispositions. Their lives condition the soil for the reception of the seed. The imperceptible power of their good example opens men's hearts to the word of God. But it is not the only influence at work. In a last frenetic effort, symptomatic of the imminent end of his domination, Satan endeavours to prevent the seed taking root. He can work through the bad example of Christians or through a person's own evil desires, through the pressures of an atheist state or through the lying miracles of Antichrist, but he will succeed in blinding only those who have already closed their hearts to the truth and who, in consequence, have been given over by God to his influence.

But in him whom God has chosen, whose heart he has prepared by the infusion of the love of truth, and whose spirit he has renewed, the seed finds the soil of generous love in which it germinates, bearing its recipient on the way of salvation.

NOTES

1. Two recent studies (H. Riesenfeld, "Le langage parabolique dans les épîtres de Saint Paul", in A. Descamps et al., *Littérature et théologie pauliniennes* (Rech. Bibl., 5), *Louvain* (1960), 47–59; D. M. Stanley, "Pauline Allusions to the Sayings of Jesus", *CBQ*, 23 (1961), 26–39, are a reaction against the opinion that Paul had no information concerning the life and teaching of Jesus, and that his preaching has as foundation only a sketchy summary of the doctrine embodied in the death and resurrection of Christ. (Cf. R. Bultmann, *Theology of the New Testament* (1952), vol. 1, 187ff.) Both authors stress the presence in his teaching of metaphors and illustrations which recall those employed by Jesus in the parables preserved in the Synoptic tradition. There is no question obviously of direct literary dependence on the Gospels, for these in their present form were written at a date subsequent to the Epistles, but the allusions occur in sufficient number to indicate that Paul was familiar with the *logia* of Jesus conserved in the oral tradition drawn on by the Synoptics. (Cf. Cerfaux, *Le Christ*, 146.) In referring 2 Cor. 9.6–10 and Gal. 6.8 to the Parable of the Sower, Riesenfeld perhaps exaggerates a little, but, granted the general familiarity, the allusion seems clear in 1 Cor. 9.11 and the present instance. See also Rigaux, *Thess.*, 160; C. Moule, *The Epistles ... to the Colossians and to Philemon*, Cambridge (1958), 51.

2. The preacher appears as of consequence only in view of the word, cf. 1 Thess. 5.13. Note the "what" of 1 Cor. 3.4 where in reference to persons one would expect "who".

3. D. M. Stanley, "Become Imitators of Me—the Pauline Conception of Apostolic Tradition", *Biblica*, 40 (1959), 865.

4. This will be further developed in the next section.

5. "A servant of the Lord must ... be gentle towards all, a capable teacher ... correcting opponents with meekness in case God should grant them repentance unto knowledge of truth." (2 Tim. 2.24–5.) Sarcasm and intolerance could be obstacles to the working of grace in his hearers.

6. The same idea of mediate imitation is found in 1 Thess. 1.5–6, "Our gospel reached you, not as a matter of mere words, but with the power of the Spirit ... And you, in your turn, became imitators of us and of the Lord, accepting the word with joy despite great tribulation." Further exhortations to imitation occur in 2 Thess. 3.6–9: Gal 4.12: Phil. 3.17. This emphasis immediately distinguishes the Christian preacher from the Greek professor. The professor communicates a mode of thought, the preacher a way of life; and his conviction of the truth of what he preaches is manifested by his conduct, not his argumentation. The Greek disciple learns in order to teach in his turn; the Christian learns in order to live. The essence of Christianity lies not in the assimilation of doctrine but in the following of a person, Christ. (Cf. Mark 8.34: Acts 25.19.) Cf. Rengstorf, *TWNT*, vol. 4, 408, 453.

7. From Gal. 5.11 it is clear that Paul was accused of preaching circumcision when it suited him. (Acts 16.3, and possibly also Gal. 2.3–5.) His change of plan with regard to visiting Corinth (2 Cor. 1.15–16; cf. 1 Cor. 16.3) was interpreted as symptomatic of casualness and inconsistency; he was thought to trim his sails to the prevailing wind and not to be guided by the Holy Spirit. (2 Cor. 1.12.)

8. Cf. H. Chadwick, "'All Things to All Men' (1 Cor. 9.22)", *NTS*, 1 (1954–5), 263.

9. Compare the presentation to the Jews at Antioch (Acts 13.16–41) with that to the Athenians (Acts 17.22–3; cf. J. Dupont, "Le Salut des gentils et la signification théologique du livre des Actes", *NTS*, 6 (1959–60), 152–4). Chadwick's analysis ("'All Things'," 264–7) of 1 Cor. 7 demonstrates Paul's ability to first find a

point of contact with his adversaries, and only then to develop a line of reasoning that runs completely contrary to their assertions. The preoccupation of the Apostle to come into contact with the thought and tendencies of his time, whether it be to correct them or to bring to light a new dimension revealed by Christian wisdom is particularly evident in 1 Cor. (Cf. 1.18–2.16: 6.12–14: 8.1–3: 10.23–4.) This effort of adaptation cannot be taken as implying that Paul's thought simply grew out of the situation with which he was faced, i.e. that this theology was opportunist, cf. P. Benoit's criticisms of W. L. Knox, *Saint Paul and the Church of the Gentiles*, in *Vivre et Penser* [=RB, 50] 1 (1941), 146–7. The limits of adaptation are determined by God's will, and not by the whims of his audience. (1 Thess. 2.4: Gal. 1.10.)

10. The superior must verify the aptitude of the candidate for the function of presbyter (1 Tim. 3.3–12: Titus 1.6–9), which involved preaching. (1 Tim. 5.17.)

11. "What is looked for in stewards is that a man prove faithful [*pistos*]." (1 Cor. 4.2.) *Pistos*, "trustworthy, worthy of confidence", is the characteristic virtue of God's ministers, cf. Matt. 24.45: Luke 12.42: Eph. 6.21: Col. 1.7. Paul emphasises the fidelity with which he transmitted what he had received, be it from the traditions of the Church in Palestine (1 Cor. 11.2: 15.3) or from direct revelation (Gal. 1.12: 1 Cor. 11.23). Writing to Timothy, he stresses the care with which the deposit is to be preserved. (1 Tim. 6.20.)

12. Cf. Spicq. "*Pastorales (Épîtres)*", DBS, 7, 33.

13. False teachers not only know nothing (1 Tim. 1.7: 6.4), but are deceivers (Titus 1.10), impostors (2 Tim. 2.13), hypocrites (1 Tim. 4.2), motivated by greed (Titus 1.12: 1 Tim. 6.5), and incapable of any good work. (Titus 1.16.)

14. It is the constant care of the Apostle to stress his disinterestedness. To accept even the support that was his due might give the impression that his motive was personal gain. (1 Cor. 9.12: 2 Cor. 11.9.) In order not to arouse pointless suspicion and jealousy he asks

that someone be sent with him to bear the collection to Jerusalem. (2 Cor. 8.20.)

15. H. Schlier, "La Notion paulinienne de la parole de Dieu", in A. Descamps et al., *Littérature et théologie pauliniennes* (Rech. Bibl., 5), Louvain (1960), 133.

16. We could put this in more scholastic terms by saying that the "concrete manifestation of divine life in the witnesses is a sign of credibility that must accompany the normal presentation of the Gospel message. It is true that a lack of such a manifestation in the individual preacher can be supplied for his hearers by its presence elsewhere in the Church. But this remains an anomaly." (C. Davis, "The Theology of Preaching", *Clergy Review*, 45 (1960), 539.) in Graeco-Roman times the witness (*martus*)·was never a simple spectator, never limited himself just to furnishing a proof. Originally the defender and assistant of one party, he guaranteed a successful ending to the matter in which he found himself engaged. Cf. F. Pringsheim, "Le Témoinage dans la Grèce et Rome archaïque", *Revue internat. des droits de l'Antiquité*, 6 (1951), 162.

17. This verse, adapted from Prov. 3.4, forms part of Paul's exposé of the nature of "genuine charity" (*v.* 9). This charity possesses two fundamental characteristics: horror of evil, attachment to good. After drawing out the implications of this for the community of believers (*v.* 10–16), the Apostle envisages here (*v.* 7) the relationship of these believers with non-Christians (Lagrange). The truly charitable person is one who prudently chooses, in function of his love of good, actions that are *kala* (cf. below, p. 215) in the interest of souls and for the good repute of his faith.

18. In 1 Tim. 4.16 (the only other instance of its use by Paul) it has the meaning "to pay attention to, to fix the mind on", and is paralleled by Luke 14.17: Acts 3.5: Ecclus. 34.2: 2 Macc. 9.25. In Acts 19.22 the sense is "to wait".

19. *The Vocabulary of the Greek New Testament*, London (1949), 232.

20. Cf. *A-G.*, 285.

21. Benoit (*Bible de Jérusalem*), Bonnard, Ewald, Vincent etc.

22. It is used of Christ (1 Pet. 1.19: Heb. 9.14), of the Church (Eph. 5.27), and with reference to the goal intended to be achieved by divine election (Eph. 1.4) and Christ's death (Col. 1.22), namely, that we might be without blemish.

23. The clearest example is that of Zachary and Elizabeth, both of whom "were just before God, walking without blame in all the commandments and ordinances of the Lord". (Luke 1.6.) Paul describes himself as being "in the justice to be found in the Law proved without blame". (Phil. 3.6.) And the author of Hebrews says, "If the Old Covenant had been *amemptos* there would have been no place for the second" (8.7)—the implication being that the Old Covenant was incapable of fulfilling the role assigned to it. (Cf. Heb. 7.28.) Trench notes that "if *amōmos* is the 'unblemished', *amemptos* is the 'unblamed'", but admits at the same time "a constant tendency to regard the *inculpatus* as also the *inculpabilis* so that in actual usage there is a continual breaking down of the distinct and several uses of these words". (*Synonyms of the New Testament*, London (1894), 381.

24. Cf. R. Trench, *Synonyms*, 206. This is perfectly illustrated by Rom. 16.19: "uncontaminated as regards evil".

25. "That which is in its primitive state of integrity, perfection, moral innocence." (Kittel, *TWNT*, I, 209.)

26. In Gal. 4.16 (the only other New-Testament occurrence). *alētheuein* means "to speak the truth", but here, where attention is focused not immediately on false teachers but on those in danger of being misled by them (Eph. 4.14), this meaning does not seem adequate. Moreover, Abbott notes that verbs in *-euō* express the realization in action of what is signified by the corresponding substantive in *-eia*. *Alētheuein*, then, must be understood as a bodying forth of the truth

received, cf. Eph. 4.1: Phil. 1.27: 4.9. Spicq translates, "vivre en authentique croyant" (*Agapé*, vol. 2, 231), and Bultmann, "des rechten Glaubens in der Liebe leben". (*TWNT*, vol. 1, 251.)

27. Cf. I. de la Potterie, "De Sensu Vocis 'emeth' in Vetere Testamento", *VD*, 28 (1950), 35–36. On the concept of truth at Qumran, cf. O. Betz, *Offenbarung und Schriftforschung in der Qumranseckte*, Tübingen (1960), 54.

28. The response of the Corinthians to Paul's appeal for the Church in Jerusalem is be the test of the "genuineness" (*gnēsios*) of their charity (2 Cor. 8.7–8). That good works are but the normal expression of Christian charity is suggested by the evocation of the sacrifice of Christ in the succeeding verse; cf. Spicq, *Agapé*, vol. 2, 140.

29. Cf. Spicq, "Vie chrétienne et beauté", Excursus XIII, *Pastorales*, 290–97, from which we take the non-biblical references; Grundmann, *TWNT*, vol. 3, 539–558.

30. Compare 1 Tim. 1.5,19 and Heb. 13.18; .cf. 2 Cor. 13.7: Gal. 6.9: Rom. 7.18–21. In the vast majority of cases the Septuagint uses one or the other to translate the same Hebrew term *tob*.

31. Cf. R. Trench, *Synonyms*, 389–390.

32. Cf. Plato, *Lys.*, 216c; *Banquet*, 211e–212a; *Phaed.*, 250d; Philo, *Agric.*, 99; Aristotle, *Rhet.*, I, 1362a,23; I, 1364b,27; I, 1366ab. For a discussion of the Greek ideal of beauty, cf. T. Boman, *Hebrew Thought compared with Greek*, London (1961), 84–7.

33. Cf. Kittel, *TWNT*, vol. 1, 222; Rigaux, *Thess.*, 161.

34. That *akouō* is capable of including the idea of submission is clear from Matt. 18.16–17: "If he will not *listen*, take one or two others with you so that all facts may be duly established on the evidence of two or three witnesses. If he refuses to *listen* to them, report the matter to the congregation; and if he will not *listen* even to the congregation, you must then treat him as you would a pagan or a tax-gatherer."

35. Cf. Schlier, *Eph.*, 217; Cerfaux, *Le Christ*, 375.

36. Here, because of the context, the practical, moral dimension of "learning" is much in evidence; cf. Rengstorf, *TWNT*, vol. 4, 412.

37. Schlier, Abbott.

38. *Hē pistis ek akoēs, hē de akoē dia rhēmatos Christou.* *Akoē* in the citation from Isa. 53.1 which immediately precedes this verse certainly means "preaching", and since Paul draws a conclusion from it, the assumption is that in *v.* 17 he uses the term in the same sense. In view, however, of the connection with *v.* 18 and with the thought of *v.* 14, a shading off of the meaning towards the active sense of *akoē*, i.e., "hearing", seems indicated (Sanday-Headlam). Hence we translate: "Faith comes through hearing [the Gospel], and hearing [is] through the instrumentality of the words of Christ." This brings out more strongly the idea underlying *v.* 14, namely, the identification of the words of the authorized preacher with those of Christ.

39. Cf. above, p. 231.

40. Cf. above, p. 251.

41. Upheld by Kittel, *TWNT*, vol. 1, 222.

42. Cf. Heb. 4.2 in which Bonsirven sees a "sort of play on words opposing those who have listened to the word and those who have really heard it".

43. *Gnosis*, 12, *n.* 1. On *epignōsis alētheias*, cf. ch. 5 (p. 239).

44. *Pneuma* is also used by Paul as a synonym for *psychē* (1 Cor. 5.5), especially in its union with the body (1 Cor. 7.34), and for *nous.* (1 Cor. 2.11.)

45. Cf. Spicq, *Dieu*, 159.

46. Cf. Delling, *TWNT*, vol. 4, 14.

47. In the Old Testament the objects of *manthanō* in a religious context are "the fear of God" (Deut. 4.10 etc), "the commandments" (Ps. 119.71,73), "justice" (Isa. 26.9), "doing good" (Isa. 1.17). "To learn" in these contexts is to submit oneself to the will of God as manifested in the Law. A more intellectual element evident in the Sapiential literature (Ecclus. 8.9: 16.24: Wisd. 6.2:

7.13) was accentuated by later Judaism, the rabbis using *lmd* for the *study* of the Law (cf. B. Gerhardsson, *Memory and Manuscript*, Uppsala (1961), 126–9), but even then it was ideally learning for the sake of doing, cf. Rengstorf, *TWNT*, vol. 4, 402–3. In some instances Paul employs *manthanō* in a purely Greek sense, e.g., 1 Cor. 14.31,35: Gal. 3.2.

48. It is difficult to decide whether "faith" is here subjective (the act of adhesion to Christ) or objective (a body of doctrine). Lagrange considers the subjective value of the genitive the more probable: "... the obedience that is faith". (*Rom.*, 10.) As we shall see, the Pauline concepts of faith and of obedience to the word are coextensive.

49. Bultmann ("Glossen in Römerbrief", *Theologische Literaturzeitung* 72 (1947), 202) and Leenhardt deny the authenticity of this verse on the sole grounds that it interrupts the flow of thought. This is entirely unfounded, cf. F. W. Beare, "On the Interpretation of Rom. 6.17", *NTS*, 5 (1958–9), 206–10; K. Lee, "Words Denoting 'Pattern' in the New Testament", *NTS*, 8 (1961–2), 170.

50. It does not seem necessary to show again that *typos didachēs* does not denote an antithesis either with other forms of Christian teaching or with Jewish teaching, cf. F. W. Beare, "Rom. 6.17"; J. Kurzinger, "*Typos didachēs* und der Sinn von Röm 6.17", *Biblica* 39 (1958), 156–76.

51. Cf. W. D. Stacey, *The Pauline View of Man*, London (1956), 194–7.

52. In the immediate context only the liberty of this submission is explicit. It will not be out of place, however, to note that some texts insinuate the identification of the "heart" with the "infused spirit" as the point of reception of divine gifts, notably faith (Eph. 3.17) and charity (2 Thess. 3.5: Rom. 5.5: 1 Tim. 1.5). Compare Gal. 4.7 and Rom. 8.15–16. Cf. Spicq. *Dieu*, 162. Comparison with 1 Cor. 2.14–15 (above, p. 224) suggests that the "heart" from which obedience flows in Rom.

6.17 has already been enlightened and strengthened by the Spirit. There are a number of other illuminating parallels. "Lydia was listening and the Lord opened her heart to respond to what Paul said." (Acts 16.14.) "I will give them a heart to know that I am Yahweh." (Jer. 24.7.) "May he open your heart to his Law." (Isa. 50.5.)

53. The purpose of preaching within the community is the preservation of this basic attitude. The object of Paul's reproaches is "that your obedience be perfect". (2 Cor. 10.6.)

54. Cf. *A-G*, 845.

55. This is given by Kittel as the primary meaning (*TWNT*, vol. 1, 224.)

56. This precise point is emphasized in Romans where everlasting life is promised to those who persevere in good works (2.7), but "for those who disobey the truth, but obey wickedness, there will be wrath and fury". (2.8.) The motive inspiring such disobedience is *eritheia* "selfishness, selfish ambition". (So *A-G*, which admits that the meaning in our literature is a matter of conjecture.)

57. Cf. Prat, *Theol.*, vol. 1, 250; Lagrange, *Rom.*, 245.

58. St Thomas glosses *v.* 10b: "Culpa et poena est eorum seductio: unde dicit *mittet*, id est, permittet illis venire operationem erroris" (*In Epistola ad Thess. Secunda*, ch. 2, lect. 3, *n.* 54). St Paul, however, speaks of a divine action bearing those who refuse the light, through belief in the lie, to their inevitable and well-merited (*kai dia touto*) condemnation. "The whole movement of the phrase shows that this eternal damnation punishes, not so much the adhesion to the lie and submission to Antichrist, as the first refusal of the light." (Spicq, *Agapé*, vol. 2, 38.)

59. *Anth'hōn* is used by Paul only in this passage, but its explicative value (i.e. as indicating logical consequence) is attested to by Luke 1.20: 19.44: Acts 12.23. For the usage in the papyri, cf. Spicq, *Agapé*, vol. 2, 34, *n.* 1.

60. Cf. the section on "Receiving" (above, p. 222).

61. That "truth" here has a pronounced moral dimension is evident from the fact that it is placed in opposition to "wickedness" (*adikia*), which is for Paul the state diametrically opposed to justification (Rom. 6.13). Note the contrast in *v.* 12.

62. The reception of the "love of truth" puts one on the way of salvation since it is "unto their salvation". In 1 Cor. 1.18–24 only "those being saved" receive the Gospel.

63. This conclusion finds confirmation in a recent study on the "anointing" of the Christian in 2 Cor. 1.21–2. The text runs: "He who confirms us together with you in Christ and has anointed us, is God, who also set his seal upon us and gave us the pledge of the Spirit in our hearts." The four divine actions (expressed in Greek by participles) are grouped in pairs, each pair having but one article. This separation of the two groups suggests that confirming and anointing precede sealing and granting of the pledge. It has been shown in ch. 1 (p. 18) that sealing here is an allusion to baptism. Hence the anointing precedes baptism. The parallelism with Eph. 1.13 reveals the nature of this anointing, the only difference between the two texts being the point of view adopted; 2 Cor. views things from the point of view of God, and Eph. from the point of view of the believer.

2 Cor.	Eph.
(a) He who has anointed us is God,	(a) You also heard the word of truth ... and having believed it,
(b) who also set his seal upon us and gave us in our hearts	(b) you also were sealed by the Holy Spirit,
(c) the pledge	(c) that Spirit who is
(d) of the Spirit.	(d) the pledge of our inheritance.

Because of the exact parallel between the second and third members, namely, the sealing and the reception of the pledge, the anointing must be the divine activity that is the counterpart of the human acts of hearing and believing. The divine anointing, then, must be God's action arousing faith in the elect who hear the word. Cf. I. de la Potterie. "L'Onction du chrétien par la foi", *Biblica*, 40 (1959), 14–25.

64. St Thomas, *In Epistola ad Romanos*, ch. 10, lect. 2, *n*. 842.

65. Cf. above, p. 234.

66. Cf. above, p. 225.

67. St Thomas, *In Epistola ad Romanos*, ch. 10, lect. 2, *n*. 844.

68. The succeeding genitive always indicates the object of this knowledge: God (Col. 1.10: Eph. 1.17), the Son of God (Eph. 4.13), the mystery of God (Col. 2.2), the will of God (Col. 1.9), "every good that is in us" (Philem. 6). An explicit object is lacking in Rom. 1.28: 10.2: Phil. 1.9 and Col. 3.10, but the context in each case enables us to supply one. The force of the pre-position *epi*, then, appears as similar to its significance in the corresponding verb, where it does not indicate addition, in the sense of more advanced knowledge, but rather direction: "Thus *ginōskein* means 'to know' in the fullest sense that can be given to the word "knowledge"; *epignōskein* directs attention to some particular point in regard to which knowledge is affirmed." (J. A. Robinson, "On the Meaning of *Epignōsis*", in his *Saint Paul's Epistle to the Ephesians*, London (1928), 249.)

69. *TWNT*, vol. 1, 707.

70. "And this is my prayer that your charity may more and more abound in knowledge [*en epignōsei*] and all discernment." (Phil. 1.9.) It is impossible to see how Bultmann can say that there is no difference in meaning between this knowledge which is a flowering of charity, and the charismatic *gnōsis* of 1 Cor. 1.5, concerning which the Corinthians had so many erroneous ideas.

71. Cf. 2 Thess. 2.12–13: 2 Cor. 4.2: 1 Tim. 6.5: Titus 1.14: 2 Tim. 2.18: 3.8: 4.4: "word of truth", 2 Cor. 6.7: Col. 1.5: 1.13.

72. Cf. Spicq, *Pastorales*, 362.

73. This is also illustrated by the case of those women whose desire for knowledge was rooted in a purely intellectual curiosity: "... those women who are laden with sins and are led about by all kinds of desires, ever learning and never able to come to knowledge of truth" (2 Tim. 3.6–7). The *entire* movement towards faith is both God's and man's. Faith is to be sought by man (2 Tim. 2.22) and is at the same time the effect of the divine action in the soul. (Phil. 1.29: Eph. 3.17.) Paul sees no contradiction in exhorting his readers to do something and at the same time suggesting that God does it in them. Compare, for example, Phil. 1.27 (Eph. 4.1) and 2 Thess. 1.11 (living the Gospel): Phil. 2.15 and 1 Thess. 3.13 (blamelessness).

74. Cf. Bultmann, *TWNT*, vol. 1, 697.

75. For Bultmann (*TWNT*, vol. 1, 698) election pertains to divine knowledge as such. After an analysis of the passages on which he bases this assertion (Gen. 18.19: Exod. 3.12: Amos 3.2: Os. 13.5: Jer. 1.5) Dupont concludes that this is to give the idea of knowledge a precision that it did not possess in the minds of the Old-Testament writers. (*Gnosis*, 75–80.)

76. Cf. A. Richardson, *An Introduction to the Theology of the New Testament*, London (1958), 276.

77. Cf. S. Lyonnet, *Quaestiones in Epistola ad Romanos*, Series Altera, Rome (1956), 13.

78. Lagrange notes *à propos* of Rom. 9.11: "The question considered directly by Paul is not at all that of predestination and reprobation, but solely that of the call of the Gentiles to the grace of Christianity, having as antithesis the incredulity of the Jews. . . . Great care, then, must be exercised in applying what is said of the call to Christianity to eternal predestination and reprobation." (*Rom.*, 247.)

79. Cf. 1 Tim. 1.19: 5.15: 6.10,21: 2 Tim. 4.4: 1 Cor. 5 etc.

80. A. Richardson, *Introduction*, 275.

81. A permissive sense is the only one possible in texts such as Ezek. 39.7: "I will no longer pollute my holy name." God polluting his name at any time is inconceivable; the meaning is, "I will no longer permit my holy name to be defiled." The Old Testament displays a consistent disregard for secondary causes, for the Semitic mentality easily refers all causality immediately to the First Cause. This outlook is aided and abetted by a language that does not clearly distinguish the various forms of causality. (Cf. P. G. Duncker, *Compendium Grammaticae Linguae Hebraicae Biblicae*, Rome (1948), 53; A. Condamin, *Le livre d'Isaïe*, Paris (1905), 46.) God was considered to do that which he foresaw and could have impeded, but which he, in fact, only permitted.

82. The little allegory of Heb. 6.7–8 perfectly expresses Paul's thought: "A soil which has drunk in the abundant rain that has fallen on it, and yields a useful crop to those for whom it is cultivated, receives a blessing from God, but if it bears thorns and thistles, it is worthless and is nigh unto a curse and the end thereof is burning." The faithful soul, in making use of the graces showered on it to produce the fruit of virtue, disposes itself to receive from God further gifts. Note again that it is God who holds the entire initiative, yet man's co-operation is mandatory (Phil. 2.12). On the other hand, the soul can make itself impermeable to grace (according to Heb. 3.13 the seduction of sin has a hardening effect), and thus fit itself for nothing but punishment.

83. Cf. St Thomas, *In Epistola ad Romanos*, ch. 8, lect. 6, *n*. 707.

84. The New Testament designates the powers of evil by a great many titles (at least 28), but examination shows them to be to a great extent interchangeable. This, coupled with the very fact of the multiplicity of

names, suggests we have to deal with a single subject not adequately described by any one name. "Fundamentally we are dealing with a single phenomenon which is diffused, and which concerns us in various manifestations.... These powers have revealed themselves as manifestations of a spirit who is a person." (H. Schlier, *Principalities and Powers in the New Testament,* Freiburg-London (1961), 17, 21.)

85. The demonological element in the Gospels and Epistles is not an accidental factor, a current mode of thought that imperceptibly influenced the New-Testament writers, and which they adopted without attaching much significance to it. Its importance for a true understanding of redemption has long been recognized by Catholic exegetes and recently a number of Protestants have insisted on its value, for example, Fridrichsen, Manson, Brunner, and Cullman. Cf. T. Ling, *The Significance of Satan,* London (1961).

86. Schlier, *Principalities and Powers,* 29.

87. The devil works through false teachers (2 Cor. 11.14–15: 1 Tim. 4.1) and through the pagan idols (1 Cor. 10.20: 12.2). Historical situations (2 Thess. 2.8), as well as human institutions are his instruments. Cullmann suggests that, for Paul, demonic activity is well exemplified in the activities of the totalitarian anti-Christian state (*Christ and Time,* London (1951), 199–200: cf. G. H. C. MacGregor, "Principalities and Powers", *NTS,* 1 (1954–5), 24–7.

88. Cf. F. Prat, "Le Triomphe du Christ sur les principautés et les puissances", *RSR,* 3 (1912), 201–229.

89. "Let not the sun go down upon your anger and give no place to the devil." (Eph. 4.26–7.)

90. This is the opinion of St Thomas, Allo, Plummer, Spicq.

91. Cornely, *2 Cor.,* 113. The term *apistos* is applied indiscriminately to all who have not received the Gospel, whether heard or not (1 Cor. 7.12–14: 10.27: 14.22–4: 1 Tim. 5.8), sometimes associated with the idea of moral fault (1 Cor. 6.6: 2 Cor. 6.14–15: Titus

1.15). To designate those who have positively refused to believe, Paul uses *hoi apeitheis*. (Titus 1.16.)

91a. It is not entirely certain whether 2 Tim. 2.25–6 should be considered in this section. The passage concerns the impossibility of access to the truth because of an obstacle placed by the devil, but the context suggests that the individuals in question once possessed this truth and later culpably abandoned it.

92. Paul's zeal was sincere and lacked this *arrière-pensée*. Consequently he was found worthy of confidence. (1 Tim. 1.12.)

93. Styled "doctors of the law" (1 Tim. 1.7), they distinguish pure and impure foods (1 Tim. 4.3: Titus 1.15), and "disputes about the Law" absorb their attention equally with Jewish fables. (Titus 1.14: 3.9.)

94. *Epistamai* (1 Tim. 6.4) appears to have been deliberately chosen by Paul in the technical sense of its substantive, i.e., clear, assured knowledge, presupposing a patient effort of acquisition (Spicq). We have already noted that *epignōsis alētheias* is always found with a particle of motion, suggesting the movement of the human spirit involved in its assimilation.

95. *Diaphtheirō* (1 Tim. 6.5) is used of the corruption worked by rust on iron (cf. *A-G*, 189).

96. Cf. Rom. 1.28–31: Col. 3.5–8: Titus 3.3.

PREACHING: A LITURGICAL ACT[1]

Among the many passages which permit us to share, in some degree, Paul's concept of the preacher, one stands out as unique because it suggests that by his preaching the preacher fulfils a *priestly* function. This text, which occurs in the epilogue of the Epistle to the Romans, while singular among the passages alluding to the proclamation of the word of God, is nonetheless perfectly coherent with his general teaching concerning the liturgical dimension of the Christian life as a whole. It is in this wider context that Paul's assertion that God has given him the grace to be "a priest of Christ Jesus among the Gentiles, ministering-in-sacrifice the Gospel of God" must be viewed, if its depth of meaning is to be fully appreciated.

THE LITURGICAL DIMENSION OF THE CHRISTIAN LIFE

THE TEMPLE

In describing the pagan converts as the wild shoot grafted onto the cultivated olive (Rom.

11.24) whose root bears them (11.18), Paul sets forth his conviction that the Church is not so much an entirely new creation as it is the transformation of an existing reality. This transformation, effected by the death of Christ, marks a new stage in the religious history of the world. Paul, however, was keenly aware that the present was not a complete break with the past—the Christian is not a Jew but the believers are the "sons of Abraham" (Gal. 3.7): "If you are Christ's, then are you the seed of Abraham." (Gal. 3.29.) Therefore, the inheritance promised to Abraham and his seed is theirs. (Gal. 3.16.) The privileges going to make up this inheritance are enumerated by Paul in Rom. 9.4: "The adoption, the glory, the covenants, the legislation, the worship (*latria*), the promises...". Granted the pre-eminent place it occupied in Jewish thought, it is not surprising to find two direct references to the Temple in this list: "glory" and "worship".[2] "Glory" is intimately associated with the idea of God's presence. His taking possession of the Tabernacle and of the Temple are described in almost identical terms: the glory of Yahweh (in the form of a cloud) filled the place. (Exod. 40.32: 1 Kings 8.10–11.) Later the Temple is characterized as the house of glory. (Dan. 3.53.) In the light of this tradition it is impossible to imagine Paul conceiving "glory" as one of the privileges of Israel without direct reference to the Temple.[3] The same must be said of "worship" for, while Paul does employ this term in a purely spiritual sense (Phil. 3.3), he was aware that it could also carry the connotation of public ritual worship, its constant meaning in the Septuagint.[4] The idea of public worship evokes that of the Temple which, as the place of the divine presence, was the place of worship *par excellence*. (Cf. Wisd. 9.8.)

It may be inferred, therefore, that Paul considered the Temple, the place of the presence of God and of liturgical worship, among the privileges of Israel.[5] It must in consequence belong to the new Israel, the true inheritor of the promises. But just as Israel has been transformed by the fact of Christ, so too the Temple. No longer is it a material edifice, the focal point of the Jewish world and the proudest possession of the old Israel. Rather, the new Israel *is* a spiritual temple:

> Do you not know that you are a temple of God—that the Spirit of God dwells in you? If anyone destroy the temple of God, God will destroy him, for the temple of God is holy and you are his temple. [1 Cor. 3.16–17]

The appearance of the idea of the temple here as a step in Paul's polemic against the party spirit threatening to divide and destroy the Church at Corinth, indicates that it is applied

to the community as such and not to individuals.
Its introduction without explanation, not to
mention the words, "Do you not know", suggests
that the concept was already well known,[6] most
probably through Paul's own preaching. In
Chapter 6 of this same epistle it is the believer
who is considered a temple: "Do you not know
that your body is the temple of the Holy Spirit
who dwells in you?" (v. 19.) These two applications of the same idea are not contradictory, and
certainly not mutually exclusive. The agent of
sanctification of the "life-giving spirit" (1 Cor.
15.45) who is the risen Christ is the Spirit. He
dwells permanently in the hearts of those who
believe. (Rom. 8.9–11). It is through his presence
that they belong to Christ (Rom. 8.10) and
through his activity in baptism (Titus 3.5) that
they participate in Christ's passion and resurrection. (Rom. 6.) But the action of the Spirit
in an individual Christian also has social implications. Baptism, besides sanctifying him, makes
him a stone in the temple of the living God. (1
Pet. 2.4–5.) Thus, it is precisely the same principle, the indwelling Spirit, that makes both the
community and the individual a temple. And
while it seems that the temple-community rather
than the temple-individual is primary in Paul's
thought,[7] the two applications necessarily imply
one another. He considers the community as a
temple again in 2 Cor. 6.16. The Spirit is not

mentioned, but the assertion is supported by two passages from the Old Testament (Lev. 26.12 and Ezek. 37.27), introduced to demonstrate the presence of the "living God" within the community.

In these three passages the idea of the temple appears to have been introduced because of the note of sanctity necessarily associated with it. In other words, in Paul's mind, what is important is not the temple as such but the practical conclusion to be drawn from the fact that Christians, individually or collectively, are a dwelling-place of God in the person of the Spirit. In each case the idea of the temple is invoked to reinforce a moral exigency—Christians must at all costs avoid profaning the holy temple that they are. They must keep themselves apart from the corruption of paganism (2 Cor. 6.16) and hold fornication in abhorrence (1 Cor. 6.19): "Let us cleanse ourselves from all defilement of the flesh and of the spirit." (2 Cor. 7.1.) That profanation spells destruction because of the spirituality of the edifice is clear from 1 Cor. 3.16–17. There the destruction of the temple is connected with the activity of those who build on the foundation laid by Paul. The materials they use, to the extent that they are not the pure gold of the Gospel, tend to destroy rather than to build up the temple. Purity of doctrine, then, is essential to the sanctity of the temple, and the introduction of heterodox elements is equivalent to a profanation.

No moralizing motive underlies the introduction of the theme of the temple in Eph. 2.21. Its use there is suggested, in all probability, by the mention of "the wall" as the symbol of the spiritual barrier which, before the death of Christ, separated the pagans from the Jews. (Eph. 2.14.) The allusion is to the wall of the Temple at Jerusalem which divided the Court of the Gentiles from that of the Jews and barred the access of the former to the sanctuary. That barrier now exists no longer. The death of Christ has meant the birth of a new undivided humanity. In his crucified body Jew and Gentile have been reconciled to God "both in one body". (2.16.) It is Christ's body the Church which is here primarily in view: Christ the Redeemer and Head, imparting the life of his Spirit to Jew and Gentile, forms them into one body and leads them, now one, into the presence of his Father. (2.18.)[8] But underlying this is the concept of Christ's personal body as "an offering and sacrifice" (Eph. 5.2), for it is through his sacrificial act that the Gentiles are admitted to the "household of God". (2.19.) From the idea of "household" Paul's mind jumps easily to that of "building" (2.20), and thence to that of "temple":

(20) The building that you are is built up on the foundation of the apostles and prophets:

the corner-stone is Christ Jesus himself. (21)
In him the whole building is duly fitted together and grows into a holy temple in the
Lord; (22) in him you also are being built
together to become a divine dwelling-place
in the Spirit.

The temple in this passage is no longer an individual or a local community, but the universal
Church. What is especially significant here is
the relationship that is established between the
temple and the supreme liturgical act of Christ.
His sacrificial death *is* the formation of his body,
which is a holy temple, God's dwelling-place.
The intimate association of temple (building)
and body in Paul's mind is evidenced by his
attribution to one of what belongs exclusively
to the other: he speaks of the temple as *growing*
(Eph. 2.21) and of the body as being *built*. (Eph.
4.16.)[9]

THE TEMPLE SERVICE

Paul's conception of both the Christian, and
the body of Christ, of which he is a member, as
a temple is sufficient indication in itself that he
recognized a liturgical value in the Christian
life as a whole. A temple is God's dwelling-place,
but it is *par excellence* the place where liturgical
worship is offered him. The activity of the believer participates in the liturgical character of

his being. The sanctity of the divine dwelling-place and the purity of the cult offered therein do not, as we have seen, consist in ritual cleanliness, but in a life of union with God, in avoidance of false doctrines and in opposition to sin and to corrupt pagan influences. The worship offered by the believer consists fundamentally in the fulfilment of the duties imposed on him by his new state. What he does is done in the presence of God. He is a priest officiating in the temple of his own body[10]: "Glorify [*doxasate*] God in your bodies." (1 Cor. 6.20.)[11] Paul frequently alludes to this activity in liturgical terms.

To the Romans he says:

I exhort you therefore, brethren, to present your bodies as a living sacrifice [*thusian zōsan*] holy and pleasing to God, your rational worship [*logikēn latreian*]. [Rom. 12.1]

The worship demanded of man does not merely consist in the offering of what he possesses. Because endowed with intellect, he can appreciate that there is but one God "from whom [come] all things and to whom we [tend]" (1 Cor. 8.6), and, consequently, can recognize that the worship God desires must include the offering of himself.[12] This offering of one's whole person, particularly as expressed in external activity (*v.* 2), is not a momentary affair, because the existence of the victim is not terminated, as it is in a material immolation. Man must present himself as a "*living* sacrifice". "Life" here is not natural human existence, but the new life conferred on man in baptism: "Offer yourselves to God as men come to life from the dead." (Rom. 6.13; cf. 8.13.) The living sacrifice is the continuing satisfaction of the exigencies of that gift. The renewal effected by baptism affects the whole person, but in the order of virtuous activity, it first perfects the mind (1 Cor. 2.15), enabling it to perceive what is pleasing to God. (*v.* 2.) To foster this discernment in his readers, Paul describes God's will in more concrete detail in subsequent verses (*vv.* 9–21) whose substance is summed up in the initial nominal phrase, which dominates the section almost as a chapter heading[12]: "[Let] charity [be] without hypocrisy."

In Eph. 5.1–2 this charity which animates the living sacrifice is described in liturgical terms expressly related to the sacrifice of the Cross:

> Be then imitators of God as beloved children and walk in love as Christ also loved us and gave himself up for us as an offering and sacrifice to God as a sweet perfume [*prosphoran kai thusian tō theō eis osmen euōdias*].

Since Christians are truly sons of God, their life is defined as an imitation of him. But how are

they to imitate him whom they have never seen?
In answer to this unspoken question, Paul presents Christ, the Beloved Son *par excellence*
(Eph. 1.5: Col. 1.13), as a concrete model. To
live up to their calling (Eph. 1.4), to "walk in
love", the believers have only to love as Christ
loved. And it is highly significant that Paul
evokes the love of Christ in its supreme expression—his death on the Cross. The terms used
convey not only the freedom and immensity of
this gift of self but also its liturgical character.[14]
To live as a Christian, then, is to be animated
by a sacrificial love as spontaneous and as generous as that of the crucified Christ. As a result,
Paul can speak of the "sacrifice and liturgy of
your faith". (Phil. 2.17.) It is generally agreed
that the genitive "of your faith" is explanatory[15];
the sacrifice offered by the Philippians *is* their
faith. The addition of "liturgy" (*leitourgia*) as
a qualification of "sacrifice"[16] accentuates the
ritual character of the offering, because while
this term can simply mean "service", it was most
frequently employed in the Septuagint for a
sacred service and in particular for that of the
Temple.[17] This suggests the public character of
the sacrifice. Consequently, "faith" should be
understood not merely as an internal attitude,
but as the full living out of the obligations assumed at baptism, which is the basic mandatory
expression of faith. It is the equivalent of the

"activity of faith" (1 Thess. 1.3: 2 Thess. 1.11),
"the sum total of the moral activity of the
Christian as such, that is, acting under the light
and inspiration of faith".[18] This is confirmed by
the fact that Paul speaks of the gift made to him
by the Philippians, the expression of their faith
and love, as "a sweet savour, an acceptable sacrifice pleasing to God". (Phil. 4.18.)[19] In an analogous passage of the Pastoral Epistles elderly
women are counselled to comport themselves
with the dignity and reverence befitting pries-
tesses officiating in a temple. (*Hieroprēpēs*, Titus
2.3.)[20]

The liturgical character of the Christian life
flows immediately from the fact that believers
are the dwelling place of God, his temple. We
have also noted that the existence of the temple
is related immediately to the death of Christ,
which Paul conceives as a liturgical offering,
and that the love of Christians is to be modelled
on the love displayed in this sacrifice. The ultimate source of the liturgical quality of the believer's existence, however, is the permanent,
mystical (but nonetheless real) participation in
the death of Christ effected by baptism. (Rom.
6.6.) The sufferings of the believer are those of
Christ (2 Cor. 1.5;[21] cf. Rom. 8.17), whose very
dying is continued daily in his ministers:
". . . bearing about always in our body the putting to death of Jesus". (2 Cor. 4.10; cf. Col.

1.24.) It is this putting on of Christ in the
supreme liturgical act of his sacrifice that stamps
the Christian life at its deepest level with its
liturgical character. "In the death of Christ
Christians have already been presented in sacrifice to God; the Christian life is the working out
in daily living of this oblation of Christ's."[22]

"GOD'S GOSPEL FOR MY PRIESTLY CHARGE"

If the Christian life as such is liturgical in
character, so too must be the activity of the
Apostle. If the ordinary believer offers worship
in fulfilling the duties of his new state, no less
can be said of the preacher.[23] His primary obligation is to preach the Gospel (1 Cor. 1.17), and
this he does in the "House of God" (1 Tim. 3.15)
and in God's presence. (2 Cor. 2.17.) "In preaching the Gospel of his Son I offer God spiritual
worship." (Rom. 1.9.)[24] Preaching is a liturgical
act because it is an essential component of the
"living sacrifice" of one who has been commissioned as God's minister.

This quality is also clearly implied in two
passages which relate preaching to the construction and to the preservation of the temple. In
them the preachers appear as both the foundation of the temple (Eph. 2.20) and those who lay
this foundation (1 Cor. 3.10).

This latter passage compares the community

at Corinth to a building constructed by the
activity of "servants", among whom figure Paul
and Apollos:

> Like a skilful architect I laid a foundation
> according to the divine grace given me. But
> let each one take care how he builds upon it,
> for no-one can lay any other foundation than
> that which is laid, which is Jesus Christ ...
> Do you not know that you are a temple of
> God and that the Spirit of God dwells in you?
> If anyone destroy the temple of God, God will
> destroy him, for the temple of God is holy
> and you are his temple. [1 Cor. 3.10–17]

The temple, which is the community, comprises
a superstructure resting on a foundation. To
these parts of the building there corresponds the
activity of Paul's successors and of Paul himself.
The expressions must not be interpreted in too
material a sense, however, because the spiritual
edifice exists in its entirety from the time of the
placing of its foundation. It would be absurd to
imagine Paul's successors as adding anything
essential. All the Apostle intends to convey is
that they work on the materials he has provided
(Rom. 15.20), and in so doing characterizes his
own activity as the laying of the foundation.
That foundation is Jesus Christ. Since Paul's
activity at Corinth consisted in speaking the
language of the Cross (1.18), that is, in pro-

claiming Jesus Christ crucified (1.23: 2.2), he laid the foundation by engendering faith which leads to baptism. Anything endangering this faith threatens the entire structure; to corrupt it is to undermine an edifice whose very existence is a liturgical offering. Faith, which is the foundation, is a sacrifice, an act of worship. Without the preaching of the Apostle none of this new liturgy could have existed.

Its continued dependence on his action is more clearly indicated in Eph. 2.20, where the holy temple is said to be "built up on the foundation of the apostles and prophets". The genitive "of the apostles and prophets" has been variously interpreted as indicating, (1) *possession:* the foundation is that on which the apostle-prophets themselves rest; (2) *origin:* the foundation laid by the apostle-prophets; (3) *explanation:* the foundation which is the apostle-prophets.[25] As Pfammatter points out, the defenders of interpretations (1) and (2) are influenced by a desire to harmonize this passage with the above (1 Cor. 3.11) and in their view the foundation here is also *Christ.*[26] Grammatically such an interpretation is possible, but the context, in distinguishing Christ as corner-stone (*akrogōniaios*) from the foundation (*themelios*), is decidedly against it. The foundation, then, must be the apostle-prophets,[27] and this does not at all conflict with 1 Cor. 3.11. Christ is the foundation of the temple in so far as he is preached. But in preaching Christ, the apostles themselves become the foundation because the apostolate is inseparable from the preached Christ.[28] The body of Christ, which is the temple, was formed virtually on the Cross (Eph. 2.16) but, as Eph. 3.4–6 shows, the Gentiles actually enter into Christ and are built up on him through the preaching of the Gospel in which his Spirit is active. The apostle-prophets are the foundation not in their persons but in the exercise of the function as the official bearers of the revelation of Christ.[29] The spiritual temple is inconceivable apart from preaching. It is only natural, therefore, that preaching should share its liturgical character.

We are now in a position to appreciate Paul's most significant expression of this idea. In a few words in the epilogue of the Epistle to the Romans he states clearly what has already been inferred from other passages. The brevity of this statement should not tempt us to dismiss it lightly. That Paul considered it important and not a casual aside may be gleaned from its place in a passage where the Apostle is concerned to vindicate his right to write to the Romans, and in the severe tone he has had to adopt, by an appeal to the divine character of his mission. He says:

But I write to you somewhat more boldly, as again putting you in mind of things, in virtue of the grace given me by God to be a priest [*leitourgos*] of Christ Jesus to the Gentiles, ministering-in-sacrifice [*hierourgounta*] the gospel of God, that [*hina*] the offering [*prosphora*] of the Gentiles may be acceptable being sanctified in the Holy Spirit. [Rom. 15.15–16]

Despite its obvious relationship to *leitourgia*, which is used by the Septuagint as a technical term for the exercise of the priestly office,[30] *leitourgos* is employed but rarely to designate a priest. (Isa. 61.6: Neh. 10.39: Ecclus. 7.31.) Apart from these three instances, its meaning in the Old Testament is always that of "servant", and apparently a servant who was also a freeman.[31] This usage is reflected in the New Testament, where the exact value to be given the term must be determined in each case from the context, for while it can mean a true priest (Heb. 8.2), it is also used of those whose activity is only very remotely ordered to a religious end. (Rom. 13.6: Phil. 2.25.) In itself, therefore, the term has no special liturgical value. Here, however, it is determined by *hierourgounta*, the present participle of *hierourgeō*. This verb, which does not occur in the Septuagint, means "to perform a sacred function, especially, to sacrifice" and consequently, "to act as a priest with regard to

something".[32] Its sense is admirably rendered by
Alan Richardson's translation which we have
adopted. It is precisely in performing a priestly
act, then, that Paul is a *leitourgos* of Christ and
we may legitimately translate it by "priest". The
sacrifice offered by Paul is his activity. Asting
cannot be correct in considering the Apostle to
be a sacrificing priest in so far as he mediates a
heavenly gift (divine revelation) to men.[33] The
movement in revelation is from God to man, in
sacrifice and worship from man to God. Others,
with slightly more reason, consider the sacrifice,
which Paul offers, to be the Gentiles as sanctified
in the Spirit.[34] These commentators, as a rule,
simply assume that the genitive "of the Gentiles"
has an explanatory value (the offering *which is*
the Gentiles). By way of exception, Lagrange
does offer two parallels from the Septuagint in
this sense, Ps. 39(40).7 and Ecclus. 46.19. It must
be pointed out, however, that the Septuagint
also provides examples in which the genitive
qualifying "offering" has certainly the value of
a *genitivus auctoris*: "The Most High does not
accept the offerings of the impious" (Ecclus.
34.23); "The offering of the just man rejoices
the altar." (Ecclus. 35.8.) And it would be much
more in accord with the rest of Paul's liturgical
expressions to take "the offering of the Gentiles"
as the offering *made by* the Gentiles.[35] This offering which, because of the absence of any limita-

tion, we understand as their whole existence, becomes pleasing to God in being sanctified by the Holy Spirit. This sanctification is effected by baptism, but the passage under consideration relates the acceptability of the Gentiles' offering to Paul's preaching (*hina*). This difficulty disappears when we recollect the extremely close association between preaching and baptism in Paul's mind. Without the faith which comes through preaching (Rom. 10.17) there are no sacraments; full obedience to the Gospel, which Paul goes on to mention as the object of his commission (15.18), includes submission to the rite of baptism. Therefore, it is through the Apostle that the Gentiles are brought into contact with the Spirit, because what he has accomplished has been achieved by the Spirit's power 15.19). Although every element in the Christian life obviously must not be attributed to preaching as its cause, preaching is the foundation on which it rests. The liturgy that is the believer's Spirit-filled existence in Christ, is rooted in the liturgy that is the preaching of the word of God.[36]

It is difficult to assess the exact value of the liturgical terms used by Paul to describe both preaching and the Christian life. Are they mere metaphors or do they express a mystical reality? One would be tempted to see them as metaphors pure and simple were it not for the idea of the spiritual temple, for this notion, as applied to the Church or to an individual, is certainly more than a metaphor. The edifice erected by the Jews was the Temple because God dwelt therein. Now, through his Spirit, God dwells in both the body of Christ and in its members, and is more perfectly present in them than he was in the Temple. The presence of God of which the Old Testament speaks was a presence of action; God was considered to dwell where his action was most constant and favourable.[37] God now dwells in the Christian by transforming him into the image of his beloved Son through a grace which is a participation of his own nature.[38] The most essential element in the Old-Testament notion of the Temple is, therefore, realized in an eminent way in the case of the Christian. Paul, in spiritualizing the idea, perfects rather than destroys it. This being so, it seems impossible to deny a real (as opposed to a metaphorical) value to the other liturgical expressions whose use flows naturally from the acceptance of the idea of the temple. If the Christian is a temple in a real sense, then his activity is in some sense really liturgical. The coherence among themselves of the ideas expressed, together with the fact that Paul introduces them without a word of explanation and refers to them as to a doctrine already known and understood, tends to confirm the impression that it is a question of something more than a succession of metaphors. Then, too, it must not be forgotten that through baptism the believer participates in the supreme liturgical act of Christ, his sacrificial death, which leaves its stamp on his whole existence.

The matter is slightly less clear when preaching is considered. Unquestionably, all that is true of the Christian is true of the preacher. The extremely close relationship of his activity to the existence and preservation of the spiritual temple suggests also that the liturgical quality attributed to this activity is intrinsic to it. Finally, in deliberately choosing a rare term like *hierourgeō*[39] to characterize his activity does not Paul intend to underline the realism of his expressions?[40]

NOTES

1. The term "liturgical" is not ideal because it may be misleading. As used throughout this chapter all overtones of solemn religious exercises governed by rubrics are suppressed and only the connotation of *worship* remains. The French *cultuel* (as distinguished from *liturgique*) renders the idea perfectly.

2. The Temple is mentioned among the privileges of Israel in 1 Kings 8.33–7: Isa. 56.3–7: Ecclus. 24.8–12, but perhaps the best indication of the primordial position accorded it, is that the construction of a new glorious temple formed part of the messianic hope of Israel, cf. Ezek. 43.18–44.26; Schrenk, *TWNT*, vol. 3, 239–340. M. Baillet concludes his study of the fragments

of an Aramaic MS discovered at Qumran: "It is tempting to see it as a liturgical construction inspired by the
Temple at Jerusalem, but referring probably to the
Israel to come." ("Fragments Araméens de Qumrân 2;
description de la Jérusalem Nouvelle", *RB*, 62 (1955),
244). See also O. Betz, "Le Ministère cultuel dans la
secte de Qumrân et dans le christianisme primitif", in
J. van der Ploeg et al., *La secte de Qumrân et les
origines du christianisme* (Rech. Bibl., 4), Louvain
(1959), 166.

3. Lagrange, Sanday-Headlam, Sickenberger.

4. "*Latreuein*, therefore, signifies precisely cultic service, cultic worship, above all through sacrifice ... The
use of *latreia*, then, in the Septuagint is exactly parallel
to that of *latreuein*" (Strathmann, *TWNT*, vol. 4, 60,
61).

5. Cf. M. Fraeyman, "La Spiritualisation de l'idée du
Temple dans les épîtres pauliniennes", *ETL*, 23 (1947),
382.

6. According to Cerfaux (*L'Église*, 115–117), Paul
found the idea of the community as a spiritual temple
already in existence in the primitive Church. The
seminal expression of the idea was undoubtedly the
teaching of Christ concerning the destruction of the
Temple (Mark 14.58: Matt. 24.1–2) and the new worship
in spirit and in truth. (John 4.23; cf. 2.19.) But under
what influence did its elaboration take place? No contribution, apparently, came from orthodox Jewish
thought, for the glorious temple of the messianic age
was always conceived as a *material* reality. However,
we can no longer say, as Fraeyman did ("La Spiritualisation", 406), that the idea of a spiritual temple was
unknown to the Jews. K. G. Kuhn ("Les Rouleaux de
cuivre de Qumran", *RB*, 61 (1954), 203) has drawn
attention to the existence of this concept at Qumran. A
passage from the *Manual of Discipline* (1QS) enunciates
a doctrine similar to Paul's on many points:

When these things come to pass in Israel—the council
of the community being established in truth—an

eternal plant, *a holy house* consisting of Israel and a most holy congregation consisting of Aaron true witnesses about uprightness, chosen by [divine] pleasure to atone for the earth... *a most holy dwelling* consisting of Aaron with eternal knowledge of this covenant of uprightness, offering up a sweet odour. [1QS VIII, 5–9; cf. XI, 8: trans. of P. Wernberg-Møller, *The Manual of Discipline*, Leiden, 1957, 33, who also shows that these lines refer to the community and not just to the council.]

Despite the striking resemblances, there are important differences to be noted between the doctrine of the sectaries and that of Paul: (1) Both accept that the lives of the members of the community have a sacrificial value (Rom. 12.1: Phil. 2.30: 1QS IX, 3–5), but for Paul this value is a consequence of the Christian's being a temple, whereas for the sectaries it is rather the reason why they are a temple. In other words, for the Apostle, God dwells within the Christians collectively and individually, therefore they are a temple, therefore their lives have a liturgical value. The point of view at Qumran was different. The existence of the community there is explained by the extreme importance they attached to ritual purity. They felt that they could no longer associate themselves with the meaningless worship (CD VI, 17–20), offered in a profaned sanctuary (CD V, 6), by unclean ministers (CD IV, 17: V, 6–11). Only in the new Israel of the perfect (the community) was God truly worshipped by the sacrifice of a perfect life and the sacrifice of prayer. (1QS IX, 3–6.) This was the line of thought that led the sectaries to the conception of the community as the true (spiritual) temple, cf. D. Barthélemy, "La Sainteté selon la communauté de Qumrân et selon l'évangile", in J. van der Ploeg et al., *La Secte de Qumrân* (Rech. Bibl., 4), Louvain (1959), 210. This conception is closer to that of Peter, for whom the temple is primarily the place of sacrifice (1 Pet. 2.5), than to that of Paul, who emphasizes the fact of God's presence. (2) The sectaries considered their spiritual liturgy as preferable to that of the Temple actually existing in Jerusalem, but did not regard it as intrinsically superior to the offering of bloody victims. They lived hoping intensely for the day when, in the Temple of the New Jerusalem, God would be honoured by pure sacrifices, offered in conformity with the prescriptions of the Law. Cf. J. Carmignac, "L'Utilité ou l'inutilité des sacrifices sanglants dans la *Règle de la Communauté* de Qumrân", *RB*, 63 (1956), 530; O. Betz, "Le Ministère cultuel", 168. (3) Finally, for Paul, the temple is holy because God is present there (cf. Ezek. 42.13: 44.2: Ps. 5.8). The sanctity of the temple-community at Qumran is due to the presence of the holy angels in the congregation (1QSa II, 8–9.)

7. Cf. Michel, *TWNT*, vol. 5, 129; Cerfaux, *L'Église*, 113, *n. 3*, but, as Congar points out, there is no systematic and exclusive priority between the Church and the Christian. (*Le Mystère du Temple*, Paris (1958), 184.)

8. Cf. C. J. Kearns, *The Church the Body of Christ according to Saint Paul*, Dublin (1960), 32–3.

9. Robinson, *Eph.*, 71; J. Pfammatter, *Die Kirche als Bau*, Rome (1960), 103.

10. Cf. Cerfaux, *L'Église*, 114.

11. In the Septuagint *doxazō* is used to express a liturgical act (Lev. 10.3: Ps. 50.23), cf Fraeyman, "La Spiritualisation", 399.

12. Simply to translate *logikos* by "spiritual" (Lyonnet in the *Bible de Jérusalem*) is to lose a shade of meaning. Were this Paul's idea he could have used *pneumatikos* (Lagrange, Sickenberger). Lagrange and Viard paraphrase "the cult that your reason demands of you". This offering of self consisting in virtuous activity is a spiritual cult when compared with the offering of animals.

13. Cf. Spicq, *Agapé*, vol. 2, 142.

14. The couple *prosphora-thusia* is also found in the citation from Ps. 40.7 in Heb. 10.5,8, and it is not impossible that this psalm should have influenced their association here (Abbott). *Prosphora* is the more

generic term, meaning simply "offering". In the Septuagint it is used of the daily sacrifice taken as a whole (Ecclus. 50.13–14), but also of the sacrificial victim itself. (Ecclus. 34.21: 35.4: 46.9.) The phrase *osmē euōdias* occurs so frequently in the Septuagint in a liturgical context as to be a stereotyped designation of a sacrifice as pleasing to God (e.g., Gen. 8.21: Exod. 29.18: Lev. 1.9,13,17: 2.12). "*Osmē euōdias* is but another expression for the idea of sacrifice." (Delling, *TWNT*, vol. 5, 494; cf. Stumpff, *TWNT*, vol. 2, 808.)

15. Dibelius, Vincent, Seidensticker (*Lebendiges Opfer*. Münster im Westf. (1954), 229), Denis ("La Fonction apostolique et la liturgie nouvelle en esprit", *RSPT*, 42 (1958), 629).

16. With Denis ("Fonction apostolique", 629) we take *leitourgia* as a hendiadys.

17. Cf. Num. 16.9: 1 Chron. 6.48: 9.13: 23.24: 2 Macc. 3.3. "Just like *leitourgein, leitourgia* became a technical term for the priestly cult." (Strathmann, *TWNT*, vol. 4, 227.) Cf. J. Bonsirven, *Le Judaïsme palestinien au temps de Jésus-Christ*, vol. 2, Paris (1935), 106, 114.

18. Spicq, *Agapé*, vol. 2, 11. Cf. Rigaux on 1 Thess. 1.3. The allusion to the sacrifice of the Philippians follows on a passage which considers them, by reason of their virtuous activity, as "holding forth the word of life".

19. Note the similarity to the terms used to express the sacrifice of Christ (Eph. 5.2), cf. above, *n.* 14.

20. *Hieroprepēs* occurs only here in the whole Bible and means "what is in accord with the *hieron*, with the Temple and its service, with the sacred action, with religious things, in a word, with the divinity, and which, for this reason, is holy and honourable". (Schrenk. *TWNT*, vol. 3, 253.) From its use in describing the conduct of a priest, it acquired a specialized meaning "like a priest" (*A-G*, 373), and in the light of Paul's penchant for describing the Christian life in liturgical terms, it is probable that this is the meaning intended here (Spicq).

Schrenk (*TWNT*, vol. 3, 254, *n.* 3) approves Dibelius' rendering, "priestly".

21. "The sufferings of Christ overflow on us." Allo comments: "Christians have to bear them in imitation of Christ, because of Christ, and in Christ, who suffers, so to speak, in them, or who communicates his sufferings to them in order to assimilate them to himself, body and soul." Reference might be made to 1 Cor. 12.12,26. Tribulation (*thlipsis*) is a permanent quality of the believer's being, a condition that he cannot escape. (1 Thess. 3.3–4; cf. Acts 14.21.)

22. A. Richardson, *An Introduction to the Theology of the New Testament*, London (1958), 300. Cf. Seiden-sticker, *Lebendiges Opfer*, 224.

23. Cf. K. Weiss, "Paulus—Priester der christlichen Kultgemeinde", *Theologische Literaturzeitung*, 79 (1954), 355–64; A. M. Denis, "La Fonction apostolique et la liturgie nouvelle en esprit", *RSPT*, 42 (1958), 401–36, 617–56.

24. So Lyonnet (*Bible de Jérusalem*), but Lagrange, Cornely, Viard, Sickenberger, content themselves with the meaning "serve", and understand *pneuma* in the sense of St Thomas, "not solely with the external service of the body but especially with the internal service of the spirit". Sanday-Headlam and Strathmann (*TWNT*, vol. 4, 64–5) admit a liturgical nuance, but because of the mention of prayer.

25. The various authors holding these opinions are listed in Pfammatter, *Die Kirche als Bau*, 80.

26. *Die Kirche als Bau*, 81.

27. This is by far the most common opinion, number-ing among its adherents Abbott, Benoit (*Bible de Jérusalem*), Schlier, Schmidt (*TWNT*, vol. 3, 63) etc.

28. "He poses the foundation, Christ, in his gospel—the foundation is the 'preached' Christ (2 Cor. 1.19)—which cannot be separated from the apostle and his apostolate. There is no access to Christ other than through the apostles and prophets, who have preached him, and who themselves become and remain, in their preaching, the foundation." (Schlier, *Eph.*, 142.)

29. Cf. ch. 2, n. 2.

30. Cf. above n. 17.

31. Cf. Strathmann, *TWNT*, vol. 4, 237.

32. Cf. Schrenk, *TWNT*, vol. 3, 252: *A-G*, 374: Sanday-Headlam.

33. *Die Verkündigung des Wortes in Urchristentum*. Stuttgart (1938), 354, 394.

34. Lagrange, Sanday-Headlam, Sickenberger, Schrenk (*TWNT*, vol. 3, 252), Weiss ("Paulus", 357), Lyonnet (*Bible de Jérusalem*), *Westminster Version, New English Bible*.

35. Viard, Denis, "Fonction apostolique", 406.

36. Similar to Rom. 15.15–16 in structure is Phil. 2.17, where Paul, speaking of his own position relative to that of the Philippians, characterizes both in liturgical terms: "Even if I am to be poured out in libation [*spendomai*] on the sacrifice and cult of your faith, I rejoice." *Spendō* occurs elsewhere in the New Testament only once (2 Tim. 4.6), and in a religious context can have but one meaning, "to offer a libation or drink-offering". Evidently this could be an allusion to Paul's martyrdom (Vincent, Bonnard, Bauer), but neither in profane Greek nor in the Septuagint is *spendō* ever used in the sense of "to pour out blood in sacrifice" (cf. Denis, "Fonction apostolique", 633, 639). Consequently, it is more probable that the allusion is to the humiliating circumstances of Paul's imprisonment. (Phil. 1.12.) In neither hypothesis is there any reference to preaching. But the text has its importance in so far as it underlines the close relationship of the preacher and his converts, for in the liturgy of the Temple the libation of wine and the holocaust formed a single liturgical act. (Cf. Denis, 645.)

37. Cf. Lagrange, *Le Judaïsme avant Jésus-Christ*, Paris (1931), 447.

38. Cf. Spicq, *Dieu*, 204.

39. It is not found elsewhere in the New Testament nor in the Septuagint.

40. Cf. Denis, "Fonction apostolique", 407.

CONCLUSION

THE structure of this study was determined by the fact that Paul nowhere gives us a formal explicit treatment of preaching. What we find in his epistles is a series of scattered statements for the most part concerning his own personal obligations in the matter or those of his delegates, and conditioned by the circumstances in which they found themselves. There are, however, many little touches which indicate that each time he is applying a general idea to a particular situation. The harmony among themselves of numerous partial insights and the striking consistency of the emergent picture suggest very strongly that Paul had a very clear concept of what the preacher's function is.

The preacher is never an absolute. To conceive him as an autonomous agent is impossible —he is supremely a man of God. He is chosen for his office by God in the person of Christ; he receives divine aid in its exercise; his word is the word of God. He achieves only what God wishes him to achieve, because those who respond to his message do so because moved by God. The divine causality is all-pervasive. Yet the reality of the preacher's contribution to the

execution of the plan of salvation is never called
in doubt. His role is devoid of all significance
for he is only an instrument, but this, paradoxically, is his greatest glory, since it is God who
speaks through him. The preacher is *God's co-
worker*. In thus co-operating with God he exercises a priestly function, and his activity possesses
the quality of a liturgical offering. In the last
analysis this is so because preaching is but a
particular modality of the Christian life which,
when perfectly lived, is a living sacrifice. We
may note in passing that as far as the ordinary
Christian is concerned the converse is true; if
his life possesses this liturgical quality it is a
form of preaching.

Because his theology centres on the idea of
salvation through sacrificial expiation of sin, the
preacher's message, according to Paul, is essentially the word of the Cross, the proclamation
of the plan of salvation as revealed and actualized
in Jesus Christ. The message is inevitably "personalized" in delivery, but the dynamism which
makes it "the power of God for salvation" (Rom.
1.16) is not dependent on the science or eloquence of the preacher. These have a definite
value, but the saving efficacy of his words stems
from his mission, which is closely integrated
with the temporal missions of the Son and the
Holy Spirit. Because he is God's chosen servant
his activity is impregnated by the redemptive

interaction of Christ and the Spirit. The
preacher disposes of the power of the Spirit, the
effect of which is to realize a presence of Christ.

The presence of Christ in the word of his
minister obviously differs from his presence on
earth and his definitive presence at the *parousia*.
In opposition to these immediate presences, his
presence in the word is mediate and veiled. This
veiled presence differs also from his presence
in the Eucharist. Christ is substantially present
under the consecrated species. In his word he is
present only in the saving power proper to the
risen messianic Lord. The *fact* of this presence
is conditioned by the preacher, its *efficacy* by
the dispositions of his audience.

Christ will not be present if the word of his
minister is not God's word, nor will he be
present if God's word is not also his minister's.
The preacher is an instrument but a free one,
and in consequence great stress is laid on his
fidelity. It should be the natural accompaniment
of the spirit of charity given him, but he can
resist this grace and "falsify" the word of God.
In which case the doctrine he proffers will be
but profitless human speculation and not the
power of salvation. But even if the doctrine he
preaches is authentic revelation, it will not be
the saving presence of Christ unless the preacher
possesses the mind of Christ, unless he has really
put on Christ. God's word must also be the

preacher's, the manifestation of an intense personal conviction. It will not be this, unless Christ operative in the word is being permitted to transform him into his own image. Since his mission is a prolongation of that of Christ, he must himself be an *alter Christus*. The preacher does not really bear witness to Christ if his testimony is a matter of words alone. His whole existence must witness to the saving power of the Gospel.

In order that the saving power of Christ present in the word be effective the word must be heard. This acceptance is not just a simple intellectual acquiescence in the truth proposed, although this is certainly included. Paul describes true reception of the word of God as an "obedience", a positive commitment of the whole personality. This total commitment (faith) demands a divinely-given illumination and change of heart, accorded only to those who have corresponded with the grace of the love of truth. These are the elect. For them the Gospel is the efficacious expression of a divine choice. It puts into effect an eternal decision, for in receiving the Gospel they are saved. The word, when received, remains active in the believers and its fruits are manifest in obedience to the preacher's subsequent counsels and directives. In turn, this conduct adds lustre to the word of God and is, in effect, a wordless sermon.

Those who reject the word do so because blinded by Satan. He can work through the bad example of others or through man's own inordinate desires, but he succeeds in blinding only those who have already refused the love of truth and who, in consequence, have been handed over to his influence.

Preaching, finally, is penetrated through and through by love. The plan of salvation was motivated and conceived in love; the means chosen for its execution was an epiphany of love; the end desired is love. Preaching enters into this scheme as the revelation of Love Incarnate and as the initial communication to men of the fruits of that love.

BIBLIOGRAPHY

(This list is limited to works cited in abbreviation in the notes)

ABBOT, T. K., *A Critical and Exegetical Commentary on the Epistles to the Ephesians and to the Colossians*, Edinburgh (1909).

ALLO, E. B., *Saint Paul. Première Épître aux Corinthiens*, Paris (1956).

————, *Saint Paul. Seconde Épitre aux Corinthiens*, Paris (1956).

AQUINAS, ST THOMAS, *Super Epistolas S. Pauli Lectura*, ed. R. Cai, Taurini, Rome (1953).

BONNARD, P., *L'Épître de Saint Paul aux Philippiens*, Neuchâtel-Paris (1950).

BURTON, E. DE WITT, *A Critical and Exegetical Commentary on the Epistle to the Galatians*, Edinburgh (1921).

CERFAUX, L., *La Théologie de l'Église suivant saint Paul*, Paris (1948).

————, *Le Christ dans la théologie de saint Paul*, Paris (1954).

CORNELY, R., *Prior Epistola ad Corinthios*, Paris (1890).

————, *Epistola ad Corinthios Altera et ad Galatas*, Paris (1892).

————, *Epistola ad Romanos*, Paris (1896).

DIBELIUS, M., *An die Thessaloniker I, II. An die Philipper*, Tübingen (1925).

————, *An die Kolosser, Epheser, Philemon*, Tübingen (1927).

DUPONT, J., *Gnosis, la connaissance religieuse dans les épîtres de S. Paul*, Louvain (1949).

EWALD, P., *Die Briefe des Paulus an die Epheser, Kolosser und Philemon*, Leipzig (1910).

FRAME, J. E., *A Critical and Exegetical Commentary on the Epistle of Saint Paul to the Thessalonians*, Edinburgh (1912).

GODET, F., *Commentaire sur l'épître aux Romains*, Paris, 1 (1879), II (1890).

LAGRANGE, M. J., *Saint Paul. Épître aux Galates*, Paris (1950).

————, *Saint Paul. Épître aux Romains*, Paris (1922).

LEENHARDT, F. J., *L'Épître de S. Paul aux Romains*, Neuchâtel-Paris (1957).

LIGHTFOOT, J. B., *St Paul's Epistles to the Colossians and to Philemon*, London (1892).

MASSON, C., *L'Épître de Saint Paul aux Colossiens*, Neuchâtel-Paris (1950).

————, *L'Épître de Saint Paul aux Éphésiens*, Neuchâtel-Paris (1953).

————, *Les deux Épîtres aux Thessaloniciens*, Neuchâtel-Paris (1957).

MICHEL, O., *Der Brief an die Römer*, Gottingen (1955).

PRAT, F., *The Theology of Saint Paul*, trans. by J. Stoddard, Westminster, Maryland (1956).

RIGAUX, B., *Saint Paul. Les Épîtres aux Thessaloniciens*, Paris (1956).

ROBERTSON, A. and PLUMMER, A., *A Critical and Exegetical Commentary on the First Epistle of St Paul to the Corinthians*, Edinburgh (1914).

SANDAY, W. and HEADLAM, A. C., *A Critical and Exegetical Commentary on the Epistle to the Romans*, Edinburgh (1958).

SCHLIER, H., *Der Brief an die Epheser*, Düsseldorf (1957).

——, *Le Temps de l'Église*, trans. by F. Corin, Tournai (1961).

SICKENBERGER, J., *Die Briefe des Heiligen Paulus an die Korinther und Römer*, Bonn (1932).

SPICQ, C., *Saint Paul. Les Épîtres pastorales*, Paris (1947).

——, *Épîtres aux Corinthiens* (P-C XIb), Paris (1951).

——, *L'Épître aux Hébreux*, vol. 1, Paris (1952), vol. 2, Paris (1953).

——, *Agapé dans le Nouveau Testament. Analyse des Textes*, vol. 1, Paris (1958), vol. 2 and 3, Paris (1959).

——, *Dieu et l'homme selon le Nouveau Testament*, Paris (1961).

STABB, K. and FREUNDORFER, J., *Die Thessalonicherbriefe, die Gefangenschaftsbriefe und die Pastoralbriefe*, Regensburg (1950).

STEINMANN, A., *Die Briefe an die Thessalonicher und Galater*, Bonn (1935).

VIARD, A., *Épître aux Romains* (P-C XIb), Paris (1951).

VINCENT, M. R., *A Critical and Exegetical Commentary on the Epistles to the Philippians and to Philemon*, Edinburgh (1902).

VOSTÉ, J. M., *Commentarius in Epistulam ad Ephesios*, Rome-Paris (1932).

WOHLENBERG, G., *Der erste und zweite Thessalonicherbrief*, Leipzig (1909).

INDEX

INDEX OF SCRIPTURE REFERENCES

(This list is limited to the passages of the Pauline
Epistles commented on)